Charles S. Robinson

Calvary Selection of Spiritual Songs with Music

for use in social meetings

Charles S. Robinson

Calvary Selection of Spiritual Songs with Music
for use in social meetings

ISBN/EAN: 9783337265809

Printed in Europe, USA, Canada, Australia, Japan

Cover: Foto ©Thomas Meinert / pixelio.de

More available books at **www.hansebooks.com**

THE CALVARY SELECTION

OF

SPIRITUAL SONGS

WITH MUSIC

FOR USE IN SOCIAL MEETINGS.

SELECTED AND ARRANGED BY

REV. CHARLES S. ROBINSON, D. D.

AND

REV. ROBERT S. MacARTHUR, D. D.

THE CENTURY CO. NEW-YORK.

PREFACE.

THIS collection consists of hymns and tunes taken from the "Calvary Selection of Spiritual Songs," for use in Baptist churches, selected by the same compilers, and issued by the same publishers.

One reason why the music in many prayer-meetings gives so little assistance is found in the worn-out familiarity of the hymns and tunes employed. There is no growth in the exercise. What is wanted is a wider range and a fresher adaptation. But there is no adequate chance for increase, unless the experience of the Sabbath successes can be taken into the week-day monotony.

Then, on the other hand, one reason why the music on the Lord's Day often has so feeble à force is found in its exclusiveness as a thing of high art. It remains too far out of reach of the people. What is wanted is that the tunes should be learned, and the hymns should be rendered usable by frequent repetition.

Both of these ends will best be secured by the employment of manuals similar in spirit and form for all the services, even including the sessions of the Sunday-school. Then the skill of the choir will tell upon the social meetings, and the education of the people, old and young, in the more familiar assemblies, will react favorably upon the singing in the public worship.

The "Calvary Selection of Spiritual Songs," in its larger form for the church and choir, as well as in this, its smaller form, for the social meetings, is designed to furnish just this sort of help. In making this choice of pieces, the compilers have borne in mind also that there may be some churches which would prefer a book of this size more portable and less costly which may be used in all their services.

The compilers offer this manual of worship to the churches in the hope that it may prove helpful to them in their service of song, and may thus contribute to the glory of their great Head.

CHARLES S. ROBINSON,
ROBERT S. MacARTHUR.

NEW-YORK, March, 1880.

TABLE OF CONTENTS.

SPIRITUAL SONGS.

DALSTON. S. P. M.   A. WILLIAMS.

1. How pleased and blest was I, To hear the peo-ple cry, "Come, let us seek our God to - day!"

Yes, with a cheerful zeal, We haste to Zi-on's hill, And there our vows and honors pay.

1   *Psalm 122.*   I. WATTS.

How PLEASED and blest was I,
To hear the people cry,
"Come, let us seek our God to-day!"
Yes, with a cheerful zeal,
We haste to Zion's hill,
And there our vows and honors pay.

2 Zion—thrice happy place—
Adorned with wondrous grace,
While walls of strength embrace thee round:
In thee our tribes appear,
To pray, and praise, and hear
The sacred gospel's joyful sound.

3 May peace attend thy gate,
And joy within thee wait,
To bless the soul of every guest:
The man who seeks thy peace,
And wishes thine increase,
A thousand blessings on him rest !

4 My tongue repeats her vows,
"Peace to this sacred house !"
For here my friends and kindred dwell;
And since my glorious God
Makes thee his blest abode,
My soul shall ever love thee well.

1

HENDON. 7s.   C. H. A. MALAN.

1. Lord, we come be - fore thee now, At thy feet we hum-bly bow; Oh, do not our

suit dis - dain! Shall we seek thee, Lord, in vain? Shall we seek thee, Lord, in vain?

2   *"Thy face we seek."*   W. HAMMOND.

LORD, we come before thee now,
At thy feet we humbly bow;
Oh, do not our suit disdain!
Shall we seek thee, Lord, in vain?

2 Lord, on thee our souls depend,
In compassion now descend;
Fill our hearts with thy rich grace,
Tune our lips to sing thy praise.

3 In thine own appointed way,
Now we seek thee; here we stay;
Lord, we know not how to go,
Till a blessing thou bestow.

4 Comfort those who weep and mourn;
Let the time of joy return;
Those that are cast down lift up;
Make them strong in faith and hope.

5 Grant that all may seek and find
Thee a God supremely kind;
Heal the sick; the captive free;
Let us all rejoice in thee.

3   *Jesus intercedes.*   J. MONTGOMERY.

To THY temple we repair—
Lord, we love to worship there,
When within the vail we meet
Thee upon the mercy-seat.

2 While thy glorious name is sung,
Tune our lips—unloose our tongue;
Then our joyful souls shall bless
Thee, the Lord our Righteousness.

3 While to thee our prayers ascend,
Let thine ear in love attend;
Hear us, for thy Spirit pleads—
Hear, for Jesus intercedes.

4 While thy word is heard with awe,
While we tremble at thy law,
Let thy gospel's wondrous love
Every doubt and fear remove.

5 From thy house when we return,
Let our hearts within us burn;
That at evening we may say—
"We have walked with God to-day."

CHAPEL. 7s.   GERMAN CHORAL.

1. To thy temple we re-pair—Lord, we love to worship there, When within the vail we meet Thee up-on the mercy - seat.

WILBERFORCE. 7s. 6l.

C. C. CONVERSE, arr.

1. {Je - sus, Sun of Righteousness, Brightest beam of love di - vine, }
   {With the ear - ly morn-ing rays Do thou on our dark-ness shine, } And dispel with

purest light All our night,—all our night.

4   *The melted heart.*   J. BORTHWICK.

JESUS, Sun of Righteousness,
  Brightest beam of love divine,
With the early morning rays
  Do thou on our darkness shine,

And dispel with purest light
All our night,—all our night.

2 Like the sun's reviving ray,
  May thy love, with tender glow,
All our coldness melt away,
  Warm and cheer us forth to go;
Gladly serve thee and obey,
All the day,—all the day.

3 Thou, our only Life and Guide,
  Never leave us nor forsake;
In thy light may we abide
  Till the eternal morning break;
Moving on to Zion's hill,
Homeward still,—homeward still.

JESUS, MY ALL. 6s, 4s.

A. BOIELDIEU.

1. {Lord, at thy mer - cy-seat, Hum-bly I fall;}
   {Pleading thy promise sweet, Lord, hear my call;} Now let thy work begin, Oh, make me pure with- [in,

Cleanse me from every sin, Je-sus, my all.

5   *"Jesus, my all."*   F. C. VAN ALSTYNE.

LORD, at thy mercy-seat,
  Humbly I fall;
Pleading thy promise sweet,
  Lord, hear my call;
Now let thy work begin,
Oh, make me pure within,
Cleanse me from every sin,
  Jesus, my all.

2 Hark! how the words of love
  Tenderly fall,
Ere to the realms above,
  Heard is my call;
Now every doubt has flown,
Broken my heart of stone,
Lord, I am thine alone,
  Jesus, my all.

3 Still at thy mercy-seat
  Humbly I fall;
Pleading thy promise sweet,
  Heard is my call.
Faith wings my soul to thee;
This all my hope shall be,
Jesus has died for me,
  Jesus, my all.

555

4

LOVE DIVINE. 8s, 7s. D. — JOHN ZUNDEL.

1. Love di-vine, all love ex-cell-ing,—Joy of heaven, to earth come down! Fix in us thy humble dwelling;
D. S.—Vis-it us with thy sal-va-tion,

FINE.
All thy faithful mercies crown. Je-sus! thou art all com-pas-sion, Pure, unbounded love thou art;
En-ter ev-ery trembling heart.

D. S.

6 — C. WESLEY.
"Finish thy new creation."

Love divine, all love excelling,—
 Joy of heaven, to earth come down!
Fix in us thy humble dwelling,
 All thy faithful mercies crown:
Jesus! thou art all compassion,
 Pure, unbounded love thou art;
Visit us with thy salvation,
 Enter every trembling heart.

2 Breathe, oh, breathe thy loving Spirit
 Into every troubled breast!
Let us all in thee inherit,
 Let us find the promised rest:

Come, almighty to deliver,
 Let us all thy life receive!
Speedily return, and never,
 Never more thy temples leave!

3 Finish then thy new creation.
 Pure, unspotted may we be:
Let us see our whole salvation
 Perfectly secured by thee:
Changed from glory into glory,
 Till in heaven we take our place;
Till we cast our crowns before thee,
 Lost in wonder, love, and praise.

BAYLEY. 8s, 7s. D. — J. P. HOLBROOK, arr.

1. { Love di-vine, all love ex-cell-ing,—Joy of heaven, to earth come down! }
   { Fix in us thy hum-ble dwelling, All thy faith-ful (Omit).......... } mer-cies crown:
D.C.—Vis-it us with thy sal-va-tion, En-ter ev-ery (Omit).......... trem-bling heart.

D. C.

Je-sus! thou art all com-pas-sion, Pure, un-bound-ed love thou art:

WHAT A FRIEND. 8s, 7s, D. C. C. CONVERSE.

1. What a Friend we have in Jesus, All our sins and griefs to bear! What a priv-i-lege to car-ry
D. S.—All because we do not car-ry

FINE. D. S.

Ev-ery thing to God in prayer! Oh, what peace we often for-feit, Oh, what needless pain we bear,
Ev-ery thing to God in prayer!

7   *What a Friend.*   H. BONAR.

WHAT a Friend we have in Jesus,
  All our sins and griefs to bear!
What a privilege to carry
  Every thing to God in prayer!
Oh, what peace we often forfeit,
  Oh, what needless pain we bear,
All because we do not carry
  Every thing to God in prayer!

2 Have we trials and temptations?
  Is there trouble anywhere?
We should never be discouraged,—
  Take it to the Lord in prayer.
Can we find a friend so faithful,
  Who will all our sorrows share?
Jesus knows our every weakness—
  Take it to the Lord in prayer.

8   *The Pilgrim.*   T. HASTINGS.

GENTLY, Lord, oh, gently lead us,
  Through this lonely vale of tears;
Through the changes thou'st decreed us,
  Till our last great change appears.
When temptation's darts assail us,
  When in devious paths we stray,
Let thy goodness never fail us,
  Lead us in thy perfect way.

2 In the hour of pain and anguish,
  In the hour when death draws near,
Suffer not our hearts to languish,
  Suffer not our souls to fear.
And when mortal life is ended,
  Bid us in thine arms to rest,
Till by angel bands attended,
  We awake among the blest.

9   *God's Welcome.*   F. W. FABER.

THERE's a wideness in God's mercy,
  Like the wideness of the sea:
There's a kindness in his justice,
  Which is more than liberty.
There is welcome for the sinner,
  And more graces for the good;
There is mercy with the Saviour;
  There is healing in his blood.

2 For the love of God is broader
  Than the measure of man's mind;
And the heart of the Eternal
  Is most wonderfully kind.
If our love were but more simple,
  We should take him at his word;
And our lives would be all sunshine
  In the sweetness of our Lord.

BELMONT. C M.
S. WEBBE.

1. Lord, thou on earth didst love thine own, Didst love them to the end;

Oh, still from thy ce - les - tial throne, Let gifts of love de - scend.

10 *"One as we are one."* RAY PALMER.

LORD, thou on earth didst love thine own,
  Didst love them to the end;
Oh, still from thy celestial throne,
  Let gifts of love descend.

2 The love the Father bears to thee,
  His own eternal Son,
Fill all thy saints, till all shall be
  In pure affection one.

3 As thou for us didst stoop so low,
  Warmed by love's holy flame,
So let our deeds of kindness flow
  To all that bear thy name.

4 One blessèd fellowship of love,
  Thy living church should stand,
Till, faultless, she at last above
  Shall shine at thy right hand.

5 Oh, glorious day, when she, the Bride,
  With her dear Lord appears!
Then, robed in beauty at his side,
  She shall forget her tears!

11 1 John 4 : 21. J. SWAIN.

HOW SWEET, how heavenly is the sight,
  When those who love the Lord
In one another's peace delight,
  And so fulfill his word!

2 When each can feel his brother's sigh,
  And with him bear a part!
When sorrow flows from every eye,
  And joy from heart to heart!

3 When, free from envy, scorn, and pride,
  Our wishes all above,
Each can his brother's failings hide,
  And show a brother's love!

4 Let love, in one delightful stream,
  Through every bosom flow;
And union sweet, and dear esteem
  In every action glow.

5 Love is the golden chain that binds
  The happy souls above;
And he's an heir of heaven who finds
  His bosom glow with love.

EVAN. C. M.
W. H. HAVERGAL, arr.

1. How sweet, how heavenly is the sight, When those who love the Lord In one another's peace delight, And so fulfill his word!

HENLEY. 10s, 11s.

LOWELL MASON.

1. We would see Je - sus— for the shadows lengthen Across this litt - tle landscape of our life;

We would see Je - sus, our weak faith to strengthen For the last weariness—the fi - nal strife.

12   *"We would see Jesus."*   ANON.

WE would see Jesus—for the shadows lengthen
Across this little landscape of our life;
We would see Jesus, our weak faith to strengthen
For the last weariness—the final strife.

2 We would see Jesus—the great Rock Foundation,
Whereon our feet were set with sovereign grace;
Not life, nor death, with all their agitation,
Can thence remove us, if we see his face.

3 We would see Jesus—other lights are paling,
Which for long years we have rejoiced to see;
The blessings of our pilgrimage are failing,
We would not mourn them, for we go to thee.

4 We would see Jesus—this is all we're needing,
Strength, joy, and willingness come with the sight;
We would see Jesus, dying, risen, pleading,
Then welcome day, and farewell mortal night!

13   *Trust, strength, calmness.*   S. JOHNSON, alt.

SAVIOUR, in thy mysterious presence kneeling,
Fain would our souls feel all thy kindling love;
For we are weak, and need some deep revealing
Of trust, and strength, and calmness from above.

2 Lord, we have wandered forth through doubt and sorrow,
And thou hast made each step an onward one;
And we will ever trust each unknown morrow,—
Thou wilt sustain us till its work is done.

3 In the heart's depths a peace serene and holy
Abides, and when pain seems to have its will,
Or we despair,—oh, may that peace rise slowly,
Stronger than agony, and we be still!

4 Now, Saviour, now, in thy dear presence kneeling,
Our spirits yearn to feel thy kindling love;
Now make us strong, we need thy deep revealing
Of trust, and strength, and calmness from above.

ITALIAN HYMN. 6s, 4s. _　　　　　　　　　　　F. GIARDINI._

1. Come, thou almighty King, Help us thy name to sing, Help us to praise: { Father! all-glorious, O'er all vic-to-rious, } Come, and reign over us, Ancient of Days!

14　　_"One in Three."_　　C. WESLEY.

Come, thou almighty King,
Help us thy name to sing,
　Help us to praise:
Father! all-glorious,
O'er all victorious,
Come, and reign over us,
　Ancient of Days!

2 Come, thou incarnate Word,
Gird on thy mighty sword;
　Our prayer attend;
Come, and thy people bless,
And give thy word success;
Spirit of holiness!
　On us descend

3 Come, holy Comforter!
Thy sacred witness bear,
　In this glad hour:
Thou, who almighty art,
Now rule in every heart,
And ne'er from us depart,
　Spirit of power!

4 To the great One in Three,
The highest praises be,
　Hence evermore!
His sovereign majesty
May we in glory see,
And to eternity
　Love and adore.

BREAD OF LIFE. 6s, 4s.　　　　　　　　　WM. F. SHERWIN.

1. Break thou the bread of life, Dear Lord, to me, As thou didst break the loaves Beside the sea;

Be-yond the sacred page I seek thee, Lord; My spirit pants for thee, O liv-ing Word!

15　　_"By Galilee."_　　M. A. LATHBURY.

Break thou the bread of life,
　Dear Lord, to me,
As thou didst break the loaves
　Beside the sea;
Beyond the sacred page
　I seek thee, Lord;
My spirit pants for thee,
　O living Word!

2 Bless thou the truth, dear Lord,
　To me—to me—
As thou didst bless the bread
　By Galilee;
Then shall all bondage cease,
　All fetters fall;
And I shall find my peace,
　My All-in-All!

LEIGHTON. S. M.

H. W. GREATOREX.

1. Mine eyes and my de - sire Are ev - er to the Lord;

I love to plead his prom - is - es, And rest up - on his word.

16   *Psalm 25.*   I. WATTS.

MINE eyes and my desire
  Are ever to the Lord;
I love to plead his promises,
  And rest upon his word.

2 Lord, turn to thee my soul;
  Bring thy salvation near:
When will thy hand release my feet
  From sin's destructive snare?

3 When shall the sovereign grace
  Of my forgiving God
Restore me from those dangerous ways
  My wandering feet have trod?

4 Oh, keep my soul from death,
  Nor put my hope to shame!
For I have placed my only trust
  In my Redeemer's name.

5 With humble faith I wait
  To see thy face again;
Of Israel it shall ne'er be said,
  He sought the Lord in vain.

17   *Psalm 60.*   T. KELLY.

ARISE, ye saints, arise!
  The Lord our Leader is;
The foe before his banner flies,
  And victory is his.

2 We follow thee, our Guide,
  Our Saviour, and our King!
We follow thee, through grace supplied
  From heaven's eternal spring.

3 We soon shall see the day
  When all our toils shall cease;
When we shall cast our arms away,
  And dwell in endless peace.

4 This hope supports us here;
  It makes our burdens light;
'T will serve our drooping hearts to cheer,
  Till faith shall end in sight.

5 Till, of the prize possessed,
  We hear of war no more;
And ever with our Leader rest,
  On yonder peaceful shore.

18   *Psalm 31.*   H. F. LYTE.

MY spirit on thy care,
  Blest Saviour, I recline;
Thou wilt not leave me to despair,
  For thou art love divine.

2 In thee I place my trust;
  On thee I calmly rest:
I know thee good, I know thee just,
  And count thy choice the best.

3 Whate'er events betide,
  Thy will they all perform;
Safe in thy breast my head I hide,
  Nor fear the coming storm.

4 Let good or ill befall,
  It must be good for me,—
Secure of having thee in all,
  Of having all in thee.

MESSIAH. 7s. D.   GEO. KINGSLEY, *arr.*

1. Brethren, while we sojourn here, Fight we must, but should not fear; Foes we have, but we've a Friend,

One that loves us to the end: Forward, then, with courage go; Long we shall not

dwell be-low; Soon the joy-ful news will come, "Child, your Fa-ther calls—come home!"'

19   *"Come home."*   J. SWAIN.

BRETHREN, while we sojourn here,
Fight we must, but should not fear;
Foes we have, but we've a Friend,
One that loves us to the end:
Forward, then, with courage go;
Long we shall not dwell below;
Soon the joyful news will come,
"Child, your Father calls—come home!"

2 In the way a thousand snares
Lie, to take us unawares;
Satan, with malicious art,
Watches each unguarded part:

But, from Satan's malice free,
Saints shall soon victorious be;
Soon the joyful news will come,
"Child, your Father calls—come home!"

3 But of all the foes we meet,
None so oft mislead our feet,
None betray us into sin,
Like the foes that dwell within;
Yet let nothing spoil our peace,
Christ shall also conquer these;
Soon the joyful news will come,
"Child, your Father calls—come home!"

VIENNA. 7s.   W. H. HAVERGAL.

1. Children of the heavenly King, As ye journey, sweetly sing: Sing your Saviour's worthy praise, Glorious in his works and ways.

THEODORA. 7s.   FROM HANDEL.

1. Ev-erlasting arms of love Are beneath, around, above; He who left his throne of light, And unnumbered angels bright;—

20   *"The everlasting arms."*   ANON.

EVERLASTING arms of love
Are beneath, around, above;
He who left his throne of light,
And unnumbered angels bright;—

2 He who on the accursèd tree
Gave his precious life for me;
He it is that bears me on,
His the arm I lean upon.

3 All things hasten to decay,
Earth and sea will pass away;
Soon will yonder circling sun
Cease his blazing course to run.

4 Scenes will vary, friends grow strange,
But the Changeless cannot change:
Gladly will I journey on,
With his arm to lean upon.

PLEYEL'S HYMN. 7s.   I. PLEYEL.

1. Children of the heavenly King, As ye journey, sweetly sing; Sing your Saviour's worthy praise, Glorious in his works and ways.

21   *Isaiah 35: 8—10.*   J. CENNICK.

CHILDREN of the heavenly King,
As ye journey, sweetly sing;
Sing your Saviour's worthy praise,
Glorious in his works and ways.

2 Ye are traveling home to God
In the way the fathers trod;
They are happy now, and ye
Soon their happiness shall see.

3 Shout, ye little flock, and blest!
You on Jesus' throne shall rest;
There your seat is now prepared;
There your kingdom and reward.

4 Fear not, brethren; joyful stand
On the borders of your land;
Jesus Christ, your Father's Son,
Bids you undismayed go on.

5 Lord, submissive make us go,
Gladly leaving all below;
Only thou our Leader be,
And we still will follow thee.

22   *Redeeming Love.*   M. MADAN.

Now begin the heavenly theme,
Sing aloud in Jesus' name;
Ye who Jesus' kindness prove,
Triumph in redeeming love.

2 Ye who see the Father's grace
Beaming in the Saviour's face,
As to Canaan on ye move,
Praise and bless redeeming love.

3 Mourning souls, dry up your tears;
Banish all your guilty fears;
See your guilt and curse remove,
Canceled by redeeming love.

4 Welcome, all by sin opprest,
Welcome to his sacred rest;
Nothing brought him from above,
Nothing but redeeming love.

5 Hither, then, your music bring,
Strike aloud each joyful string;
Mortals, join the host above,
Join to praise redeeming love.

PRINCE. L. M.
FELIX MENDELSSOHN-BARTHOLDY.
FINE.

1. Come, gracious Spir - it, heaven - ly Dove, With light and comfort from a - bove:
D. S.—O'er every thought and step pre - side.

D.S.

Be thou our guardian, thou our guide!

23 *Invocation.* S. BROWNE, alt.

Come, gracious Spirit, heavenly Dove,
With light and comfort from above:
Be thou our guardian, thou our guide!
O'er every thought and step preside.

2 To us the light of truth display,
And make us know and choose thy way;
Plant holy fear in every heart,
That we from God may ne'er depart.

3 Lead us to holiness—the road
That we must take to dwell with God;
Lead us to Christ, the living way,
Nor let us from his precepts stray.

4 Lead us to God, our final rest,
To be with him for ever blest;
Lead us to heaven, its bliss to share—
Fullness of joy for ever there!

ZEPHYR. L. M.
W. B. BRADBURY.

1. Sure the blest Comforter is nigh, 'Tis he sustains my fainting heart; Else would my hopes forever die, And every cheering ray depart.

24 *The Spirit near.* A. STEELE.

Sure the blest Comforter is nigh,
'Tis he sustains my fainting heart;
Else would my hopes for ever die,
And every cheering ray depart.

2 Whene'er, to call the Saviour mine,
With ardent wish my heart aspires,—
Can it be less than power divine,
That animates these strong desires?

3 And, when my cheerful hope can say,—
I love my God and taste his grace,—
Lord! is it not thy blissful ray,
That brings this dawn of sacred peace?

4 Let thy good Spirit in my heart
For ever dwell, O God of love!

And light and heavenly peace impart,—
Sweet earnest of the joys above.

25 *Giver of Rest.* STEWART.

Come, Holy Spirit! calm my mind,
And fit me to approach my God;
Remove each vain, each worldly thought,
And lead me to thy blest abode.

2 Hast thou imparted to my soul
A living spark of holy fire?
Oh, kindle now the sacred flame;
Make me to burn with pure desire.

3 A brighter faith and hope impart,
And let me now my Saviour see;
Oh, soothe and cheer my burdened heart
And bid my spirit rest in thee.

J. P. HOLBROOK.

1. My soul, how love - ly is the place, To which thy God re - sorts!

'T is heaven to see his smil - ing face, Though in his earth - ly courts.

26   *Psalm 84.*   I. WATTS.

My soul, how lovely is the place,
  To which thy God resorts!
'T is heaven to see his smiling face,
  Though in his earthly courts.

2 There the great Monarch of the skies
  His saving power displays;
And light breaks in upon our eyes,
  With kind and quickening rays.

3 With his rich gifts the heavenly Dove
  Descends and fills the place;
While Christ reveals his wondrous love,
  And sheds abroad his grace.

4 There, mighty God, thy words declare
  The secrets of thy will;
And still we seek thy mercy there,
  And sing thy praises still.

27   *Psalm 25 : 14.*   C. WESLEY, *alt.*

SPEAK to me, Lord, thyself reveal,
  While here on earth I rove;
Speak to my heart, and let me feel
  The kindling of thy love.

2 With thee conversing, I forget
  All time and toil and care;
Labor is rest, and pain is sweet,
  If thou, my God, art here.

3 Thou callest me to seek thy face;
  Thy face, O God, I seek,—
Attend the whispers of thy grace,
  And hear thee inly speak. .

4 Let this my every hour employ,
  Till I thy glory see,
Enter into my Master's joy,
  And find my heaven in thee.

PETERBORO'. C. M.

R. HARRISON.

1. My soul, how love - ly is the place To which thy God re - sorts!

'T is heaven to see his smil - ing face, Though in........ his earth - ly courts.

2

ST. THOMAS. S. M.　　　　　　　　　HANDEL. A. WILLIAMS' COLL.

1. How charm-ing is the place Where my Re-deem-er, God,

Un-vails the beau-ty of his face, And sheds his love a-broad!

28　　*The Sanctuary.*　　S. STENNETT.

How CHARMING is the place
　Where my Redeemer, God,
Unvails the beauty of his face,
　And sheds his love abroad!

2 Not the fair palaces,
　To which the great resort,
Are once to be compared with this,
　Where Jesus holds his court.

3 Here on the mercy-seat,
　With radiant glory crowned,
Our joyful eyes behold him sit
　And smile on all around.

4 Give me, O Lord, a place
　Within thy blest abode,
Among the children of thy grace,
　The servants of my God.

29　　*Psalm 63.*　　I. WATTS.

My God! permit my tongue
　This joy, to call thee mine;
And let my early cries prevail
　To taste thy love divine.

2 My thirsty fainting soul
　Thy mercy doth implore;
Not travelers, in desert lands,
　Can pant for water more.

3 For life, without thy love,
　No relish can afford;
No joy can be compared to this,—
　To serve and please the Lord.

4 In wakeful hours at night,
　I call my God to mind;
I think how wise thy counsels are,
　And all thy dealings kind.

5 Since thou hast been my help,
　To thee my spirit flies;
And, on thy watchful providence,
　My cheerful hope relies.

6 The shadow of thy wings
　My soul in safety keeps;
I follow where my Father leads,
　And he supports my steps.

30　　*Psalm 84.*　　I. WATTS.

WELCOME, sweet day of rest,
　That saw the Lord arise!
Welcome to this reviving breast,
　And these rejoicing eyes!

2 The King himself comes near,
　And feasts his saints to-day;
Here may we sit and see him here,
　And love, and praise, and pray.

3 One day, amid the place
　Where my dear Lord hath been,
Is sweeter than ten thousand days
　Within the tents of sin.

4 My willing soul would stay
　In such a frame as this,
And sit and sing herself away
　To everlasting bliss.

GLORY. S. M.

RALPH HARRISON.

1. Come, we who love the Lord, And let our joys be known; Join

in a song with sweet ac - cord, And thus sur - round the throne.

31 *"Immanuel's ground."* I. WATTS.

COME, we who love the Lord,
 And let our joys be known;
Join in a song of sweet accord,
 And thus surround the throne.

2 Let those refuse to sing
 Who never knew our God;
But children of the heavenly King
 May speak their joys abroad.

3 The men of grace have found
 Glory begun below;
Celestial fruits on earthly ground
 From faith and hope may grow.

4 The hill of Zion yields
 A thousand sacred sweets
Before we reach the heavenly fields,
 Or walk the golden streets.

5 Then let our songs abound,
 And every tear be dry;
We're marching through Immanuel's ground
 To fairer worlds on high.

32 Rev. 15:3. W. HAMMOND.

AWAKE, and sing the song
 Of Moses and the Lamb;
Wake, every heart and every tongue
 To praise the Saviour's name.

2 Sing of his dying love;
 Sing of his rising power;
Sing, how he intercedes above
 For those whose sins he bore.

3 Ye pilgrims! on the road
 To Zion's city, sing!
Rejoice ye in the Lamb of God,—
 In Christ, the eternal King.

4 Soon shall we hear him say,—
 "Ye blessèd children! come;"
Soon will he call us hence away,
 And take his wanderers home.

5 There shall each raptured tongue
 His endless praise proclaim;
And sweeter voices tune the song
 Of Moses and the Lamb.

LISBON. S. M.

DANIEL READ.

1. Welcome, sweet day of rest, That saw the Lord a - rise. Welcome to this re - viving breast, And these rejoic - ing eyes.

PACKINGTON. S. M.   J. BLACK.

1. With joy we lift our eyes To those bright realms above, That glorious temple in the skies, Where dwells e-ternal Love.

33   *Hymn of praise.*   T. JERVIS.

WITH joy we lift our eyes
  To those bright realms above,
That glorious temple in the skies,
  Where dwells eternal Love.

2 Before thy throne we bow,
  O thou almighty King;
Here we present the solemn vow,
  And hymns of praise we sing.

3 While in thy house we kneel,
  With trust and holy fear,
Thy mercy and thy truth reveal,
  And lend a gracious ear.

4 Lord, teach our hearts to pray,
  And tune our lips to sing;
Nor from thy presence cast away
  The sacrifice we bring.

34   *Christian outlook.*   P. DODDRIDGE.

NOW LET our voices join
  To raise a sacred song;
Ye pilgrims! in Jehovah's ways,
  With music pass along.

2 See—flowers of paradise,
  In rich profusion, spring;
The sun of glory gilds the path,
  And dear companions sing.

3 See—Salem's golden spires,
  In beauteous prospect, rise;
And brighter crowns than mortals wear,
  Which sparkle through the skies.

4 All honor to his name,
  Who marks the shining way,—
To him who leads the pilgrims on
  To realms of endless day.

STATE STREET. S. M.   J. C. WOODMAN.

1. I love thy kingdom, Lord, The house of thine a-bode, The Church our blest Redeemer saved With his own precious blood.

35   *Psalm 137.*   T. DWIGHT.

I LOVE thy kingdom, Lord,
  The house of thine abode,
The Church our blest Redeemer saved
  With his own precious blood.

2 I love thy Church, O God!
  Her walls before thee stand,
Dear as the apple of thine eye,
  And graven on thine hand.

3 For her my tears shall fall,
  For her my prayers ascend;

To her my cares and toils be given,
  Till toils and cares shall end.

4 Beyond my highest joy
  I prize her heavenly ways,
Her sweet communion, solemn vows,
  Her hymns of love and praise.

5 Sure as thy truth shall last,
  To Zion shall be given
The brightest glories earth can yield,
  And brighter bliss of heaven.

EVENING PRAISE. P. M.   WM. F. SHERWIN.

1. Day is dy-ing in the West; Heav'n is touching earth with rest: Wait and worship while the night

CHORUS.

Sets her evening lamps alight Thro' all the sky.   Holy, holy, ho-ly, Lord God of Hosts!

Heav'n and earth are full of thee! Heav'n and earth are praising thee, O Lord most high!

36   "Day is dying."   M. A. LATHBURY.

DAY is dying in the West;
Heaven is touching earth with rest:
Wait and worship while the night
Sets her evening lamps alight
  Through all the sky.
Holy, holy, holy, Lord God of Hosts!
Heaven and earth are full of thee!
Heaven and earth are praising thee,
  O Lord most high!

2 Lord of life, beneath the dome
Of the Universe, thy home,
Gather us who seek thy face
To the fold of thy embrace,
  For thou art nigh.
Holy, holy, holy, Lord God of Hosts!
Heaven and earth are full of thee!
Heaven and earth are praising thee,
  O Lord most high!

SOLITUDE. 7s.   L. T. DOWNES.

1. Je - sus, Je-sus! vis-it me; How my soul longs after thee! When, my best, my dearest Friend! Shall our sepa - ra-tion end?

37   "Jesus, visit me."   R. P. DUNN, tr.

JESUS, Jesus! visit me;
How my soul longs after thee!
When, my best, my dearest Friend!
Shall our separation end?

2 Lord! my longings never cease;
Without thee I find no peace;
'Tis my constant cry to thee,—
Jesus, Jesus! visit me.

3 Mean the joys of earth appear,
All below is dark and drear;
Naught but thy beloved voice
Can my wretched heart rejoice.

4 Thou alone, my gracious Lord!
Art my shield and great reward;
All my hope, my Saviour thou,—
To thy sovereign will I bow.

ROLLAND. L. M.

W. B. BRADBURY.

1. How pleasant, how di - vine-ly fair,   O Lord of hosts! thy dwellings are! With long desire my

spir - it faints, To meet th' assemblies of thy saints, To meet th' assemblies of thy saints.

38   *Psalm 84.*   I. WATTS.

How PLEASANT, how divinely fair,
O Lord of hosts! thy dwellings are!
With long desire my spirit faints,
To meet the assemblies of thy saints.

2 My flesh would rest in thine abode,
My panting heart cries out for God;
My God! my King! why should I be
So far from all my joys, and thee?

3 Blest are the saints who sit on high,
Around thy throne of majesty;
Thy brightest glories shine above,
And all their work is praise and love.

4 Blest are the souls who find a place
Within the temple of thy grace;
There they behold thy gentler rays,
And seek thy face, and learn thy praise.

5 Cheerful they walk with growing strength,
Till all shall meet in heaven at length;
Till all before thy face appear,
And join in nobler worship there.

39   *Psalm 84.*   I. WATTS.

GREAT God! attend, while Zion sings
The joy that from thy presence springs;
To spend one day with thee on earth
Exceeds a thousand days of mirth.

2 Might I enjoy the meanest place
Within thy house, O God of grace!
Nor tents of ease, nor thrones of power,
Should tempt my feet to leave thy door.

3 God is our sun, he makes our day;
God is our shield, he guards our way
From all the assaults of hell and sin,
From foes without, and foes within.

4 All needful grace will God bestow,
And crown that grace with glory, too;
He gives us all things, and withholds
No real good from upright souls.

5 O God, our King, whose sovereign sway
The glorious hosts of heaven obey,
Display thy grace, exert thy power,
Till all on earth thy name adore!

40   *Morning Hymn.*   J. CHANDLER,   *tr.*

O CHRIST! with each returning morn
Thine image to our hearts be borne;
And may we ever clearly see
Our God and Saviour, Lord, in thee!

2 All hallowed be our walk this day;
May meekness form our early ray,
And faithful love our noontide light,
And hope our sunset, calm and bright.

3 May grace each idle thought control,
And sanctify our wayward soul;
May guile depart, and malice cease,
And all within be joy and peace.

4 Our daily course, O Jesus, bless;
Make plain the way of holiness:
From sudden falls our feet defend,
And cheer at last our journey's end.

MELCOMBE. L. M.   SAMUEL WEBBE.

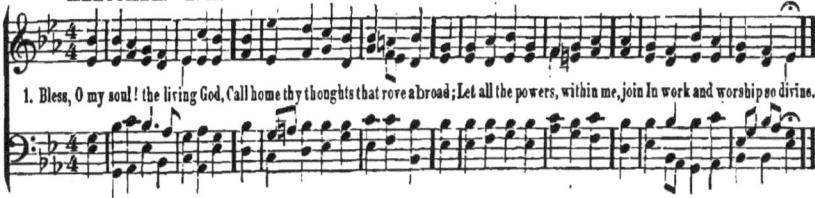

1. Bless, O my soul! the living God, Call home thy thoughts that rove abroad; Let all the powers, within me, join In work and worship so divine.

41   *Psalm 103.*   I. WATTS.

BLESS, O my soul! the living God,
Call home thy thoughts that rove abroad;
Let all the powers, within me, join
In work and worship so divine.

2 Bless, O my soul! the God of grace;
His favors claim thy highest praise:
Why should the wonders he hath wrought
Be lost in silence and forgot?

3 'Tis he, my soul! who sent his Son
To die for crimes which thou hast done:
He owns the ransom, and forgives
The hourly follies of our lives.

4 Let the whole earth his power confess,
Let the whole earth adore his grace;

The Gentile with the Jew shall join
In work and worship so divine.

42   *Psalm 135.*   I. WATTS.

PRAISE ye the Lord; exalt his name,
   While in his earthly courts ye wait,
Ye saints, that to his house belong,
   Or stand attending at his gate.

2 Praise ye the Lord, the Lord is good;
   To praise his name is sweet employ:
Israel he chose of old, and still
   His church is his peculiar joy.

3 Bless ye the Lord who taste his love,
   People and priests exalt his name;
Among his saints he ever dwells;
   His church is his Jerusalem.

MIGDOL. L. M.   LOWELL MASON.

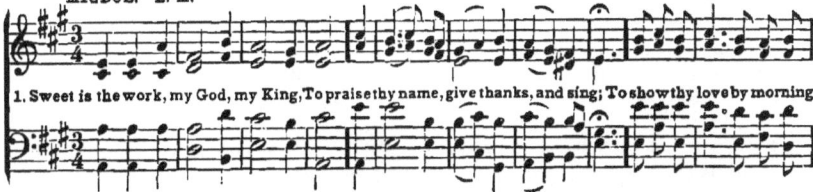

1. Sweet is the work, my God, my King, To praise thy name, give thanks, and sing; To show thy love by morning

light, And talk of all thy truth at night.

43   *Psalm 92.*   I. WATTS.

SWEET is the work, my God, my King,
To praise thy name, give thanks and sing;
To show thy love by morning light,
And talk of all thy truth at night.

2 Sweet is the day of sacred rest;
No mortal care shall seize my breast;

Oh, may my heart in tune be found,
Like David's harp of solemn sound!

3 My heart shall triumph in my Lord,
And bless his works and bless his word;
Thy works of grace, how bright they shine!
How deep thy counsels! how divine!

4 Lord, I shall share a glorious part,
When grace hath well refined my heart,
And fresh supplies of joy are shed,
Like holy oil to cheer my head.

5 Then shall I see, and hear, and know
All I desired or wished below;
And every power find sweet employ,
In that eternal world of joy.

AZMON. C. M.   LOWELL MASON, arr.

1. Come, let us join our cheerful songs With angels round the throne; Ten thousand thousand are their tongues, But all their joys are one.

44   *"Worthy the Lamb!"*   I. WATTS.

COME, let us join our cheerful songs
  With angels round the throne;
Ten thousand thousand are their tongues,
  But all their joys are one.

2 " Worthy the Lamb that died," they cry,
  "To be exalted thus!"
"Worthy the Lamb!" our lips reply,
  "For he was slain for us."

3 Jesus is worthy to receive
  Honor and power divine;
And blessings, more than we can give,
  Be, Lord, for ever thine!

4 Let all that dwell above the sky,
  And air, and earth, and seas,
Conspire to lift thy glories high,
  And speak thine endless praise.

5 The whole creation join in one,
  To bless the sacred name
Of him who sits upon the throne,
  And to adore the Lamb!

45   *Reconciliation.*   I. WATTS.

COME, let us lift our joyful eyes,
  Up to the courts above,
And smile to see our Father there,
  Upon a throne of love.

2 Now we may bow before his feet,
  And venture near the Lord:
No fiery cherub guards his seat,
  Nor double flaming sword.

3 The peaceful gates of heavenly bliss
  Are opened by the Son;
High let us raise our notes of praise,
  And reach the almighty throne.

4 To thee ten thousand thanks we bring,
  Great Advocate on high,
And glory to the eternal King,
  Who lays his anger by.

46   *Christ, our Priest.*   A. PIRRIE.

COME, let us join our songs of praise
  To our ascended Priest;
He entered heaven with all our names
  Engraven on his breast.

2 Below he washed our guilt away,
  By his atoning blood;
Now he appears before the throne,
  And pleads our cause with God.

3 Clothed with our nature still, he knows
  The weakness of our frame,
And how to shield us from the foes
  Which he himself o'ercame.

4 Nor time, nor distance, e'er shall quench
  The fervor of his love;
For us he died in kindness here,
  For us he lives above.

5 Oh! may we ne'er forget his grace,
  Nor blush to bear his name;
Still may our hearts hold fast his faith—
  Our lips his praise proclaim.

47   *"Crowned with honor."*   T. KELLY.

THE head that once was crowned with thorns,
  Is crowned with glory now;
A royal diadem adorns
  The mighty Victor's brow.

2 The highest place that heaven affords,
  Is his by sovereign right;
The King of kings, and Lord of lords,
  He reigns in glory bright;—

3 The joy of all who dwell above,
  The joy of all below,
To whom he manifests his love,
  And grants his name to know.

4 To them the cross with all its shame,
  With all its grace, is given;
Their name—an everlasting name,
  Their joy—the joy of heaven.

BOYLSTON. S. M.   LOWELL MASON,

1. Blest be the tie that binds Our hearts in Christian love: The fellow-ship of kindred minds Is like to that a - bove.

48   *"Christian Love."*   J. FAWCETT.

BLEST be the tie that binds
  Our hearts in Christian love:
The fellowship of kindred minds
  Is like to that above.

2 Before our Father's throne
  We pour our ardent prayers;
Our fears, our hopes, our aims are one,
  Our comforts and our cares.

3 We share our mutual woes,
  Our mutual burdens bear;
And often for each other flows
  The sympathizing tear.

4 When we asunder part,
  It gives us inward pain;
But we shall still be joined in heart,
  And hope to meet again.

5 This glorious hope revives
  Our courage by the way;
While each in expectation lives,
  And longs to see the day.

6 From sorrow, toil, and pain,
  And sin, we shall be free,
And perfect love and friendship reign
  Through all eternity.

WOOD. S. M.   D. E. JONES.

1. Je - sus, we look to thee, Thy promised presence claim; Then in the midst of us shalt be, As - sembled in thy name.

49   *Christ's Presence.*   C. WESLEY.

JESUS, we look to thee,
  Thy promised presence claim;
Thou in the midst of us shalt be,
  Assembled in thy name.

2 Not in the name of pride
  Or selfishness we meet;
From nature's paths we turn aside,
  And worldly thoughts forget.

3 We meet the grace to take,
  Which thou hast freely given;
We meet on earth for thy dear sake,
  That we may meet in heaven.

4 Present we know thou art,
  But, oh, thyself reveal!
Now, Lord, let every bounding heart
  Thy mighty comfort feel.

5 Oh, may thy quickening voice
  The death of sin remove;
And bid our inmost souls rejoice,
  In hope of perfect love.

50   *Christian Union.*   D. BEDDOME.

LET party names no more
  The Christian world o'erspread;
Gentile and Jew, and bond and free,
  Are one in Christ their head:

2 Among the saints on earth,
  Let mutual love be found;
Heirs of the same inheritance,
  With mutual blessings crowned.

3 Thus will the church below
  Resemble that above;
Where streams of pleasure ever flow,
  And every heart is love.

51 *Spiritual Songs*, p. 30. W. W. WALFORD.
SWEET hour of prayer! sweet hour of prayer!
That calls me from a world of care,
And bids me, at my Father's throne,
Make all my wants and wishes known:
In seasons of distress and grief,
My soul has often found relief,
And oft escaped the tempter's snare,
By thy return, sweet hour of prayer!
2 Sweet hour of prayer! sweet hour of prayer!
Thy wings shall my petition bear
To him whose truth and faithfulness
Engage the waiting soul to bless:
And, since he bids me seek his face,
Believe his word, and trust his grace,
I'll cast on him my every care,
And wait for thee, sweet hour of prayer!

52 *Spiritual Songs*, p. 225. ANON.
My life flows on in endless song;
Above earth's lamentation,
I catch the sweet, though far-off, hymn
That hails a new creation;
Through all the tumult and the strife,
I hear the music ringing;
It finds an echo in my soul—
How can I keep from singing?
2 What though my joys and comforts die?
The Lord my Saviour liveth;
What though the darkness gather round?
Songs in the night he giveth;
No storm can shake my inmost calm,
While to that refuge clinging;
Since Christ is Lord of heaven and earth,
How can I keep from singing?
3 I lift my eyes; the cloud grows thin;
I see the blue above it;
And day by day this pathway smooths,
Since first I learned to love it;
The peace of Christ makes fresh my heart,
A fountain ever springing;
All things are mine since I am his—
How can I keep from singing?

53 *Spiritual Songs*, p. 171. E. CODNER.
LORD, I hear of showers of blessing
Thou art scattering full and free;
Showers the thirsty soul refreshing;
Let some dropings fall on me!
REF.—Even me, even me—
Let thy blessing fall on me.

2 Pass me not, O gracious Father!
Lost and sinful though I be;
Thou might'st curse me, but the rather
Let thy mercy light on me.—REF.
3 Have I long in sin been sleeping,—
Long been slighting, grieving thee?
Has the world my heart been keeping?—
Oh, forgive and rescue me!—REF.
4 Pass me not, O mighty Spirit!
Thou canst make the blind to see;
Testify of Jesus' merit,
Speak the word of peace to me.—REF.

54 *Spiritual Songs*, p. 54. A. WARNER.
ONE more day's work for Jesus,
One less of life for me!
But heaven is nearer, And Christ is dearer,
Than yesterday, to me;
His love and light
Fill all my soul to-night.
REF.—One more day's work for Jesus,
One more day's work for Jesus,
One more day's work for Jesus,
One less of life for me.
2 One more day's work for Jesus!
How sweet the work has been,
To tell the story, To show the glory,
Where Christ's flock enter in!
How did it shine
In this poor heart of mine!—REF.
3 Oh, blesséd work for Jesus!
Oh, rest at Jesus' feet!
There toil seems pleasure, My wants are
And pain for him is sweet. [treasure,
Lord, if I may,
I'll serve another day!—REF.

55 *Spiritual Songs*, p. 265. E. MOTE.
My hope is built on nothing less
Than Jesus' blood and righteousness;
I dare not trust the sweetest frame,
But wholly lean on Jesus' name:
REF.—On Christ, the solid rock, I stand;
All other ground is sinking sand.
2 When darkness seems to vail his face,
I rest on his unchanging grace;
In every high and stormy gale,
My anchor holds within the vail:—REF.
3 His oath, his covenant, and blood,
Support me in the whelming flood:
When all around my soul gives way,
He then is all my hope and stay:—REF.

HORTON. 7s. XAVIER SCHNYDER VON WARTENSEE.

1. Earth has nothing sweet or fair, Lovely forms or beauties rare, But be-fore my eyes they bring Christ, of beauty Source and Spring

56 *"Altogether lovely."* F. E. COX, tr.
EARTH has nothing sweet or fair,
Lovely forms or beauties rare,
But before my eyes they bring
Christ, of beauty Source and Spring.

2 When the morning paints the skies,
When the golden sunbeams rise,
Then my Saviour's form I find
Brightly imaged on my mind.

3 When the star-beams pierce the night,
Oft I think on Jesus' light;
Think how bright that light will be,
Shining through eternity.

57 *"Who first loved us."* J. E. LEESON.
SAVIOUR! teach me, day by day,
Love's sweet lesson to obey;
Sweeter lesson cannot be,—
Loving him who first loved me.

2 With a childlike heart of love,
At thy bidding may I move;
Prompt to serve and follow thee,
Loving him who first loved me.

3 Teach me all thy steps to trace,
Strong to follow in thy grace;
Learning how to love from thee,
Loving him who first loved me.

58 *Hymn at Parting.* ANON.
THOU, from whom we never part,
Thou, whose love is everywhere,
Thou, who seest every heart,
Listen to our evening prayer.

2 Father, fill our hearts with love,
Love unfailing, full and free;
Love that no alarm can move,
Love that ever rests on thee.

3 Heavenly Father! through the night
Keep us safe from every ill;

Cheerful as the morning light,
May we wake to do thy will.

59 *Spiritual Songs*, p. 176. F. C. VAN ALSTYNE.
JESUS, keep me near the Cross,
There a precious fountain,
Free to all—a healing stream,
Flows from Calvary's mountain.
REF.—In the Cross, in the Cross,
Be my glory ever;
Till my raptured soul shall find
Rest beyond the river.

2 Near the Cross, a trembling soul,
Love and mercy found me:
There the bright and morning star
Shed its beams around me.—REF.

3 Near the Cross, O Lamb of God,
Bring its scenes before me;
Help me walk from day to day,
With its shadow o'er me.—REF.

60 *Spiritual Songs*, p. 170. F. C. VAN ALSTYNE.
PASS me not, O gentle Saviour,
Hear my humble cry;
While on others thou art smiling,
Do not pass me by.
REF.—
Saviour, Saviour, hear my humble cry!
While on others thou art calling,
Do not pass me by.

2 Let me at thy throne of mercy
Find a sweet relief;
Kneeling there in deep contrition,
Help my unbelief.—REF.

3 Trusting only in thy merit,
Would I seek thy face;
Heal my wounded, broken spirit,
Save me by thy grace.—REF.

DALLAS. 7s.   FROM M. L. CHERUBINI.

1. Come, my soul, thy suit pre-pare, Je-sus loves to an-swer prayer;

He him-self has bid thee pray, There-fore will not say thee nay.

61   *A Prayer in Need.*   J. NEWTON.

COME, my soul, thy suit prepare,
Jesus loves to answer prayer ;
He himself has bid thee pray,
Therefore will not say thee nay.

2 With my burden I begin:— .
Lord ! remove this load of sin;
Let thy blood, for sinners spilt,
Set my conscience free from guilt.

3 Lord ! I come to thee for rest;
Take possession of my breast:

There, thy blood-bought right maintain,
And, without a rival, reign.

4 While I am a pilgrim here,
Let thy love my spirit cheer;
As my Guide, my Guard, my Friend,
Lead me to my journey's end.

5 Show me what I have to do,
Every hour my strength renew;
Let me live a life of faith,
Let me die thy people's death.

DIJON. 7s.   GERMAN EVENING HYMN.

1. Lord! I can-not let thee go, Till a blessing thou bestow; Do not turn away thy face, Mine's an urgent, pressing case.

62   *The Case Argued.*   J. NEWTON.

LORD ! I cannot let thee go,
Till a blessing thou bestow;
Do not turn away thy face,
Mine's an urgent, pressing case.

2 Once a sinner, near despair,
Sought thy mercy-seat by prayer;
Mercy heard and set him free—
Lord ! that mercy came to me.

3 Many days have passed since then,
Many changes I have seen;

Yet have been upheld till now;
Who could hold me up but thou?

4 Thou hast helped in every need—
This emboldens me to plead;
After so much mercy past,
Canst thou let me sink at last?

5 No—I must maintain my hold;
'Tis thy goodness makes me bold;
I can no denial take,
Since I plead for Jesus' sake.

DIX. 7s. 6l.   WILLIAM HENRY MONK, *arr.*

1. { As with gladness men of old Did the guiding star behold;
As with joy they hailed its light, Leading onward, beaming bright; } So, most gracious Lord, may we Evermore be led to thee.

63   *The Guiding Star.*   W. C. DIX.

As WITH gladness men of old
Did the guiding star behold,
As with joy they hailed its light,
Leading onward, beaming bright;
So, most gracious Lord, may we
Evermore be led to thee.

2 As with joyful steps they sped,
Saviour, to thy manger bed,
There to bend the knee before
Thee whom heaven and earth adore;
So may we with willing feet
Ever seek the mercy-seat.

3 As they offered gifts most rare
At thy cradle rude and bare,
So may we with holy joy,
Pure and free from sin's alloy,
All our costliest treasures bring,
Christ, to thee our heavenly King.

4 Holy Jesus, every day
Keep us in the narrow way;
And, when earthly things are past,
Bring our ransomed souls at last
Where they need no star to guide,
Where no clouds thy glory hide.

HEROLD. 7s.   A. J. F. HEROLD

1. They who seek the throne of grace Find that throne in ev - ery place;
If we live a life of prayer, God is pres - ent ev - ery - where.

64   *God everywhere.*   ANON.

THEY who seek the throne of grace
Find that throne in every place;
If we live a life of prayer,
God is present everywhere.

2 In our sickness and our health,
In our want, or in our wealth,
If we look to God in prayer,
God is present everywhere.

3 When our earthly comforts fail,
When the foes of life prevail,
'Tis the time for earnest prayer;
God is present everywhere.

4 Then, my soul, in every strait,
To thy Father come, and wait;
He will answer every prayer:
God is present everywhere.

WOODSTOCK. C. M.   D. DUTTON.

1. I love to steal a - while a - way From ev - ery cum - bering care,

And spend the hours of set - ting day In hum - ble, grate - ful prayer.

65 *Retirement.* P. H. BROWN.

I LOVE to steal awhile away
From every cumbering care,
And spend the hours of setting day
In humble, grateful prayer.

2 I love in solitude to shed
The penitential tear,
And all his promises to plead,
Where none but God can hear.

3 I love to think on mercies past,
And future good implore,

And all my cares and sorrows cast
On him whom I adore.

4 I love by faith to take a view
Of brighter scenes in heaven;
The prospect doth my strength renew,
While here by tempests driven.

5 Thus, when life's toilsome day is o'er,
May its departing ray
Be calm as this impressive hour,
And lead to endless day.

SOUTHPORT. C. M.   GEORGE KINGSLEY.

1. Hail, tranquil hour of closing day! Begone, disturbing care! And look, my soul, from earth away, To him who heareth prayer.

66 *"Tranquil hour."* L. BACON.

HAIL, tranquil hour of closing day!
Begone, disturbing care!
And look, my soul, from earth away,
To him who heareth prayer.

2 How sweet the tear of penitence,
Before his throne of grace,
While, to the contrite spirit's sense,
He shows his smiling face.

3 How sweet, thro' long remembered years,
His mercies to recall;

And, pressed with wants, and griefs, and
To trust his love for all.   [fears,

4 How sweet to look, in thoughtful hope,
Beyond this fading sky,
And hear him call his children up
To his fair home on high.

5 Calmly the day forsakes our heaven
To dawn beyond the west;
So let my soul, in life's last even,
Retire to glorious rest.

BYEFIELD. C. M.   THOS. HASTINGS.

1. Prayer is the soul's sincere desire. Ut-tered or un-expressed; The motion of a hidden fire That trembles in the breast.

67 *What prayer is.* J. MONTGOMERY.

PRAYER is the soul's sincere desire,
  Uttered or unexpressed;
The motion of a hidden fire
  That trembles in the breast.

2 Prayer is the burden of a sigh,
  The falling of a tear,
The upward glancing of an eye,
  When none but God is near.

3 Prayer is the simplest form of speech
  That infant lips can try;
Prayer the sublimest strains that reach
  The Majesty on high.

4 Prayer is the Christian's vital breath,
  The Christian's native air:
His watchword at the gates of death—
  He enters heaven with prayer.

5 Prayer is the contrite sinner's voice,
  Returning from his ways;
While angels in their songs rejoice,
  And cry—"Behold he prays!"

6 O thou, by whom we come to God—
  The Life, the Truth, the Way;
The path of prayer thyself hast trod;
  Lord! teach us how to pray.

68 *"The sacred fire."* B. BEDDOME.

PRAYER is the breath of God in man,
  Returning whence it came;
Love is the sacred fire within,
  And prayer the rising flame.

2 It gives the burdened spirit ease,
  And soothes the troubled breast;
Yields comfort to the mourning soul,
  And to the weary rest.

3 When God inclines the heart to pray,
  He hath an ear to hear;
To him there's music in a sigh,
  And beauty in a tear.

4 The humble suppliant cannot fail
  To have his wants supplied,
Since He for sinners intercedes,
  Who once for sinners died.

COLCHESTER. C. M.   H. PURCELL.

1. Prayer is   the breath of   God   in   man,   Re - turn - ing whence it   came;

Love is   the   sa - cred fire   with - in,   And   prayer the   ris - ing flame.

69 THE LORD'S PRAYER.

LOWELL MASON.

Our Father who art in heaven, hallow-ed be thy name; thy kingdom come: thy will be

done on earth as it is in heaven. Give us this day our dai-ly bread: and for-give us our

tres-passes, as we for-give them that tres-pass a-gainst us. And lead us not

in-to temp-ta-tion, but de-liv-er us from e-vil; for thine is the

kingdom, and the pow-er, and the glo-ry: for-ev-er and ev-er. A-men.

LANGTON. S. M.   C. STREETFIELD, arr.

1. Jesus, who knows full well The heart of every saint, Invites us all our grief to tell, To pray and never faint.

70 *Importunity.*   J. NEWTON.

JESUS, who knows full well
  The heart of every saint,
Invites us all our grief to tell,
  To pray and never faint.

2 He bows his gracious ear,—
  We never plead in vain ;
Then let us wait till he appear,
  And pray, and pray again.

3 Jesus, the Lord, will hear
  His chosen when they cry;
Yes, though he may a while forbear,
  He'll help them from on high.

4 Then let us earnest cry,
  And never faint in prayer;
He sees, he hears, and, from on high,
  Will make our cause his care.

SHIRLAND. S. M.   S. STANLEY.

1. Our heavenly Father calls, And Christ invites us near; With both, our friendship shall be sweet, And our communion dear.

71 *"God pities."*   P. DODDRIDGE.

OUR heavenly Father calls.
  And Christ invites us near;
With both, our friendship shall be sweet,
  And our communion dear.

2 God pities all our griefs:
  He pardons every day;
Almighty to protect our souls,
  And wise to guide our way.

3 How large his bounties are !
  What various stores of good,
Diffused from our Redeemer's hand,
  And purchased with his blood !

4 Jesus, our living Head,
  We bless thy faithful care;
Our Advocate before the throne,
  And our Forerunner there.

5 Here fix, my roving heart !
  Here wait, my warmest love !
Till the communion be complete,
  In nobler scenes above.

  3

72 *"The throne of grace."*   J. NEWTON.

BEHOLD the throne of grace !
  The promise calls me near;
There Jesus shows a smiling face,
  And waits to answer prayer.

2 That rich atoning blood,
  Which sprinkled round I see,
Provides for those who come to God
  An all-prevailing plea.

3 My soul ! ask what thou wilt;
  Thou canst not be too bold:
Since his own blood for thee he spilt,
  What else can he withhold ?

4 Thine image, Lord, bestow,
  Thy presence and thy love;
I ask to serve thee here below,
  And reign with thee above.

5 Teach me to live by faith;
  Conform my will to thine:
Let me victorious be in death,
  And then in glory shine.

RETREAT. L. M.   THOS. HASTINGS.

1. From every stormy wind that blows, From every swelling tide of woes, There is a calm, a

sure retreat, 'T is found beneath the mercy-seat.

73   *The mercy-seat.*   H. STOWELL.

FROM every stormy wind that blows,
From every swelling tide of woes,
There is a calm, a sure retreat;
'T is found beneath the mercy-seat.

2 There is a place where Jesus sheds
The oil of gladness on our heads,—

A place than all besides more sweet;
It is the blood-bought mercy-seat.

3 There is a scene where spirits blend,
Where friend holds fellowship with friend;
Though sundered far, by faith they meet
Around one common mercy-seat.

4 There, there, on eagle wings we soar,
And sense and sin molest no more,
And heaven comes down our souls to greet,
And glory crowns the mercy-seat.

5 Oh, let my hand forget her skill,
My tongue be silent, cold, and still,
This throbbing heart forget to beat,
If I forget the mercy-seat.

LINWOOD. L. M.   GIOACCHIMO ROSSINI.

1. Je - sus, where'er thy peo - ple meet, There they be - hold thy mer - cy - seat;

Where'er they seek thee thou art found, And ev - ery place is hal - lowed ground.

74   *The mercy-seat.*   W. COWPER.

JESUS, where'er thy people meet,
There they behold thy mercy-seat;
Where'er they seek thee thou art found,
And every place is hallowed ground.

2 For thou, within no walls confined,
Inhabitest the humble mind;
Such ever bring thee where they come,
And going, take thee to their home.

3 Great Shepherd of thy chosen few,
Thy former mercies here renew;
Here to our waiting hearts proclaim
The sweetness of thy saving name.

4 Here may we prove the power of prayer,
To strengthen faith and sweeten care,
To teach our faint desires to rise,
And bring all heaven before our eyes.

OBERLIN. L. M.　　　　　　　　THOS. HASTINGS, arr.

1. Where high the heavenly tem-ple stands, The house of God not made with hands,

A great High Priest our na-ture wears,—The Guardian of man-kind ap-pears.

75 *"The evil hour."* M. BRUCE.

WHERE high the heavenly temple stands,
The house of God not made with hands,
A great High Priest our nature wears,—
The Guardian of mankind appears.

2 Though now ascended up on high,
He bends on earth a brother's eye;
Partaker of the human name,
He knows the frailty of our frame.

3 Our Fellow-sufferer yet retains
A fellow-feeling of our pains;
And still remembers, in the skies,
His tears, his agonies, and cries.

4 In every pang that rends the heart,
The Man of Sorrows had a part;
He sympathizes with our grief,
And to the sufferer sends relief.

5 With boldness, therefore, at the throne,
Let us make all our sorrows known;
And ask the aid of heavenly power,
To help us in the evil hour.

76 *"What thou wilt."* J. NEWTON.

AND dost thou say, "Ask what thou wilt?"
Lord, I would seize the golden hour:
I pray to be released from guilt,
And freed from sin and Satan's power.

2 More of thy presence, Lord, impart;
More of thine image let me bear:
Erect thy throne within my heart,
And reign without a rival there.

3 Give me to read my pardon sealed,
And from thy joy to draw my strength:
Oh, be thy boundless love revealed
In all its height and breadth and length.

4 Grant these requests—I ask no more,
But to thy care the rest resign:
Sick, or in health, or rich, or poor,
All shall be well, if thou art mine.

77 *Prayers hindered.* W. COWPER.

WHAT various hindrances we meet
In coming to a mercy-seat!
Yet who that knows the worth of prayer
But wishes to be often there?

2 Prayer makes the darkened cloud with-
draw;
Prayer climbs the ladder Jacob saw,
Gives exercise to faith and love,
Brings every blessing from above.

3 Restraining prayer, we cease to fight;
Prayer makes the Christian's armor bright;
And Satan trembles when he sees
The weakest saint upon his knees.

4 Have you no words? ah! think again;
Words flow apace when you complain,
And fill a fellow-creature's ear
With the sad tale of all your care.

5 Were half the breath thus vainly spent
To heaven in supplication sent,
Our cheerful song would oftener be,
"Hear what the Lord hath done for me!"

OLD HUNDRED. L. M.   GUILLAUME FRANC.

1. Be - fore Je - ho - vah's aw - ful throne, Ye na - tions! bow with sa - cred joy:

Know that the Lord is God a - lone: He can cre - ate, and he de - stroy.

78   *Psalm 100.*   I. WATTS.

BEFORE Jehovah's awful throne,
  Ye nations! bow with sacred joy:
Know that the Lord is God alone:
  He can create, and he destroy.

2 His sovereign power, without our aid,
  Made us of clay, and formed us men;
And when, like wandering sheep, we strayed,
  He brought us to his fold again.

3 We are his people, we his care,—
  Our souls, and all our mortal frame:
What lasting honors shall we rear,
  Almighty Maker! to thy name?

4 We'll crowd thy gates with thankful songs,
  High as the heavens our voices raise;
And earth, with her ten thousand tongues,
  Shall fill thy courts with sounding praise.

5 Wide as the world is thy command,
  Vast as eternity, thy love;
Firm as a rock thy truth must stand,
  When rolling years shall cease to move.

79   *Psalm 100.*   W. KETHE.

ALL people that on earth do dwell,
  Sing to the Lord with cheerful voice:
Him serve with mirth, his praise forth tell,
  Come ye before him and rejoice.

2 Know that the Lord is God indeed;
  Without our aid he did us make:
We are his flock, he doth us feed,
  And for his sheep he doth us take.

3 Oh, enter then his gates with praise,
  Approach with joy his courts unto:
Praise, laud, and bless his name always,
  For it is seemly so to do.

4 For why? the Lord our God is good,
  His mercy is for ever sure;
His truth at all times firmly stood,
  And shall from age to age endure.

80   *Doxology.*   T. KEN.

PRAISE God, from whom all blessing flow,
Praise him, all creatures here below;
Praise him above, ye heavenly host;
Praise Father, Son, and Holy Ghost.

81   *Doxology.*   I. WATTS.

To GOD the Father, God the Son,
And God the Spirit, Three in One.
Be honor, praise, and glory given,
By all on earth, and all in heaven

82   *Psalm 117.*   I. WATTS.

FROM all that dwell below the skies,
Let the Creator's praise arise:
Let the Redeemer's name be sung,
Through every land, by every tongue.

2 Eternal are thy mercies, Lord!
Eternal truth attends thy word:
Thy praise shall sound from shore to shore,
Till suns shall rise and set no more.

WARE. L. M.   GEO. KINGSLEY.

1. Now to the Lord a no-ble song! A-wake, my soul! a-wake my tongue!,

Ho-san-na to th'e-ter-nal name, And all his boundless love pro-claim.

83   *God's grace.*   I. WATTS.

Now to the Lord a noble song!
Awake, my soul! awake, my tongue!
Hosanna to the eternal name,
And all his boundless love proclaim.

2 See where it shines in Jesus' face,—
The brightest image of his grace!
God, in the person of his Son,
Hath all his mightiest works outdone.

3 Grace!—'tis a sweet, a charming theme:
My thoughts rejoice at Jesus' name:
Ye angels! dwell upon the sound:
Ye heavens! reflect it to the ground.

4 Oh, may I reach that happy place,
Where he unvails his lovely face,
Where all his beauties you behold,
And sing his name to harps of gold.

84   *Psalm 36.*   I. WATTS.

High in the heavens, eternal God!
Thy goodness in full glory shines;
Thy truth shall break through every cloud
That vails and darkens thy designs.

2 For ever firm thy justice stands,
As mountains their foundations keep:
Wise are the wonders of thy hands,
Thy judgments are a mighty deep.

3 My God, how excellent thy grace!
Whence all our hope and comfort springs;
The sons of Adam, in distress,
Fly to the shadow of thy wings.

4 From the provisions of thy house
We shall be fed with sweet repast;
There, mercy like a river flows,
And brings salvation to our taste.

5 Life, like a fountain rich and free,
Springs from the presence of my Lord;
And in thy light our souls shall see
The glories promised in thy word.

85   *"Te Deum."*   T. COTTERILL, alt.

Lord God of Hosts, by all adored!
Thy name we praise with one accord;
The earth and heavens are full of thee,
Thy light, thy love, thy majesty.

2 Loud hallelujahs to thy name
Angels and seraphim proclaim;
Eternal praise to thee is given
By all the powers and thrones in heaven.

3 The apostles join the glorious throng,
The prophets aid to swell the song,
The noble and triumphant host
Of martyrs make of thee their boast.

4 The holy church in every place
Throughout the world exalts thy praise;
Both heaven and earth do worship thee,
Thou Father of eternity!

5 From day to day, O Lord, do we
Highly exalt and honor thee;
Thy name we worship and adore,
World without end for evermore.

1. Holy Father, hear my cry; Holy Saviour, bend thine ear; Holy Spirit, come thou nigh: Father, Saviour, Spirit, hear!

Father, save me from my sin; Saviour, I thy mer-cy crave; Gracious Spirit, make me clean: Father, Son, and Spirit, save!

86   *The Trinity.*   H. BONAR.

HOLY, Father, hear my cry;
  Holy Saviour, bend thine ear;
Holy Spirit, come thou nigh:
  Father, Saviour, Spirit, hear!
Father, save me from my sin;
  Saviour, I thy mercy crave;
Gracious Spirit, make me clean:
  Father, Son, and Spirit, save!

2 Father, let me taste thy love;
  Saviour, fill my soul with peace;
Spirit, come my heart to move:
  Father, Son, and Spirit, bless!
Father, Son, and Spirit—thou
  One Jehovah, shed abroad
All thy grace within me now;
  Be my Father and my God!

87   *"Holy, holy, holy."*   J. MONTGOMERY.

HOLY, holy, holy Lord
  God of Hosts! when heaven and earth,
Out of darkness, at thy word
  Issued into glorious birth,
All thy works before thee stood,
And thine eye beheld them good,
While they sung with sweet accord,
Holy, holy, holy Lord!

2 Holy, holy, holy! thee,
  One Jehovah evermore,
Father, Son, and Spirit! we,
  Dust and ashes, would adore:

Lightly by the world esteemed,
From that world by thee redeemed,
Sing we here with glad accord,
Holy, holy, holy Lord!

3 Holy, holy, holy! all
  Heaven's triumphant choir shall sing,
While the ransomed nations fall
  At the footstool of their King:
Then shall saints and seraphim,
Harps and voices, swell one hymn,
Blending in sublime accord,
Holy, holy, holy Lord!

88   *Divine Presence.*   R. GRANT.

LORD of earth! thy forming hand
Well this beauteous frame hath planned;
Woods that wave, and hills that tower,
Ocean rolling in his power:
Yet, amid this scene so fair,
Should I cease thy smile to share,
What were all its joys to me?
Whom have I on earth but thee?

2 Lord of heaven! beyond our sight
Shines a world of purer light;
There in love's unclouded reign
Parted hands shall meet again:
Oh, that world is passing fair!
Yet, if thou wert absent there,
What were all its joys to me?
Whom have I in heaven but thee?

LAUD. C. M.   JOHN B. DYKES.

1. O God! we praise thee, and con-fess That thou the on-ly Lord

And ev-er-last-ing Fa-ther art, By all the earth a-dored.

89   "Te Deum."   TATE—BRADY.

O God! we praise thee, and confess
That thou the only Lord
And everlasting Father art,
By all the earth adored.

2 To thee all angels cry aloud;
To thee the powers on high,
Both cherubim and seraphim,
Continually do cry:—

3 O holy, holy, holy Lord,
Whom heavenly hosts obey,
The world is with the glory filled
Of thy majestic sway!

4 The apostles' glorious company,
And prophets crowned with light,
With all the martyrs' noble host,
Thy constant praise recite.

5 The holy church throughout the world,
O Lord, confesses thee,
That thou the eternal Father art,
Of boundless majesty.

90   Eternity.   I. WATTS.

Great God! how infinite art thou!
What worthless worms are we!
Let the whole race of creatures bow,
And pay their praise to thee.

2 Thy throne eternal ages stood,
Ere seas or stars were made;
Thou art the ever-living God,
Were all the nations dead.

3 Eternity, with all its years,
Stands present in thy view;
To thee there's nothing old appears—
Great God! there's nothing new.

4 Our lives through various scenes are drawn,
And vexed with trifling cares;
While thine eternal thought moves on
Thine undisturbed affairs.

5 Great God! how infinite art thou!
What worthless worms are we!
Let the whole race of creatures bow,
And pay their praise to thee.

DUNDEE. C. M.   GUILLAUME FRANC.

1. Great God! how in-fi-nite art thou! What worthless worms are we! Let the whole race of creatures bow, And pay their praise to thee.

AUTOMN. 8s, 7s. D.   SPANISH; FROM MARECHIO.

1. Mighty God! while angels bless thee, May a mortal lisp thy name? Lord of men, as well as an-gels!
D. 8.—Sounded thro' the wide crea-tion,

FINE.   D. 8.

Thou art every creature's theme: Lord of ev - 'ry land and nation! Ancient of e-ternal days!
Be thy just and awful praise.

91   *Christ is God.*   R. ROBINSON.

Mighty God! while angels bless thee,
  May a mortal lisp thy name?
Lord of men, as well as angels!
  Thou art every creature's theme:
Lord of every land and nation!
  Ancient of eternal days!
Sounded through the wide creation
  Be thy just and awful praise.

2 For the grandeur of thy nature,—
  Grand, beyond a seraph's thought;
For the wonders of creation,
  Works with skill and kindness wrought;
For thy providence, that governs
  Through thine empire's wide domain,
Wings an angel, guides a sparrow;
  Blesséd be thy gentle reign.

3 For thy rich, thy free redemption,
  Bright, though vailed in darkness long,
Thought is poor, and poor expression;
  Who can sing that wondrous song?
Brightness of the Father's glory!
  Shall thy praise unuttered lie?
Break, my tongue! such guilty silence,
  Sing the Lord who came to die:—

4 From the highest throne of glory,
  To the cross of deepest woe,
Came to ransom guilty captives!—
  Flow, my praise! for ever flow:

Re-ascend, immortal Saviour!
  Leave thy footstool, take thy throne;
Thence return and reign for ever;—
  Be the kingdom all thine own!

92   *"Lo, Jehovah!"*   W. GOODE.

Crown his head with endless blessing,
  Who, in God the Father's name,
With compassions never ceasing,
  Comes salvation to proclaim.
Hail, ye saints, who know his favor,
  Who within his gates are found;
Hail, ye saints, the exalted Saviour,
  Let his courts with praise resound.

2 Lo, Jehovah, we adore thee;
  Thee our Saviour! thee our God!
From his throne his beams of glory
  Shine through all the world abroad.
In his word his light arises,
  Brightest beams of truth and grace;
Bind, oh, bind your sacrifices,
  In his courts your offerings place.

3 Jesus, thee our Saviour hailing,
  Thee our God in praise we own;
Highest honors, never failing,
  Rise eternal round thy throne;
Now, ye saints, his power confessing,
  In your grateful strains adore;
For his mercy, never ceasing,
  Flows, and flows for evermore.

SILVER STREET. S. M.   I. SMITH.

1. Come, sound his praise a-broad, And hymns of glo-ry sing:

Je-ho-vah is the sov-'reign God, The u-ni-ver-sal King.

93   *Psalm 95.*   I. WATTS.

Come, sound his praise abroad,
  And hymns of glory sing:
Jehovah is the sovereign God,
  The universal King.

2 He formed the deeps unknown;
  He gave the seas their bound;
The watery worlds are all his own,
  And all the solid ground.

3 Come, worship at his throne,
  Come, bow before the Lord:
We are his work, and not our own,
  He formed us by his word.

4 To-day attend his voice,
  Nor dare provoke his rod;
Come, like the people of his choice,
  And own our gracious God.

94   *Psalm 81.*   H. F. LYTE.

Sing to the Lord, our Might,
  With holy fervor sing;
Let hearts and instruments unite
  To praise our heavenly King.

2 The Sabbath to our sires
  In mercy first was given;
The Church her Sabbaths still requires
  To speed her on to heaven.

3 We still, like them of old,
  Are in the wilderness;
And God is still as near his fold,
  To pity and to bless.

4 Then let us open wide
  Our hearts for him to fill;
And he, that Israel then supplied,
  Will help his Israel still.

BARBER. S. M.   JOHANN C. W. A. MOZART.

1. Sing to the Lord, our Might, With ho-ly fer-vor sing:

Let hearts and in-stru-ments u-nite To praise our heavenly King.

CORONATION. C. M.

OLIVER HOLDEN.

1. All hail the power of Jesus' name! Let angels prostrate fall! Bring forth the royal di-a-dem, And

crown him Lord of all; Bring forth the royal di-a-dem, And crown him Lord of all.

95   *"Lord of all."*   E. PERRONET.

ALL hail the power of Jesus' name !
  Let angels prostrate fall;
Bring forth the royal diadem,
  And crown him Lord of all.

2 Crown him, ye martyrs of our God,
  Who from his altar call;
Extol the stem of Jesse's rod,
  And crown him Lord of all.

3 Ye chosen seed of Israel's race,
  Ye ransomed from the fall;
Hail him, who saves you by his grace,
  And crown him Lord of all.

4 Sinners, whose love can ne'er forget
  The wormwood and the gall;
Go, spread your trophies at his feet,
  And crown him Lord of all.

5 Let every kindred, every tribe,
  On this terrestrial ball,
To him all majesty ascribe,
  And crown him Lord of all.

6 Oh, that with yonder sacred throng,
  We at his feet may fall;
We'll join the everlasting song,
  And crown him Lord of all.

MILES LANE. C. M.

W. SHRUBSOLE.

1. All hail the power of Je-sus' name! Let an-gels prostrate fall; Bring forth the royal

di-a-dem, And crown him, crown him, crown him, crown him Lord of all.

PORTUGUESE HYMN. L. M.　　J. READING.

1. O Christ, the Lord of heaven! to thee, Clothed with all ma-jes-ty di - vine, E - ternal power and glo - ry be! E - ter - nal praise, of right, is thine, E - ter - nal praise, of right, is thine.

96 *"Lord of heaven."*　RAY PALMER.

O CHRIST, the Lord of heaven! to thee,
Clothed with all majesty divine,
Eternal power and glory be!
　Eternal praise, of right, is thine.

2 Reign, Prince of life! that once thy brow
Didst yield to wear the wounding thorn;
Reign, throned beside the Father now,
　Adored the Son of God first-born.

3 From angel hosts that round thee stand,
With forms more pure than spotless snow,
From the bright burning seraph band,
　Let praise in loftiest numbers flow.

4 To thee, the Lamb, our mortal songs,
Born of deep fervent love, shall rise;
All honor to thy name belongs,
　Our lips would sound it to the skies.

5 "Jesus!"—all earth shall speak the word;
"Jesus!"—all heaven resound it still;
Immanuel, Saviour, Conqueror, Lord!
　Thy praise the universe shall fill.

97　*Psalm 45.*　I. WATTS.

Now BE my heart inspired to sing
The glories of my Saviour King,—
Jesus the Lord; how heavenly fair
His form! how bright his beauties are!

2 O'er all the sons of human race,
He shines with a superior grace:
Love from his lips divinely flows,
And blessings all his state compose.

3 Thy throne, O God, for ever stands;
Grace is the sceptre in thy hands;
Thy laws and works are just and right;
Justice and grace are thy delight.

4 God, thine own God, has richly shed
His oil of gladness on thy head;
And with his Sacred Spirit blessed
His first-born Son above the rest.

98　*"King, Creator, Lord."*　RAY PALMER, *tr.*

O CHRIST! our King, Creator, Lord!
Saviour of all who trust thy word!
To them who seek thee ever near,
Now to our praises bend thine ear.

2 In thy dear cross a grace is found,—
It flows from every streaming wound,—
Whose power our inbred sin controls,
Breaks the firm bond, and frees our souls.

3 Thou didst create the stars of night;
Yet thou hast vailed in flesh thy light,
Hast deigned a mortal form to wear
A mortal's painful lot to bear.

4 When thou didst hang upon the tree,
The quaking earth acknowledged thee;
When thou didst there yield up thy breath,
The world grew dark as shades of death

5 Now in the Father's glory high,
Great Conqueror! never more to die,
Us by thy mighty power defend,
And reign through ages without end.

LUTZEN. C. M.   NICHOLAUS HERMANN.

1. The Lord, our God, is full of might, The winds o-bey his will; He speaks,-and, in his heavenly height, The rolling sun stands still.

99   *Power.*   H. K. WHITE.

THE Lord, our God, is full of might,
  The winds obey his will;
He speaks,—and, in his heavenly height,
  The rolling sun stands still.

2 Rebel, ye waves, and o'er the land
  With threatning aspect roar;
The Lord uplifts his awful hand,
  And chains you to the shore.

3 Howl, winds of night, your force combine;
  Without his high behest,
Ye shall not, in the mountain pine,
  Disturb the sparrow's nest.

4 His voice sublime is heard afar,
  In distant peals it dies;
He yokes the whirlwind to his car,
  And sweeps the howling skies.

5 Ye nations, bend—in reverence bend;
  Ye monarchs, wait his nod,
And bid the choral song ascend
  To celebrate your God.

100   *Providence.*   I. WATTS.

KEEP silence, all created things!
  And wait your Maker's nod;
My soul stands trembling, while she sings
  The honors of her God.

2 Life, death, and hell, and worlds unknown,
  Hang on his firm decree;
He sits on no precarious throne,
  Nor borrows leave to be.

3 His providence unfolds the book,
  And makes his counsels shine;
Each opening leaf, and every stroke,
  Fulfills some deep design.

4 My God! I would not long to see
  My fate, with curious eyes—
What gloomy lines are writ for me,
  Or what bright scenes may rise.

5 In thy fair book of life and grace,
  Oh, may I find my name
Recorded in some humble place,
  Beneath my Lord, the Lamb.

ST. ANN'S. C. M.   WM. CROFT.

1. The Lord, our God, is full of might, The winds o - bey his will;

He speaks,—and, in his heaven-ly height, The roll - ing sun stands still.

ONIDO. 7s, D.

LOWELL MASON, arr.

1. God e-ter-nal, Lord of all! Lowly at thy feet we fall: All the world doth worship thee;

We a-midst the throng would be. All the ho-ly an-gels cry, Hail, thrice-ho-ly,

God most high! Lord of all the heavenly pow'rs, Be the same loud anthem ours.

101   *"Te Deum."*   J. E. MILLARD, *tr.*

God eternal, Lord of all!
Lowly at thy feet we fall:
All the world doth worship thee;
We amidst the throng would be.
All the holy angels cry,
Hail, thrice-holy, God most high!
Lord of all the heavenly powers,
Be the same loud anthem ours.

2 Glorified apostles raise,
Night and day, continual praise;
Hast thou not a mission too
For thy children here to do?
With the prophets' goodly line
We in mystic bond combine;
For thou hast to babes revealed
Things that to the wise were sealed.

3 Martyrs, in a noble host,
Of thy cross are heard to boast;
Since so bright the crown they wear,
We with them thy cross would bear.
All thy church, in heaven and earth,
Jesus! hail thy spotless birth;—
Seated on the judgment-throne,
Number us among thine own!

102   *"In Excelsis."*   C. WESLEY.

Glory be to God on high,—
God, whose glory fills the sky;
Peace on earth to man forgiven,—
Man, the well-beloved of heaven.
Sovereign Father, Heavenly King!
Thee we now presume to sing;
Glad thine attributes confess,
Glorious all, and numberless.

2 Hail, by all thy works adored!
Hail, the everlasting Lord!
Thee with thankful hearts we prove,—
God of power, and God of love!
Christ our Lord and God we own,—
Christ the Father's only Son;
Lamb of God, for sinners slain,
Saviour of offending man.

3 Jesus! in thy name we pray,
Take, oh, take our sins away!
Powerful Advocate with God!
Justify us by thy blood.
Hear, for thou, O Christ! alone,
Art with thy great Father one;
One the Holy Ghost with thee;—
One supreme eternal Three.

LYONS. 10s, 11s. FRANCIS JOSEPH HAYDN.

FINE. D. S.

1. Ye servants of God, your Master proclaim, And publish abroad his won-der-ful name; The name all-vic-torious of Jesus ex-tol;
D. S.—His kingdom is glorious, he rules over all.

103 *"Salvation to God."* C. WESLEY.

YE servants of God, your Master proclaim,
And publish abroad his wonderful name;
The name all-victorious of Jesus extol;
His kingdom is glorious, he rules over all.

2 God ruleth on high, almighty to save;
And still he is nigh——his presence we have;
The great congregation his triumph shall sing,
Ascribing salvation to Jesus our King.

3 Salvation to God, who sits on the throne,
Let all cry aloud and honor the Son;
The praises of Jesus the angels proclaim,
Fall down on their faces and worship the
Lamb.

104 *"Worship the King."* R. GRANT.

OH, worship the King, all-glorious above,
And gratefully sing his wonderful love;
Our Shield and Defender, the Ancient of days,
Pavilioned in splendor, and girded with praise.

2 Thy bountiful care what tongue can recite?
It breathes in the air, it shines in the light,
It streams from the hills, it descends to the
plain.
And sweetly distils in the dew and the rain.

3 Frail children of dust, and feeble as frail,
In thee do we trust, nor find thee to fail;
Thy mercies how tender! how firm to the end!
Our Maker, Defender, Redeemer and Friend.

MARLOW. C. M. LOWELL MASON.

1. Come, Holy Ghost! our hearts inspire, Let us thine influence prove; Source of the old prophetic fire! Fountain of life and love!

105 *Invocation.* C. WESLEY.

COME, Holy Ghost! our hearts inspire,
Let us thine influence prove;
Source of the old prophetic fire!
Fountain of life and love!

2 Water with heavenly dew thy word,
In this appointed hour;
Attend it with thy presence, Lord,
And bid it come with power.

3 Open the hearts of them that hear,
To make the Saviour room;
Now let us find redemption near;
Let faith by hearing come.

106 *"Come, Lord!"* A. STEELE.

COME, thou Desire of all thy saints!
Our humble strains attend,
While with our praises and complaints,
Low at thy feet we bend.

2 How should our songs, like those above,
With warm devotion rise!
How should our souls, on wings of love,
Mount upward to the skies!

3 Come, Lord! thy love alone can raise
In us the heavenly flame;
Then shall our lips resound thy praise,
Our hearts adore thy name.

ARMENIA. C. M.   S. B. POND.

1. {Do not I love thee, O my Lord? Be-hold my heart, and see;}
{And turn the dearest i - dol out (Omit) ....} That dares to ri - val thee.

107   *Loving and Beloved.*   P. DODDRIDGE.

Do NOT I love thee, O my Lord?
Behold my heart, and see;
And turn the dearest idol out
That dares to rival thee.

2 Is not thy name melodious still
To mine attentive ear?
Doth not each pulse with pleasure bound,
My Saviour's voice to hear?

3 Hast thou a lamb in all thy flock
I would disdain to feed?
Hast thou a foe, before whose face
I fear thy cause to plead?

4 Thou knowést that I love thee, Lord;
But, oh, I long to soar
Far from the sphere of mortal joys,
And learn to love thee more.

108   *Sincerity.*   J. D. CARLYLE.

LORD! when we bend before thy throne,
And our confessions pour,
Oh, may we feel the sins we own,
And hate what we deplore.

2 Our contrite spirits pitying see;
True penitence impart:
And let a healing ray from thee
Beam hope on every heart.

3 Let faith each meek petition fill,
And waft it to the skies;
And teach our hearts 'tis goodness still
That grants it or denies.

109   *The Mercy-Seat.*   A. STEELE.

DEAR Father, to thy mercy-seat
My soul for shelter flies:
'Tis here I find a safe retreat
When storms and tempests rise.

2 My cheerful hope can never die,
If thou, my God, art near;

Thy grace can raise my comforts high,
And banish every fear.

3 My great Protector, and my Lord!
Thy constant aid impart;
Oh, let thy kind, thy gracious word
Sustain my trembling heart.

110   *"Hearts to Pray."*   J. NEWTON.

AGAIN our earthly cares we leave,
And to thy courts repair;
Again with joyful feet we come,
To meet our Saviour here.

2 Great Shepherd of thy people, hear!
Thy presence now display;
We bow within thy house of prayer;
Oh, give us hearts to pray!

3 Show us some token of thy love,
Our fainting hopes to raise;
And pour thy blessing from above,
To aid our feeble praise.

111   *Retirement.*   W. COWPER.

FAR from the world, O Lord, I flee,
From strife and tumult far;
From scenes where Satan wages still
His most successful war.

2 The calm retreat, the silent shade,
With prayer and praise agree;
And seem by thy sweet bounty made
For those who follow thee.

3 There, if thy Spirit touch the soul,
And grace her mean abode,
Oh, with what peace, and joy, and love,
She then communes with God.

4 Author and Guardian of my life!
Sweet source of light divine,
And—all harmonious names in one—
My Saviour—thou art mine!

HURSLEY. L. M.

W. H. MONK, arr.

1. Sun of my soul! thou Sav - iour dear, It is not night if thou be near;

Oh, may no earth-born cloud a - rise To hide thee from thy servant's eyes!

112   *"Sun of my soul!"*   J. KEBLE.

Sun of my soul! thou Saviour dear,
It is not night if thou be near:
Oh, may no earth-born cloud arise
To hide thee from thy servant's eyes!

2 When soft the dews of kindly sleep
My wearied eyelids gently steep,
Be my last thought—how sweet to rest
For ever on my Saviour's breast!

3 Abide with me from morn till eve,
For without thee I cannot live;
Abide with me when night is nigh,
For without thee I dare not die.

4 Be near to bless me when I wake,
Ere through the world my way I take;
Abide with me till in thy love
I lose myself in heaven above.

EVENING HYMN. L. M.

THOS. TALLIS.

1. Glo - ry to thee, my God, this night, For all the blessings of the light:

Keep me, oh, keep me, King of kings! Be - neath thine own al - might - y wings.

113   *Evening song.*   T. KEN.

GLORY to thee, my God, this night,
For all the blessings of the light;
Keep me, oh, keep me, King of kings!
Beneath thine own almighty wings.

2 Forgive me, Lord, for thy dear Son,
The ill which I this day have done;
That with the world, myself, and thee,
I, ere I sleep, at peace may be.

3 Teach me to live, that I may dread
The grave as little as my bed:
Teach me to die, that so I may
Rise glorious at the judgment-day.

4 Oh, let my soul on thee repose,
And may sweet sleep mine eyelids close!
Sleep, which shall me more vigorous make,
To serve my God when I awake.

J. C. H. RINK.

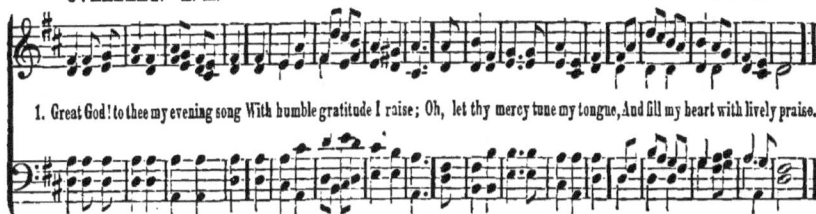

1. Great God! to thee my evening song With humble gratitude I raise; Oh, let thy mercy tune my tongue, And fill my heart with lively praise.

114   *Twilight.*   A. STEELE.

GREAT God! to thee my evening song
  With humble gratitude I raise;
Oh, let thy mercy tune my tongue,
  And fill my heart with lively praise.

2 My days unclouded as they pass,
  And every gentle, rolling hour,
Are monuments of wondrous grace,
  And witness to thy love and power.

3 Seal my forgiveness in the blood
  Of Jesus; his dear name alone
I plead for pardon, gracious God!
  And kind acceptance at thy throne.

115   *Benediction.*   J. NEWTON.

THE peace which God alone reveals,
  And by his word of grace imparts,
Which only the believer feels,
  Direct, and keep, and cheer our hearts!

2 And may the holy Three in One,
  The Father, Word, and Comforter,
Pour an abundant blessing down
  On every soul assembled here!

3 Praise God, from whom all blessings flow:
  Praise him, all creatures here below;
Praise him above, ye heavenly host!
  Praise Father, Son, and Holy Ghost.

LOWELL MASON.

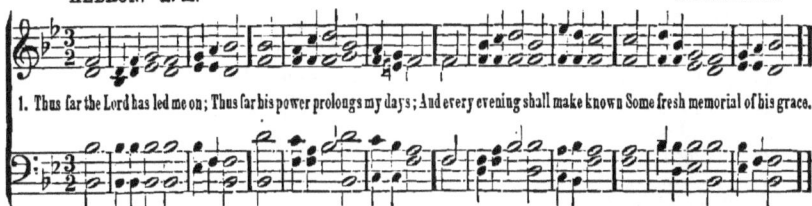

1. Thus far the Lord has led me on; Thus far his power prolongs my days; And every evening shall make known Some fresh memorial of his grace.

116   *Evening.*   I. WATTS.

THUS far the Lord has led me on;
  Thus far his power prolongs my days;
And every evening shall make known
  Some fresh memorial of his grace.

2 Much of my time has run to waste,
  And I, perhaps, am near my home,
But he forgives my follies past,
  And gives me strength for days to come.

3 I lay my body down to sleep;
  Peace is the pillow for my head;
While well-appointed angels keep
  Their watchful stations round my bed.

4 Thus when the night of death shall come,
  My flesh shall rest beneath the ground,
And wait thy voice to break my tomb,
  With sweet salvation in the sound.

117   *Dismissal.*   J. HART.

DISMISS us with thy blessing, Lord!
  Help us to feed upon thy word;
All that has been amiss, forgive,
  And let thy truth within us live.

2 Though we are guilty, thou art good;
  Wash all our works in Jesus' blood;
Give every burdened soul release,
  And bid us all depart in peace.

4

DENNIS. S. M.   LOWELL MASON, arr.

1. The swift de - clin-ing day, How fast its moments fly! While evening's broad and gloomy shade Gains on the western sky.

118   *Evening.*   P. DODDRIDGE.

THE swift declining day,
  How fast its moments fly!
While evening's broad and gloomy shade
  Gains on the western sky.

2 Ye mortals, mark its pace,
  And use the hours of light;
And know, its Maker can command
  At once eternal night.

3 Give glory to the Lord,
  Who rules the whirling sphere;
Submissive at his footstool bow,
  And seek salvation there.

4 Then shall new lustre break
  Through death's impending gloom,
And lead you to unchanging light,
  In your celestial home.

119   *"Abide with us."*   J. M. NEALE.

THE day, O Lord, is spent;
  Abide with us, and rest;
Our hearts' desires are fully bent
  On making thee our guest.

2 We have not reached that land,
  That happy land, as yet,
Where holy angels round thee stand,
  Whose sun can never set.

3 Our sun is sinking now,
  Our day is almost o'er;
O Sun of Righteousness, do thou
  Shine on us evermore!

120   *"Still with thee."*   J. D. BURNS.

STILL, still with thee, my God,
  I would desire to be:
By day, by night, at home, abroad,
  I would be still with thee.

2 With thee when dawn comes in,
  And calls me back to care,
Each day returning to begin
  With thee my God in prayer.

3 With thee when day is done,
  And evening calms the mind;
The setting, as the rising, sun
  With thee my heart would find.

4 With thee, in thee, by faith
  Abiding I would be;
By day, by night, in life, in death,
  I would be still with thee.

121   *Doxology.*   I. WATTS.

To GOD the only wise,
  Who keeps us by his word,
Be glory now and evermore,
  Through Jesus Christ our Lord.

2 Hosanna to the Word,
  Who from the Father came;
Ascribe salvation to the Lord,
  And ever bless his name.

3 The grace of Christ our Lord,
  The Father's boundless love,
The Spirit's blest ommunion, too,
  Be with us from above.

122   *The final rest.*   W. J. BLEW.

THE day is past and gone,
  Great God, we bow to thee;
Again, as shades of night steal on,
  Unto thy side we flee.

2 Oh, when shall that day come,
  Ne'er sinking in the west,
That country and that happy home,
  Where none shall break our rest;—

3 Where all things shall be peace,
  And pleasure without end,
And golden harps, that never cease,
  With joyous hymns shall blend;—

4 Where we, preserved beneath
  The shelter of thy wing,
For evermore thy praise shall breathe,
  And of thy mercy sing.

EVENING. S. M.   A. CHAPIN.

1. The day is past and gone, The evening shades appear; Oh, may we all re-member well The night of death draws near.

123   *Home Hymn.*   J. LELAND.

THE day is past and gone,
  The evening shades appear;
Oh, may we all remember well
  The night of death draws-near!

2 We lay our garments by,
  Upon our beds to rest;
So death will soon disrobe us all
  Of what we here possessed.

3 Lord, keep us safe this night,
  Secure from all our fears;
May angels guard us while we sleep,
  Till morning light appears.

4 And when we early rise,
  And view the unwearied sun,
May we set out to win the prize,
  And after glory run.

5 And when our days are past,
  And we from time remove,
Oh, may we in thy bosom rest,
  The bosom of thy love!

124   *"Closing hour."*   E. T. FITCH.

LORD, at this closing hour,
  Establish every heart
Upon thy word of truth and power,
  To keep us when we part.

2 Peace to our brethren give;
  Fill all our hearts with love;
In faith and patience may we live,
  And seek our rest above.

3 Through changes, bright or drear,
  We would thy will pursue;
And toil to spread thy kingdom here,
  Till we its glory view.

4 To God, the only wise,
  In every age adored,
. Let glory from the church arise
  Through Jesus Christ our Lord!

125   *Sabbath ended.*   A. STEELE.

THE day of praise is done;
  The evening shadows fall;
Yet pass not from us with the sun,
  True Light that lightenest all!

2 Around thy throne on high,
  Where night can never be,
The white-robed harpers of the sky
  Bring ceaseless hymns to thee.

3 Too faint our anthems here;
  Too soon of praise we tire;
But oh, the strains how full and clear
  Of that eternal choir!

4 Yet, Lord! to thy dear will
  If thou attune the heart,
We in thine angels' music still
  May bear our lower part.

5 Shine thou within us, then,
  A day that knows no end,
Till songs of angels and of men
  In perfect praise shall blend.

126   *At Dismission.*   J. HART.

ONCE more, before we part,
  Oh, bless the Saviour's name!
Let every tongue and every heart
  Adore and praise the same.

2 Lord, in thy grace we came,
  That blessing still impart;
We met in Jesus' sacred name,
  In Jesus' name we part.

3 Still on thy holy word
  Help us to feed, and grow,
Still to go on to know the Lord,
  And practice what we know.

4 Now, Lord, before we part,
  Help us to bless thy name:
Let every tongue and every heart
  Adore and praise the same.

EVENTIDE. 10s.   WM. H. MONK.

1. A-bide with me! Fast falls the ev - en - tide, The darkness deepens--Lord, with me a - bide!

When oth-er help - ers fail, and comforts flee, Help of the helpless, oh, a - bide with me!

127   *"Abide with us."*   H. F. LYTE.

ABIDE with me! Fast falls the eventide,
The darkness deepens—Lord, with me abide!
When other helpers fail, and comforts flee,
Help of the helpless, oh, abide with me!

2 Swift to its close ebbs out life's little day;
Earth's joys grow dim, its glories pass away;
Change and decay in all around I see;
O thou, who changest not, abide with me!

3 I need thy presence every passing hour,
What but thy grace can foil the tempter's power?
Who, like thyself, my guide and stay can be?
Thro' cloud and sunshine, oh, abide with me!

4 Hold thou thy cross before my closing eyes;
Shine through the gloom, and point me to the skies;
Heaven's morning breaks, and earth's vain shadows flee!
In life, in death, O Lord, abide with me!

PAX DEI. 10s.   J. B. DYKES.

1. Saviour, a - gain to thy dear name we raise With one accord our parting hymn of praise;

We rise to bless thee ere our worship cease, And now, de - parting, wait thy word of peace.

128   *"Go in peace."*   J. ELLERTON.

SAVIOUR, again to thy dear name we raise
With one accord our parting hymn of praise;
We rise to bless thee ere our worship cease,
And now, departing, wait thy word of peace,

2 Grant us thy peace upon our homeward way;
With thee began, with thee shall end the day;
Guard thou the lips from sin, the hearts from shame,
That in this house have called upon thy name.

3 Grant us thy peace, Lord, through the coming night;
Turn thou for us its darkness into light;
From harm and danger keep thy children free,
For dark and light are both alike to thee.

4 Grant us thy peace throughout our earthly life,
Our balm in sorrow, and our stay in strife;
Then, when thy voice shall bid our conflict cease,
Call us, O Lord, to thine eternal peace.

HOLLEY. 7s.   GEO. HEWS.

1. Soft - ly now the light of day Fades up - on my sight a - way;

Free from care, from la - bor free, Lord, I would com-mune with thee.

129   *Evening.*   G. W. DOANE.

SOFTLY now the light of day
Fades upon my sight away;
Free from care, from labor free,
Lord, I would commune with thee.

2 Thou, whose all-pervading eye
Naught escapes without, within,
Pardon each infirmity,
Open fault, and secret sin.

3 Soon, for me, the light of day
Shall for ever pass away;
Then, from sin and sorrow free,
Take me, Lord, to dwell with thee.

4 Thou who, sinless, yet hast known
All of man's infirmity;
Then from thine eternal throne,
Jesus, look with pitying eye.

130   *"Foretastes."*   J. MONTGOMERY.

FOR the mercies of the day,
For this rest upon our way,
Thanks to thee alone be given,
Lord of earth and King of heaven!

2 Cold our services have been,
Mingled every prayer with sin:
But thou canst and wilt forgive;
By thy grace alone we live.

3 While this thorny path we tread,
May thy love our footsteps lead;
When our journey here is past,
May we rest with thee at last.

4 Let these earthly Sabbaths prove
Foretastes of our joys above;
While their steps thy children bend
To the rest which knows no end.

SEYMOUR. 7s.   GREATOREX COLL.

1. Soft - ly now the light of day Fades up - on my sight a - way;

Free from care, from la - bor free, Lord, I would com - mune with thee.

EMMELAR. 6s, 5s.   J. BARNBY.

1. Now the day is o-ver, Night is drawing nigh, Shadows of the evening Steal across the sky.

131   *Day is over.*   S. BARING-GOULD.

Now THE day is over,
  Night is drawing nigh,
Shadows of the evening
  Steal across the sky.

2 Jesus, give the weary
  Calm and sweet repose;
With thy tenderest blessing
  May our eyelids close.

3 Grant to little children
  Visions bright of thee;

Guard the sailor tossing
  On the deep blue sea.

4 Through the long night-watches,
  May thine angels spread
Their white wings above me,
  Watching round my bed.

5 When the morning wakens,
  Then may I arise,
Pure and fresh and sinless
  In thy holy eyes.

A LITTLE WHILE. 11s, 10s.   F. L. BENJAMIN.

1. Oh, for the peace which floweth like a riv-er, Making life's desert places bloom and smile!

Oh, for the faith to grasp heav'n's bright "for ever," A-mid the shadows of earth's "little while."

132   *"A little while."*   J. CREWDSON.

Oh, for the peace which floweth like a river,
  Making life's desert places bloom and smile!
Oh, for the faith to grasp heaven's bright "for ever,"
  Amid the shadows of earth's "little while!"

2 A little while for patient vigil-keeping,
  To face the storm, to battle with the strong;
A little while to sow the seed with weeping,
  Then bind the sheaves and sing the harvest song!

3 A little while to keep the oil from failing,
  A little while faith's flickering lamp to trim;
And then, the Bridegroom's coming footsteps hailing,
  To haste to meet him with the bridal hymn!

4 And He who is himself the gift and giver,—
  The future glory and the present smile,—
With the bright promise of the glad "for ever"
  Will light the shadows of the "little while!"

LAST BEAM. P. M.   T. V. WEISENTHAL.

1. Fading, still fading, the last beam is shining; Father in heaven, the day is de - clining;

Safe-ty and innocence fly with the light, Temptation and danger walk forth with the night; From the

fall of the shade till the morning bells chime, Shield me from danger, save me from crime.

REFRAIN.   2d verse.

Father, have mercy, Father, have mercy, Father, have mercy thro' Jesus Christ our Lord. Amen.

133   *"The Last Beam."*   HUNTINGTON.

FADING, still fading, the last beam is shining,
Father in heaven, the day is declining;
Safety and innocence fly with the light,
Temptation and danger walk forth with the night:
From the fall of the shade till the morning bells chime,
Shield me from danger, save me from crime!—REF.

2 Father in heaven, oh, hear when we call!
Hear, for Christ's sake, who is Saviour of all;
Feeble and fainting, we trust in thy might;
In doubting and darkness, thy love be our light;
Let us sleep on thy breast while the night taper burns,
Wake in thine arms when morning returns.—REF.

SEGUR. 8s, 7s, 4s.   J. P. HOLBROOK.

1. Guide me, O thou great Jeho-vah, Pilgrim through this barren land ; I am weak, but thou art mighty ;

Hold me with thy powerful hand ; Bread of heaven, Bread of heaven, Feed me till I want no more.

134   *Guidance.*   W. WILLIAMS.

GUIDE me, O thou great Jehovah,
  Pilgrim through this barren land;
I am weak, but thou art mighty;
  Hold me with thy powerful hand;
    Bread of heaven,
  Feed me till I want no more.

2 Open thou the crystal fountain
  Whence the healing streams do flow;
Let the fiery, cloudy pillar
  Lead me all my journey through;
    Strong Deliverer,
  Be thou still my Strength and Shield.

3 When I tread the verge of Jordan,
  Bid my anxious fears subside;
Death of death! and hell's Destruction!
  Land me safe on Canaan's side;
    Songs of praises
  I will ever give to thee.

135   *"Lead us!"*   J. EDMESTON.

LEAD us, heavenly Father, lead us
  O'er the world's tempestuous sea;
Guard us, guide us, keep us, feed us,
  For we have no help but thee;
    Yet possessing   Every blessing,
  If our God our Father be.

2 Saviour, breathe forgiveness o'er us;
  All our weakness thou dost know;
Thou didst tread this earth before us;
  Thou didst feel its keenest woe;
    Lone and dreary,   Faint and weary,
  Through the desert thou didst go.

3 Spirit of our God, descending,
  Fill our hearts with heavenly joy;
Love with every passion blending,
  Pleasure that can never cloy;
    Thus provided,   Pardoned, guided,
  Nothing can our peace destroy.

OLIPHANT. 8s, 7s, 4s.   LOWELL MASON, arr.

1. Guide me, O thou great Jo-ho-vah, Pilgrim through this barren land ; I am weak, but thou art mighty, Hold me with thy

powerful hand : Bread of heav-en, Bread of heaven, Feed me till I want no more, Feed me till I want no more.

GREENVILLE. 8s, 7s, 4s.

J. J. ROUSSEAU.

1. Lord, dismiss us with thy blessing, Fill our hearts with joy and peace; { Let us each thy love pos - sess-ing, }
D. C. Oh, re - fresh us, Oh, re - fresh us, Traveling through this wilderness. { Tri-umph in re - deeming (omit) } grace;

136 *Dismissal.* W. SHIRLEY.

LORD, dismiss us with thy blessing,
Fill our hearts with joy and peace;
Let us each, thy love possessing,
Triumph in redeeming grace;
    Oh, refresh us,
Traveling through this wilderness.

2 Thanks we give, and adoration,
For thy gospel's joyful sound,
May the fruits of thy salvation
In our hearts and lives abound;
    May thy presence
With us evermore be found.

3 So, whene'er the signal's given,
Us from earth to call away;
Borne on angels' wings to heaven,
Glad to leave our cumbrous clay,
    May we, ready,
Rise and reign in endless day.

137 *"Keep us safe."* T. KELLY.

GOD of our salvation! hear us;
Bless, oh, bless us, ere we go;
When we join the world, be near us,
Lest we cold and careless grow.
    Saviour! keep us;
Keep us safe from every foe.

2 As our steps are drawing nearer
To our everlasting home,
May our view of heaven grow clearer,
Hope more bright of joys to come;

And, when dying,
May thy presence cheer the gloom.

138 *Benediction.* J. NEWTON.

MAY the grace of Christ our Saviour,
And the Father's boundless love,
With the Holy Spirit's favor,
Rest upon us from above!

2 Thus may we abide in union
With each other and the Lord;
And possess in sweet communion,
Joys which earth cannot afford.

139 *Evening blessing.* J. EDMESTON.

SAVIOUR, breathe an evening blessing,
Ere repose our spirits seal;
Sin and want we come confessing;
Thou canst save, and thou canst heal.

2 Though destruction walk around us,
Though the arrow near us fly,
Angel guards from thee surround us,
We are safe if thou art nigh.

3 Though the night be dark and dreary,
Darkness cannot hide from thee;
Thou art he who, never weary,
Watcheth where thy people be.

4 Should swift death this night o'ertake us,
And our couch become our tomb,
May the morn in heaven awake us,
Clad in light and deathless bloom.

STOCKWELL. 8s, 7s.

D. E. JONES.

1. Saviour, breathe an evening blessing, Ere repose our spirits seal; Sin and want we come confessing; Thou canst save, and thou canst heal.

1. The heavens declare thy glory, Lord! In every star thy wisdom shines; But, when our eyes behold thy word, We read thy name in fairer lines.

140   Psalm 19.   I. WATTS.

THE heavens declare thy glory, Lord!
In every star thy wisdom shines;
But, when our eyes behold thy word,
  We read thy name in fairer lines.

2 The rolling sun, the changing light,
And nights and days thy power confess;
But the blest volume thou hast writ
  Reveals thy justice and thy grace.

3 Sun, moon, and stars convey thy praise
Round the whole earth, and never stand;
So, when thy truth began its race,
  It touched and glanced on every land.

4 Nor shall thy spreading gospel rest,
Till through the world thy truth has run,
Till Christ has all the nations blessed,
  That see the light, or feel the sun.

5 Great Sun of righteousness! arise;
Bless the dark world with heavenly light;
Thy gospel makes the simple wise,
  Thy laws are pure, thy judgments right.

6 Thy noblest wonders here we view,
In souls renewed, and sins forgiven:
Lord! cleanse my sins, my soul renew,
  And make thy word my guide to heaven.

141   Inspiration.   I. WATTS.

'TWAS by an order from the Lord
The ancient prophets spoke his word!
His Spirit did their tongues inspire,
And warmed their hearts with heavenly fire.

2 The works and wonders which they wrought
Confirmed the messages they brought:
The prophet's pen succeeds his breath,
To save the holy words from death.

3 Great God, mine eyes with pleasure look
On the dear volume of thy book;
There my Redeemer's face I see,
And read his name who died for me.

142   The Gospel Word.   B. BEDDOME.

GOD, in the gospel of his Son,
Makes his eternal counsels known:
Where love in all its glory shines,
And truth is drawn in fairest lines.

2 Here sinners, of an humble frame,
May taste his grace, and learn his name;
May read, in characters of blood,
The wisdom, power, and grace of God.

3 The prisoner here may break his chains;
The weary rest from all his pains;
The captive feel his bondage cease; ·
The mourner find the way of peace.

4 Here faith reveals to mortal eyes
A brighter world beyond the skies;
Here shines the light which guides our way
From earth to realms of endless day.

5 Oh, grant us grace, Almighty Lord,
To read and mark thy holy word;
Its truth with meekness to receive,
And by its holy precepts live.

143   Psalm 19.   R. GRANT.

THE starry firmament on high,
And all the glories of the sky,
Yet shine not to thy praise, O Lord,
So brightly as thy written word.

2 The hopes that holy word supplies,
Its truths divine and precepts wise,
In each a heavenly beam I see,
And every beam conducts to thee.

3 Almighty Lord, the sun shall fail,
The moon forget her nightly tale,
And deepest silence hush on high
The radiant chorus of the sky;—

4 But fixed for everlasting years,
Unmoved, amid the wreck of spheres,
Thy word shall shine in cloudless day,
When heaven and earth have passed away.

CHENIES. 7s, 6s. D.

T. R. MATTHEWS.

1. O Word of God in - car - nate, O Wis-dom from on high, O Truth unchanged, un-chang - ing, O Light of our dark sky! We praise thee for the ra - diance That from the hal-lowed page, A lan - tern to our foot-steps, Shines on from age to age.

144 *The Church's Gift.* W. W. HOW.

O word of God incarnate,
　O Wisdom from on high,
O Truth unchanged, unchanging,
　O Light of our dark sky!
We praise thee for the radiance
　That from the hallowed page,
A lantern to our footsteps,
　Shines on from age to age.

2 The Church from her dear Master
　Received the gift divine,
And still that light she lifteth
　O'er all the earth to shine.
It is the golden casket
　Where gems of truth are stored,
It is the heaven-drawn picture
　Of Christ the living Word.

3 Oh, make thy Church, dear Saviour,
　A lamp of burnished gold,
To bear before the nations
　Thy true light as of old;
Oh, teach thy wandering pilgrims
　By this their path to trace,
Till, clouds and darkness ended,
　They see thee face to face.

145 *Psalm 19.* J. CONDER.

The heavens declare his glory,
　Their Maker's skill the skies;
Each day repeats the story,
　And night to night replies.
Their silent proclamation
　Throughout the earth is heard;
The record of creation,
　The page of nature's word.

2 So pure, so soul-restoring,
　Is truth's diviner ray;
A brighter radiance pouring
　Than all the pomp of day:
The wanderer surely guiding,
　It makes the simple wise;
And, evermore abiding,
　Unfailing joy supplies.

3 Thy word is richer treasure
　Than lurks within the mine;
And daintiest fare less pleasure
　Yields than this food divine.
How wise each kind monition!
　Led by thy counsels, Lord,
How safe the saints' condition,
　How great is their reward!

HAVEN. C. M.,   THOS. HASTINGS.

1. Thou love-ly Source of true de-light, Whom I un-seen a-dore!

Un-vail thy beau-ties to my sight, That I may love thee more.

146   *Christ in the Word.*   A. STEELE.

THOU lovely Source of true delight,
  Whom I unseen adore !
Unvail thy beauties to my sight,
  That I may love thee more.

2 Thy glory o'er creation shines;—
  But in thy sacred word,
I read, in fairer, brighter lines,
  My bleeding, dying Lord.

3 'Tis here, whene'er my comforts droop,
  And sin and sorrow rise,
Thy love, with cheering beams of hope,
  My fainting heart supplies.

4 But ah! too soon the pleasing scene
  Is clouded o'er with pain;
My gloomy fears rise dark between,
  And I again complain.

5 Jesus, my Lord, my life, my light!
  Oh, come with blissful ray;
Break radiant through the shades of night,
  And chase my fears away.

6 Then shall my soul with rapture trace
  The wonders of thy love:
But the full glories of thy face
  Are only known above.

147   *Psalm 119.*   J. FAWCETT

How PRECIOUS is the book divine,
  By inspiration given !
Bright as a lamp its doctrines shine,
  To guide our souls to heaven.

2 O'er all the strait and narrow way
  Its radiant beams are cast;
A light whose never weary ray
  Grows brightest at the last.

3 It sweetly cheers our drooping hearts,
  In this dark vale of tears;
Life, light, and joy it still imparts,
  And quells our rising fears.

4 This lamp, through all the tedious night
  Of life, shall guide our way,
Till we behold the clearer light
  Of an eternal day.

KNOX. C. M.   TEMPLE MELODIES.

1. How precious is the book divine, By in-spi-ra-tion given, Bright as a lamp its doctrines shine, To guide our souls to heaven.

IOLA. C. M. D. G. MASON.

1. How shall the young se-cure their hearts, And guard their lives from sin?

Thy word the choicest rules imparts To keep the conscience clean, To keep the conscience clean.

148   *Psalm 119.*   I. WATTS.

How SHALL the young secure their hearts,
  And guard their lives from sin?
Thy word the choicest rules imparts
  To keep the conscience clean.

2 When once it enters to the mind,
  It spreads such light abroad;
The meanest souls instruction find,
  And raise their thoughts to God.

3 'Tis like the sun, a heavenly light,
  That guides us all the day;
And, through the dangers of the night,
  A lamp to lead our way.

4 Thy precepts make me truly wise;
  I hate the sinner's road;
I hate my own vain thoughts that rise,
  But love thy law, my God!

5 Thy word is everlasting truth;
  How pure is every page!
That holy book shall guide our youth,
  And well support our age.

149   *Psalm 119.*   I. WATTS.

Oh, that the Lord would guide my ways
  To keep his statutes still:
Oh, that my God would grant me grace
  To know and do his will.

2 Oh, send thy Spirit down, to write
  Thy law upon my heart;
Nor let my tongue indulge deceit,
  Or act the liar's part.

3 From vanity turn off my eyes;
  Let no corrupt design,
Nor covetous desires, arise
  Within this soul of mine.

4 Order my footsteps by thy word,
  And make my heart sincere;
Let sin have no dominion, Lord!
  But keep my conscience clear.

5 Make me to walk in thy commands—
  'Tis a delightful road;
Nor let my head, or heart, or hands,
  Offend against my God.

YORK. C. M. SCOTCH PSALTER.

1. Oh, that the Lord would guide my ways To keep his statutes still; Oh, that my God would grant me grace To know and do his will.

BRATTLE STREET. C. M. D.   I. PLEYEL.

| 1st. | 2d.

While thee I seek, pro - tecting Power! Be my vain wish - es stilled;} With
1. {And may this con - se - crat-ed hour [omit.] ....}

bet - ter hopes be filled. Thy love the power of thought bestowed; To thee my tho'ts would

soar: Thy mer - cy o'er my life has flowed; That mer - cy I a - dore.

150   *Providence.*   H. M. WILLIAMS.

WHILE thee I seek, protecting Power !
  Be my vain wishes stilled;
And may this consecrated hour
  With better hopes be filled;
Thy love the power of thought bestowed;
  To thee my thoughts would soar:
Thy mercy o'er my life has flowed;
  That mercy I adore.

2 In each event of life how clear
  Thy ruling hand I see !
Each blessing to my soul more dear
  Because conferred by thee.
In every joy that crowns my days,
  In every pain I bear,
My heart shall find delight in praise
  Or seek relief in prayer.

3 When gladness wings my favored hour,
  Thy love my thoughts shall fill;
Resigned, when storms of sorrow lower,
  My soul shall meet thy will.

My lifted eye, without a tear,
  The gathering storm shall see;
My steadfast heart shall know no fear;
  That heart will rest on thee.

151   *Psalm 116.*   I. WATTS.

WHAT shall I render to my God,
  For all his kindness shown ?
My feet shall visit thine abode,
  My songs address thy throne.

2 Among the saints that fill thine house,
  My offering shall be paid;
There shall my zeal perform the vows,
  My soul in anguish made.

3 How much is mercy thy delight,
  Thou ever blessèd God !
How dear thy servants in thy sight !
  How precious is their blood !

4 How happy all thy servants are !
  How great thy grace to me !
My life, which thou hast made thy care,
  Lord, I devote to thee.

GENEVA. C. M.   J. COLE.

1. When all thy mer - cies, O........ my God! My ris-ing soul sur-veys,
When all thy mercies, O my God!

When all thy mercies, O my God!

Transport - ed with the view, I'm lost In won - der, love, and praise.

Transported with the view, I'm lost

152   *Continued help.*   J. ADDISON.

WHEN all thy mercies, O my God!
My rising soul surveys,
Transported with the view, I'm lost
In wonder, love, and praise.

2 Unnumbered comforts, to my soul,
Thy tender care bestowed,
Before my infant heart conceived
From whom those comforts flowed.

3 When, in the slippery paths of youth,
With heedless steps, I ran,
Thine arm, unseen, conveyed me safe,
And led me up to man.

4 Ten thousand thousand precious gifts
My daily thanks employ;
Nor is the least a cheerful heart,
That tastes those gifts with joy.

5 Through every period of my life,
Thy goodness I'll pursue;
And after death, in distant worlds,
The glorious theme renew.

6 Through all eternity, to thee
A joyful song I'll raise:
For, oh, eternity's too short
To utter all thy praise!

JERUSALEM. C. M. D.   FROM LOUIS SPOHR.

1. When all thy mercies, O my God! My ris-ing soul sur-veys, Transported with the view, I'm lost
D. S.—Be - fore my infant heart conceived

FINE.   D. S.

In wonder, love, and praise. 2. Unnumbered comforts, to my soul, Thy ten-der care be-stowed,
From whom those comforts flowed.

TRURO. L. M.

CHARLES BURNEY.

1. Lord! thou hast searched and seen me through; Thine eye commands with pierc - ing view,

My ris - ing and my rest - ing hours, My heart and flesh, with all their powers.

153   *Omniscience.—Ps. 139.*   I. WATTS.

LORD! thou hast searched and seen me thro';
Thine eye commands, with piercing view,
My rising and my resting hours,
My heart and flesh, with all their powers.

2 My thoughts, before they are my own,
Are to my God distinctly known;
He knows the words I mean to speak,
Ere from my opening lips they break.

3 Within thy circling power I stand;
On every side I find thy hand;
Awake, asleep, at home, abroad,
I am surrounded still with God.

4 Amazing knowledge, vast and great!
What large extent! what lofty height!
My soul, with all the powers I boast,
Is in the boundless prospect lost.

5 Oh, may these thoughts possess my breast,
Where'er I rove, where'er I rest;
Nor let my weaker passions dare
Consent to sin, for God is there.

154   *Faithfulness.*   I. WATTS.

OH, for a strong, a lasting faith
To credit what the Almighty saith!
To embrace the message of his Son!
And call the joys of heaven our own!

2 Then, should the earth's old pillars shake,
And all the wheels of nature break,
Our steady souls should fear no more
Than solid rocks when billows roar.

155   *Unsearchableness.*   R. SCOTT.

WHAT finite power, with ceaseless toil,
Can fathom the eternal Mind?
Or who the almighty Three in One
By searching, to perfection find?

2 Angels and men in vain may raise,
Harmonious their adoring songs;
The laboring thought sinks down, opprest,
And praises die upon their tongues.

3 Yet would I lift my trembling voice
A portion of his ways to sing;
And mingling with his meanest works,
My humble, grateful tribute bring.

FOREST. L. M.

A. CHAPIN.

1. What finite power, with ceaseless toil, Can fathom the eternal Mind? Or who the almighty Three in One By searching, to perfection find?

LOUVAN. L. M.   V. C. TAYLOR.

1. Lord of all be - ing; throned a - far, Thy glo - ry flames from sun and star;

Cen - tre and soul of ev - ery sphere, Yet to each lov - ing heart how near!

156 *Omnipresence.*   O. W. HOLMES.

Lord of all being; throned afar,
Thy glory flames from sun and star;
Centre and soul of every sphere,
Yet to each loving heart how near!

2 Sun of our life, thy quickening ray
Sheds on our path the glow of day;
Star of our hope, thy softened light
Cheers the long watches of the night.

3 Our midnight is thy smile withdrawn;
Our noontide is thy gracious dawn;
Our rainbow arch thy mercy's sign;
All, save the clouds of sin, are thine!

4 Lord of all life, below, above,
Whose light is truth, whose warmth is love,
Before thy ever-blazing throne
We ask no lustre of our own.

5 Grant us thy truth to make us free,
And kindling hearts that burn for thee,
Till all thy living altars claim
One holy light, one heavenly flame!

157 *Providence.*   A. STEELE.

Lord, how mysterious are thy ways!
How blind are we, how mean our praise!
Thy steps no mortal eyes explore;
'Tis ours to wonder and adore.

2 Great God! I do not ask to see
What in futurity shall be;
Let light and bliss attend my days,
And then my future hours be praise.

5

3 Are darkness and distress my share?
Give me to trust thy guardian care;
Enough for me, if love divine
At length through every cloud shall shine.

4 Yet this my soul desires to know,
Be this my only wish below;
That Christ is mine!—this great request,
Grant, bounteous God, and I am blest.

158 *Sovereignty.*   RAY PALMER.

Lord, my weak thought in vain would climb
To search the starry vault profound;
In vain would wing her flight sublime,
To find creation's outmost bound.

2 But weaker yet that thought must prove
To search thy great eternal plan,—
Thy sovereign counsels, born of love
Long ages ere the world began.

3 When my dim reason would demand
Why that, or this, thou dost ordain,
By some vast deep I seem to stand,
Whose secrets I must ask in vain.

4 When doubts disturb my troubled breast,
And all is dark as night to me,
Here, as on solid rock, I rest;
That so it seemeth good to thee.

5 Be this my joy, that evermore
Thou rulest all things at thy will:
Thy sovereign wisdom I adore,
And calmly, sweetly, trust thee still.

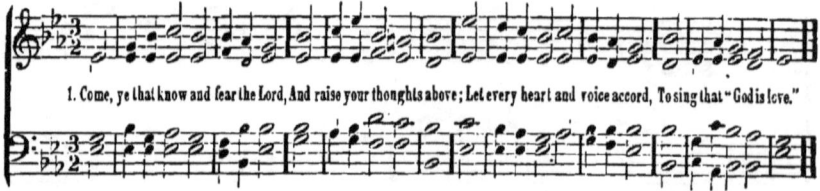

1. Come, ye that know and fear the Lord, And raise your thoughts above; Let every heart and voice accord, To sing that "God is love."

159 *Love.* G. BURDER.

COME, ye that know and fear the Lord,
And raise your thoughts above :
Let every heart and voice accord.
To sing that " God is love."

2 This precious truth his word declares,
And all his mercies prove ;
Jesus, the gift of gifts, appears,
To show that " God is love."

3 Behold his patience, bearing long
With those who from him rove ;
Till mighty grace their hearts subdues,
To teach them " God is love."

4 Oh, may we all, while here below,
This best of blessings prove ;
Till warmer hearts, in brighter worlds,
Proclaim that " God is love."

160 *Omnipresence.—Ps. 139.* I. WATTS.

IN all my vast concerns with thee,
In vain my soul would try
To shun thy presence, Lord ! or flee
The notice of thine eye.

2 Thine all-surrounding sight surveys
My rising and my rest,
My public walks, my private ways,
And secrets of my breast.

3 My thoughts lie open to the Lord,
Before they're formed within ;
And ere my lips pronounce the word.
He knows the sense I mean.

4 Oh, wondrous knowledge, deep and high.
Where can a creature hide ?
Within thy circling arms I lie,
Enclosed on every side.

5 So let thy grace surround me still.
And like a bulwark prove,
To guard my soul from every ill,
Secured by sovereign love.

161 *In Nature.* J. KEBLE.

THERE is a book that all may read,
Which heavenly truth imparts,
And all the lore its scholars need,
Pure eyes and Christian hearts.

2 The works of God above, below,
Within us and around,
Are pages in that book to show
How God himself is found.

3 The glorious sky, embracing all,
Is like the Maker's love,
Wherewith encompassed, great and small
In peace and order move.

4 The dew of heaven is like thy grace,
It steals in silence down ;
But where it lights, the favored place
By richest fruits is known.

5 Thou, who hast given me eyes to see,
And love this sight so fair,
Give me a heart to find out thee,
And read thee everywhere.

162 *Omniscience.—Ps. 139.* I. WATTS.

LORD ! where shall guilty souls retire,
Forgotten and unknown ?
In hell they meet thy dreadful fire—
In heaven thy glorious throne.

2 If, winged with beams of morning light,
I fly beyond the west,
Thy hand, which must support my flight,
Would soon betray my rest.

3 If, o'er my sins, I think to draw
The curtains of the night,
Those flaming eyes, that guard thy law,
Would turn the shades to light.

4 The beams of noon, the midnight hour,
Are both alike to thee :
Oh, may I ne'er provoke that power,
From which I cannot flee.

MANOAH. C. M.

FROM G. ROSSINI.

1. Be - gin, my tongue, some heavenly theme, And speak some boundless thing;

The might - y works, or mightier name, Of our e - ter - nal King.

163 *Faithfulness.* I. WATTS.

BEGIN, my tongue, some heavenly theme,
 And speak some boundless thing;
The mighty works or mightier name
 Of our eternal King.

2 Tell of his wondrous faithfulness,
 And sound his power abroad;
Sing the sweet promise of his grace,
 And the performing God.

3 His very word of grace is strong,
 As that which built the skies;
The voice that rolls the stars along,
 Speaks all the promises.

4 Oh, might I hear thy heavenly tongue
 But whisper, "Thou art mine!"
Those gentle words should raise my song
 To notes almost divine.

164 *Providence.* W. COWPER.

GOD moves in a mysterious way
 His wonders to perform;
He plants his footsteps in the sea,
 And rides upon the storm.

2 Deep in unfathomable mines
 Of never-failing skill,
He treasures up his bright designs,
 And works his sovereign will.

3 Ye fearful saints, fresh courage take!
 The clouds ye so much dread,
Are big with mercy, and will break
 In blessings on your head.

4 Judge not the Lord by feeble sense,
 But trust him for his grace;
Behind a frowning providence
 He hides a smiling face.

5 His purposes will ripen fast,
 Unfolding every hour;
The bud may have a bitter taste,
 But sweet will be the flower.

6 Blind unbelief is sure to err,
 And scan his work in vain;
God is his own interpreter,
 And he will make it plain.

165 *Holiness.* J. NEEDHAM.

HOLY and reverend is the name
 Of our eternal King,
Thrice holy Lord! the angels cry;
 Thrice holy! let us sing.

2 The deepest reverence of the mind,
 Pay, O my soul! to God;
Lift with thy hands a holy heart
 To his sublime abode.

3 With sacred awe pronounce his name,
 Whom words nor thoughts can reach;
A broken heart shall please him more
 Than the best forms of speech.

4 Thou holy God! preserve our souls
 From all pollution free;
The pure in heart are thy delight,
 And they thy face shall see

GOD'S LOVE. 7s, 6s. D.   WM. F SHERWIN.

1. Grander than ocean's sto-ry Or songs of forest trees— Purer than breath of morning Or

evening's gentle breeze—Clearer than mountain echoes Ring out from peaks above—Rolls on the glorious

anthem Of God's e - ter - nal love.

166   *Giving of thanks.*   W. F. SHERWIN.

GRANDER than ocean's story,
 Or songs of forest trees—
Purer than breath of morning,
 Or evening's gentle breeze—
Clearer than mountain echoes
 Ring out from peaks above—
Rolls on the glorious anthem
 Of God's eternal love.

2 Dearer than any lovings,
 The truest friends bestow;
Stronger than all the yearnings,
 A mother's heart can know;
Deeper than earth's foundation's,
 And far above all thought;
Broader than heaven's high arches—
 The love that Christ has brought.

3 Richer than all earth's treasure,
 The wealth my soul receives;
Brighter than royal jewels,
 The crown that Jesus gives;
Wondrous the condescension,
 And grace beyond degree!
I would be ever singing
 The love of Christ to me.

167   GLORIA PATRI. Irr.   CREATOREX COLL.

Glo-ry be to the Fa-ther, and to the Son, and to the Ho - ly Ghost; As it

was in the beginning, is now, and ever shall be, world without end: A-men, A-men.

MIRIAM. 7s & 6s. D.   J. P. HOLBROOK.

1. O God, the Rock of A - ges, Who ev - er-more hast been, What time the tempest ra - ges,
D. S.—To endless gen-er - a - tions,

Our dwelling-place se - rene: Be - fore thy first cre a - tions, O Lord, the same as now,
The Ev - er - last - ing thou!

168 *Everlasting.—Ps. 90.* E. BICKERSTETH.

O God, the Rock of Ages,
Who evermore hast been,
What time the tempest rages,
Our dwelling-place serene:
Before thy first creations,
O Lord, the same as now,
To endless generations,
The Everlasting thou!

2 Our years are like the shadows
On sunny hills that lie,
Or grasses in the meadows
That blossom but to die:
A sleep, a dream, a story,
By strangers quickly told,
An unremaining glory
Of things that soon are old.

3 O thou who canst not slumber,
Whose light grows never pale,
Teach us aright to number
Our years before they fail!
On us thy mercy lighten,
On us thy goodness rest,
And let thy Spirit brighten
The hearts thyself hast blessed!

169 *Omnipresent.* DUTCH HYMN.

On mountains and in valleys
Where'er we go is God;
The cottage and the palace,
Alike are his abode.

With watchful eye abiding
Upon us with delight;
Our souls, in him confiding,
He keeps both day and night.

2 Above me and beside me,
My God is ever near,
To watch, protect, and guide me,
Whatever ills appear.
Though other friends may fail me;
In sorrow's dark abode,
Though death itself assail me,
I'm ever safe with God.

170 *Sovereign Love.* J. CONDER.

'Tis not that I did choose thee,
For, Lord! that could not be;
This heart would still refuse thee;
But thou hast chosen me;—
Hast, from the sin that stained me,
Washed me and set me free,
And to this end ordained me,
That I should live to thee.

2 'Twas sovereign mercy called me,
And taught my opening mind;
The world had else enthralled me,
To heavenly glories blind.
My heart owns none above thee;
For thy rich grace I thirst;
This knowing,—if I love thee,
Thou must have loved me first.

REGENT SQUARE. 8s, 7s.   H. SMART.

1. Hark! what mean those holy voices, Sweetly warbling in the skies? Sure, th'angelic host re-joic-es,—

Loudest hal-le - lu-jahs rise, Sure, th'angelic host re-joic-es, Loudest hal - le - lu-jahs rise.

171   *"Those holy Voices."*   J. CAWOOD.

HARK! what mean those holy voices,
Sweetly warbling in the skies?
Sure, the angelic host rejoices—
Loudest hallelujahs rise.

2 Listen to the wondrous story,
Which they chant in hymns of joy;—
"Glory in the highest, glory;
Glory be to God most high!

3 "Peace on earth, good-will from heaven,
Reaching far as man is found;
Souls redeemed, and sins forgiven;—
Loud our golden harps shall sound.

4 "Christ is born, the great Anointed;
Heaven and earth his glory sing:
Glad, receive whom God appointed,
For your Prophet, Priest, and King.

5 "Hasten, mortals! to adore him,
Learn his name and taste his joy;
Till in heaven you sing before him,—
Glory be to God most high!"

6 Let us learn the wondrous story
Of our great Redeemer's birth,
Spread the brightness of his glory,
Till it cover all the earth.

ANTIOCH. C. M.   LOWELL MASON, *arr.*

1. Joy to the world—the Lord is come; Let earth receive her King; {Let eve-ry heart } {pre-pare him room,}

And heav'n and nature sing, And heav'n and nature sing,.......... And heav'n and na-ture sing.

And heav'n and nature sing, And heav'n and nature sing.

HARK. P. M. W. F. SHERWIN.

1. {Hark! hark, my soul; an-gel-ic songs are swell-ing O'er earth's green fields and
{How sweet the truth those bless-ed strains are (Omit)..........................

o-cean's wave-beat shore: } tell-ing Of that new life when sin shall be no more.

CHORUS.

An-gels of Je-sus, An-gels of light, Sing-ing to welcome the pilgrims of the night.

172 *The heavenly Host.* F. W. FABER.

HARK! hark, my soul; angelic songs are
    swelling
O'er earth's green fields and ocean's wave-
    beat shore:
How sweet the truth those blesséd strains
    are telling
Of that new life when sin shall be no
    more.—CHO.

2 Onward we go, for still we hear them sing-
    ing,
"Come, weary souls, for Jesus bids you
    come:"
And, through the dark its echoes sweetly
    ringing,
The music of the gospel leads us home.—
    CHO.

3 Far, far away, like bells at evening pealing,
The voice of Jesus sounds o'er land and sea,
And laden souls by thousands meekly steal-
    ing,
Kind Shepherd, turn their weary steps to
    thee.—CHO.

4 Angels, sing on! your faithful watches
    keeping;
Sing us sweet fragments of the songs above,
Till morning's joy shall end the night of
    weeping,
And life's long shadows break in cloud-
    less love.—CHO.

173 C.M. *Psalm 98.* I. WATTS.

Joy to the world,—the Lord is come;
    Let earth receive her King;
Let every heart prepare him room,
    And heaven and nature sing.

2 Joy to the earth,—the Saviour reigns;
    Let men their songs employ;
While fields and floods, rocks, hills and
    Repeat the sounding joy. [plains,

3 No more let sin and sorrow grow,
    Nor thorns infest the ground,
He comes to make his blessings flow,
    Far as the curse is found.

4 He rules the world with truth and grace,
    And makes the nations prove
The glories of his righteousness,
    And wonders of his love.

ORTONVILLE. C. M.

THOS. HASTINGS.

1. Ma - jes - tic sweetness sits enthroned Up-on the Saviour's brow; His head with radiant

glories crowned, His lips with grace o'er - flow, His lips with grace o'er - flow.

174 *"Altogether Lovely."* S. STENNETT.

Majestic sweetness sits enthroned
Upon the Saviour's brow;
His head with radiant glories crowned,
His lips with grace o'erflow.

2 No mortal can with him compare,
Among the sons of men;
Fairer is he than all the fair
That fill the heavenly train.

3 He saw me plunged in deep distress,
He flew to my relief;
For me he bore the shameful cross,
And carried all my grief.

4 To him I owe my life and breath,
And all the joys I have;
He makes me triumph over death,
He saves me from the grave.

5 To heaven, the place of his abode,
He brings my weary feet;
Shows me the glories of my God,
And makes my joy complete.

6 Since from his bounty I receive
Such proofs of love divine,
Had I a thousand hearts to give,
Lord! they should all be thine.

175 *"His free ways."* F. W. FABER.

Oh, see how Jesus trusts himself
Unto our childish love!
As though by his free ways with us
Our earnestness to prove.

2 His sacred name a common word
On earth he loves to hear;
There is no majesty in him
Which love may not come near.

3 The light of love is round his feet,
His paths are never dim;
And he comes nigh to us when we
Dare not come nigh to him.

4 Let us be simple with him then,
Not backward, stiff, nor cold,
As though our Bethlehem could be
What Sinai was of old.

176 *The name "Jesus."* A. STEELE.

The Saviour! oh, what endless charms
Dwell in the blissful sound!
Its influence every fear disarms,
And spreads sweet comfort round.

2 The almighty Former of the skies
Stooped to our vile abode;
While angels viewed with wondering eyes
And hailed the incarnate God.

3 Oh, the rich depths of love divine!
Of bliss a boundless store!
Dear Saviour, let me call thee mine;
I cannot wish for more.

4 On thee alone my hope relies,
Beneath thy cross I fall;
My Lord, my Life, my Sacrifice,
My Saviour, and my All!

GRIGG. C. M.   JOSEPH GRIGG.

1. Thou art the Way: to thee a-lone From sin and death we flee; And he who would the Father seek, Must seek him, Lord, by thee.

177 *"Way, Truth, and Life."*   G. W. DOANE.

THOU art the Way: to thee alone
  From sin and death we flee;
And he who would the Father seek,
  Must seek him, Lord, by thee.

2 Thou art the Truth: thy word alone
  True wisdom can impart;
Thou only canst inform the mind,
  And purify the heart.

3 Thou art the Life: the rending tomb
  Proclaims thy conquering arm;
And those who put their trust in thee
  Nor death nor hell shall harm

4 Thou art the Way, the Truth, the Life:
  Grant us that Way to know;
That Truth to keep, that Life to win,
  Whose joys eternal flow.

ELIZABETHTOWN. C. M.   GEORGE KINGSLEY.

1. Lord, as to thy dear cross we flee, And pray to be for-given, So let thy life our pattern be, And form our souls for heaven.

178   *Pattern of Forgiveness.*   J. H. GURNEY.

LORD, as to thy dear cross we flee,
  And pray to be forgiven,
So let thy life our pattern be,
  And form our souls for heaven.

2 Help us, through good report and ill,
  Our daily cross to bear;
Like thee, to do our Father's will,
  Our brother's griefs to share.

3 Let grace our selfishness expel,
  Our earthliness refine;
And kindness in our bosoms dwell
  As free and true as thine.

4 If joy shall at thy bidding fly,
  And grief's dark day come on,
We, in our turn, would meekly cry,
  "Father, thy will be done!"

5 Kept peaceful in the midst of strife,
  Forgiving and forgiven,
Oh, may we lead the pilgrim's life,
  And follow thee to heaven!

179   *"Shall we forget."*   W. MITCHELL.

JESUS! thy love shall we forget,
  And never bring to mind
The grace that paid our hopeless debt,
  And bade us pardon find?

2 Shall we thy life of grief forget,
  Thy fasting and thy prayer;
Thy locks with mountain vapors wet,
  To save us from despair?

3 Gethsemane can we forget—
  Thy struggling agony
When night lay dark on Olivet,
  And none to watch with thee?

4 Our sorrows and our sins were laid
  On thee, alone on thee;
Thy precious blood our ransom paid—
  Thine all the glory be!

5 Life's brightest joys we may forget—
  Our kindred cease to love;
But he who paid our hopeless debt,
  Our constancy shall prove.

ROOKINGHAM. L. M.

LOWELL MASON.

1. My dear Re-deemer, and my Lord, I read my du-ty in thy word; But in thy life the

law appears, Drawn out in liv-ing characters.

180 *The Divine Pattern.* I. WATTS.

My dear Redeemer, and my Lord,
I read my duty in thy word;
But in thy life the law appears,
Drawn out in living characters.

2 Such was thy truth and such thy zeal,
Such deference to thy Father's will,
Such love, and meekness so divine,
I would transcribe and make them mine.

3 Cold mountains and the midnight air
Witnessed the fervor of thy prayer;
The desert thy temptations knew,
Thy conflict and thy victory too.

4 Be thou my pattern; make me bear
More of thy gracious image here;
Then God, the Judge, shall own my name
Among the followers of the Lamb.

GERMANY. L. M.

LUDWIG VON BEETHOVEN.

1. How shall I fol-low him I serve? How shall I cop-y him I love?

Nor from those bless-ed foot-steps swerve, Which lead me to his seat a-bove.

181 *"How shall I copy?"* J. CONDER.

How SHALL I follow him I serve?
How shall I copy him I love?
Nor from those blesséd footsteps swerve,
Which lead me to his seat above?

2 Lord, should my path through suffering lie,
Forbid it I should e'er repine;
Still let me turn to Calvary,
Nor heed my griefs, remembering thine.

3 Oh, let me think how thou didst leave
Untasted every pure delight,
To fast, to faint, to watch, to grieve,
The toilsome day, the homeless night:—

4 To faint, to grieve, to die for me!
Thou camest not thyself to please:
And, dear as earthly comforts be,
Shall I not love thee more than these?

HAMBURG. L. M.   LOWELL MASON, *arr.*

1. When I survey the wondrous cross, On which the Prince of glory died, My richest gain I count but loss, And pour contempt on all my pride.

182   *"The wondrous Cross."*   I. WATTS.   **183**   *"For me."*   H. BONAR.

WHEN I survey the wondrous cross,
  On which the Prince of glory died,
My richest gain I count but loss,
  And pour contempt on all my pride.

2 Forbid it, Lord! that I should boast,
  Save in the death of Christ, my God;
All the vain things that charm me most
  I sacrifice them to his blood.

3 See, from his head, his hands, his feet,
  Sorrow and love flow mingled down;
Did e'er such love and sorrow meet,
  Or thorns compose so rich a crown?

4 His dying crimson, like a robe,
  Spreads o'er his body on the tree;
Then I am dead to all the globe,
  And all the globe is dead to me.

5 Were the whole realm of nature mine,
  That were a present far too small;
Love so amazing, so divine,
  Demands my soul, my life, my all.

JESUS, whom angel hosts adore,
  Became a man of griefs for me;
In love, though rich, becoming poor,
  That I through him enriched might be.

2 Though Lord of all, above, below,
  He went to Olivet for me:
There drank my cup of wrath and woe,
  When bleeding in Gethsemane.

3 The ever-blessèd Son of God
  Went up to Calvary for me;
There paid my debt, there bore my load,
  In his own body on the tree.

4 Jesus, whose dwelling is the skies,
  Went down into the grave for me;
There overcame my enemies,
  There won the glorious victory.

5 'Tis finished all: the vail is rent,
  The welcome sure, the access free:—
Now then, we leave our banishment,
  O Father, to return to thee!

HASLAM. L. M.   HASLAM, *arr.*

1. When I sur - vey the wondrous cross, On which the Prince of glo - ry died,

My rich - est gain I count but loss, And pour con - tempt on all my pride.

AVON. C. M.   HUGH WILSON.

1. A-las! and did my Saviour bleed, And did my Sovereign die? Would he devote that sacred head For such a worm as I?

184   *"Grace unknown."*   I. WATTS.

Alas! and did my Saviour bleed,
   And did my Sovereign die?
Would he devote that sacred head
   For such a worm as I?

2 Was it for crimes that I had done
   He groaned upon the tree?
Amazing pity! grace unknown!
   And love beyond degree!

3 Well might the sun in darkness hide,
   And shut his glories in,
When Christ, the great Creator, died
   For man, the creature's sin.

4 Thus might I hide my blushing face
   While his dear cross appears;
Dissolve my heart in thankfulness,
   And melt my eyes to tears.

5 But drops of grief can ne'er repay
   The debt of love I owe;
Here, Lord, I give myself away,
   'T is all that I can do.

185   *Suffered for sin.*   I. WATTS.

Oh, if my soul were formed for woe,
   How would I vent my sighs!
Repentance should like rivers flow
   From both my streaming eyes.

2 'Twas for my sins my dearest Lord
   Hung on the cursèd tree,
And groaned away a dying life
   For thee, my soul! for thee.

3 Oh, how I hate these lusts of mine
   That crucified my Lord;
Those sins that pierced and nailed his flesh
   Fast to the fatal wood!

4 Yes, my Redeemer—they shall die;
   My heart has so decreed;
Nor will I spare the guilty things
   That made my Saviour bleed.

5 While with a melting, broken heart,
   My murdered Lord I view,
I'll raise revenge against my sins,
   And slay the murderers too.

COMMUNION. C. M.   STEPHEN JENKS.

1. A - las! and did my Sav - iour bleed, And did my Sove - reign die?

Would he de - vote that sa - cred head For such a worm as I?

MANOAH. C. M.

FROM G. ROSSINI.

1. I saw One hang-ing on a tree, In ag-o-ny and blood;

Who fixed his lan-guid eyes on me, As near the cross I stood.

186 *The two Looks.* J. NEWTON.

I SAW One hanging on a tree,
In agony and blood;
Who fixed his languid eyes on me,
As near the cross I stood.

2 Sure, never, till my latest breath,
Can I forget that look:
It seemed to charge me with his death,
Though not a word he spoke.

3 Alas! I knew not what I did,—
But now my tears are vain;
Where shall my trembling soul be hid,
For I the Lord have slain!

4 A second look he gave, that said,
"I freely all forgive:
This blood is for thy ransom paid;
I die that thou may'st live."

5 Thus while his death my sin displays
In all its blackest hue,
Such is the mystery of grace,
It seals my pardon too!

187 *"He remembers Calvary."* I. WATTS.

How CONDESCENDING and how kind
Was God's eternal Son!
Our misery reached his heavenly mind,
And pity brought him down.

2 He sunk beneath our heavy woes,
To raise us to his throne;
There's ne'er a gift his hand bestows,
But cost his heart a groan.

3 This was compassion, like a God,
That when the Saviour knew
The price of pardon was his blood,
His pity ne'er withdrew.

4 Now, though he reigns exalted high,
His love is still as great;
Well he remembers Calvary,
Nor let his saints forget.

188 *"O Christ of God!"* RAY PALMER.

O JESUS, sweet the tears I shed,
While at thy cross I kneel,
Gaze on thy wounded, fainting head,
And all thy sorrows feel.

2 My heart dissolves to see thee bleed.
This heart so hard before;
I hear thee for the guilty plead,
And grief o'erflows the more.

3 I know this cleansing blood of thine
Was shed, dear Lord, for me:
For me, for all,—oh, grace divine!—
Who look by faith on thee.

4 O Christ of God, O spotless Lamb,
By love my soul is drawn;
Henceforth, for ever, thine I am;
Here life and peace are born.

5 In patient hope, the cross I'll bear,
Thine arm shall be my stay;
And thou, enthroned, my soul shalt spare,
On thy great judgment-day.

GERHARDT. 7s, 6s. D.   J. P. HOLBROOK.

1. O sacred Head, now wounded, With grief and shame weighed down, Now scornfully surrounded With thorns, thine on-ly crown:

O sacred Head, what glo-ry, What bliss, till now was thine! Yet, though despised and gory. I joy to call thee mine.

189   *At the Cross.*   J. W. ALEXANDER, *tr.*

O SACRED Head, now wounded,
  With grief and shame weighed down,
Now scornfully surrounded
  With thorns, thine only crown;
O sacred Head, what glory,
  What bliss, till now was thine!
Yet, though despised and gory,
  I joy to call thee mine.

2 What thou, my Lord, hast suffered
  Was all for sinners' gain:
Mine, mine was the transgression,
  But thine the deadly pain;
Lo, here I fall, my Saviour!
  'Tis I deserved thy place;
Look on me with thy favor,
  Vouchsafe to me thy grace.

3 What language shall I borrow,
  To thank thee, dearest Friend,
For this, thy dying sorrow,
  Thy pity without end?
Lord, make me thine for ever,
  Nor let me faithless prove:
Oh, let me never, never,
  Abuse such dying love.

4 Be near when I am dying,
  Oh, show thy cross to me!
And for my succor flying,
  Come, Lord, and set me free!
These eyes, new faith receiving,
  From Jesus shall not move;
For he who dies believing,
  Dies safely—through thy love.

PATNAH. 7s, 6s. D.   HASLAM, *arr.*

1. { O sacred Head, now wounded, With grief and shame weighed down,
     Now scornfully surrounded With thorns, thine on-ly crown; } O sacred Head, what glo-ry,

What bliss, till now was thine! Yet, though despised and go - ry, I joy to call thee mine.

HARWELL. 8s, 7s. D.   LOWELL MASON.

1. { Hark! ten thousand harps and voices Sound the note of praise above; } See, he sits on yonder throne;
{ Jesus reigns, and heaven rejoices; Jesus reigns, the God of love: } See, he sits

Jesus rules the world alone. Hal - le - lu - jah, Halle - lu - jah, Halle - lu - jah! A - men.
Jesus rules   the world alone.

190   "*Jesus reigns.*"   T. KELLY.

HARK! ten thousand harps and voices
Sound the note of praise above;
Jesus reigns, and heaven rejoices;
    Jesus reigns, the God of love:
See, he sits on yonder throne;
Jesus rules the world alone.

2 King of glory! reign for ever—
    Thine an everlasting crown;
Nothing, from thy love, shall sever
    Those whom thou hast made thine own;—
Happy objects of thy grace,
Destined to behold thy face.

3 Saviour! hasten thine appearing;
    Bring, oh, bring the glorious day,
When, the awful summons hearing,
    Heaven and earth shall pass away;—
Then, with golden harps, we'll sing,—
"Glory, glory to our King!"

191   *We live in Him.*   C. WORDSWORTH.

SEE, the Conqueror mounts in triumph!
    See the King in royal state,
Riding on the clouds, his chariot,
    To his heavenly palace gate!
Hark! the choirs of angel voices
    Joyful hallelujahs sing,
And the portals high are lifted
    To receive their heavenly King.

2 Who is this that comes in glory,
    With the trump of jubilee?

Lord of battles, God of armies,
    He has gained the victory;
He, who on the cross did suffer,
    He, who from the grave arose,
He has vanquished sin and Satan,
    He by death has spoiled his foes.

3 Thou hast raised our human nature,
    On the clouds to God's right hand;
There we sit in heavenly places,
    There with thee in glory stand;
Jesus reigns, adored by angels;
    Man with God is on the throne;
Mighty Lord! in thine ascension,
    We by faith behold our own.

4 Lift us up from earth to heaven,
    Give us wings of faith and love,
Gales of holy aspirations,
    Wafting us to realms above;
That, with hearts and minds uplifted,
    We with Christ our Lord may dwell,
Where he sits enthroned in glory,
    In the heavenly citadel.

5 So at last, when he appeareth,
    We from out our graves may spring,
With our youth renewed like eagles',
    Flocking round our heavenly King,
Caught up on the clouds of heaven,
    And may meet him in the air—
Rise to realms where he is reigning,
    And may reign for ever there.

RATHBUN. 8s, 7s.   I. CONKEY.

1. In the cross of Christ I glo - ry, Towering o'er the wrecks of time; All the light of

sa - cred story Gathers round its head sublime.

192   *Glorying in the Cross.*   J. BOWRING.

In the cross of Christ I glory,
　Towering o'er the wrecks of time;
All the light of sacred story
　Gathers round its head sublime.

2 When the woes of life o'ertake me,
　Hopes deceive, and fears annoy,

Never shall the cross forsake me:
　Lo! it glows with peace and joy.

3 When the sun of bliss is beaming
　Light and love upon my way,
From the cross the radiance, streaming,
　Adds more lustre to the day.

4 Bane and blessing, pain and pleasure,
　By the cross are sanctified;
Peace is there, that knows no measure,
　Joys that through all time abide.

5 In the cross of Christ I glory,
　Towering o'er the wrecks of time;
All the light of sacred story
　Gathers round its head sublime.

CARTHAGE. 8s, 7s.   G. F. ROOT, arr.

1. Christ, a - bove all glo - ry seat - ed! King e - ter - nal, strong to save!

To thee, Death, by death de - feat - ed, Tri - umph high and glo - ry gave.

193   *"Many crowns."*   ANON.

Christ, above all glory seated!
　King eternal, strong to save!
To thee, Death, by death defeated,
　Triumph high and glory gave.

2 Thou art gone where now is given
　What no mortal might could gain,
On the eternal throne of heaven,
　In thy Father's power to reign.

3 We, O Lord! with hearts adoring,
　Follow thee above the sky:
Hear our prayers thy grace imploring,
　Lift our souls to thee on high.

4 So when thou again in glory
　On the clouds of heaven shall shine,
We thy flock shall stand before thee,
　Owned for evermore as thine.

ROTHWELL. L. M. WM. TANSUR.

1. He lives! the great Redeem-er lives! What joy the blest as-surance gives! And now, be-fore his Fa-ther, God, Pleads the full merits of his blood, Pleads the full mer-its of his blood.

194 *Christ, our Advocate.* A. STEELE.

HE lives! the great Redeemer lives!
What joy the blest assurance gives!
And now, before his Father, God,
Pleads the full merits of his blood.

2 Repeated crimes awake our fears,
And justice armed with frowns appears;
But in the Saviour's lovely face
Sweet mercy smiles, and all is peace.

3 In every dark, distressful hour,
When sin and Satan join their power,
Let this dear hope repel the dart,
That Jesus bears us on his heart.

4 Great Advocate, almighty Friend!
On him our humble hopes depend;
Our cause can never, never fail,
For Jesus pleads, and must prevail.

195 *"Behold the Way!"* J. CENNICK.

JESUS, my All, to heaven is gone,
He whom I fix my hopes upon;
His track I see, and I'll pursue
The narrow way till him I view.

2 The way the holy prophets went,
The road that leads from banishment,
The King's highway of holiness,
I'll go for all his paths are peace.

3 This is the way I long had sought,
And mourned because I found it not;
My grief, my burden, long had been
Because I could not cease from sin.

4 The more I strove against its power,
I sinned and stumbled but the more;
Till late I heard my Saviour say,
"Come hither, soul, I am the Way!"

5 Lo! glad I come; and thou, dear Lamb,
Shalt take me to thee as I am,
Nothing but sin I thee can give;
Nothing but love shall I receive.

6 Then will I tell, to sinners round,
What a dear Saviour I have found;
I'll point to thy redeeming blood,
And say, "Behold the way to God!"

196 *Atonement made.* I. WATTS.

NOW to the power of God supreme
Be everlasting honors given;
He saves from hell,—we bless his name,—
He guides our wandering feet to heaven.

2 'Twas his own purpose that began
To rescue rebels doomed to die;
He gave us grace in Christ, his Son,
Before he spread the starry sky.

3 Jesus, the Lord, appears at last,
And makes his Father's counsels known;
Declares the great transactions past,
And brings immortal blessings down.

4 He dies; and in that dreadful night
Doth all the powers of hell destroy;
Rising, he brings our heaven to light,
And takes possession of the joy.

5

STEPHENS. C. M.   WM. JONES.

1. Come, Holy Spirit, heavenly Dove! With all thy quickening powers, Kindle a flame of sa-cred love In these cold hearts of ours.

197   *Invocation.*   I. WATTS.

Come, Holy Spirit, heavenly Dove!
  With all thy quickening powers,
Kindle a flame of sacred-love
  In these cold hearts of ours.

2 Look! how we grovel here below,
  Fond of these trifling toys!
Our souls can neither fly nor go
  To reach eternal joys.

3 In vain we tune our formal songs;
  In vain we strive to rise;

Hosannas languish on our tongues,
  And our devotion dies.

4 Dear Lord, and shall we ever live
  At this poor dying rate—
Our love so faint, so cold to thee,
  And thine to us so great?

5 Come, Holy Spirit, heavenly Dove!
  With all thy quickening powers;
Come, shed abroad a Saviour's love,
  And that shall kindle ours.

CHESTER. C. M.   THOS. HASTINGS.

1. O Ho-ly Ghost, the Com-fort-er, How is thy love de-spised, While the heart longs for sym-pa-thy And friends are i-dol-ized, And friends are i-dol-ized.

198   *The Comforter's love.*   ANON.

O Holy Ghost, the Comforter,
  How is thy love despised,
While the heart longs for sympathy
  And friends are idolized.

2 O Spirit of the living God,
  Brooding with dove-like wings
Over the helpless and the weak
  Among created things!

3 Where should our feebleness find strength,
  Our helplessness a stay,

Didst thou not bring us hope and help,
  And comfort, day by day?

4 Great are thy consolations, Lord.
  And mighty is thy power,
In sickness and in solitude,
  In sorrow's darkest hour.

5 Oh, if the souls that now despise
  And grieve thee, heavenly Dove,
Would seek thee, and would welcome thee.
  How would they prize thy love!

MERCY. 7s.

E. P. PARKER, arr.

1. Ho - ly Ghost! with light di - vine, Shine up - on this heart of mine:

Chase the shades of night a - way, Turn my dark - ness in - to day.

199 *All-divine.* A. REED.

HOLY Ghost! with light divine,
Shine upon this heart of mine;
Chase the shades of night away,
Turn my darkness into day.

2 Holy Ghost! with power divine,
Cleanse this guilty heart of mine;
Long hath sin, without control,
Held dominion o'er my soul.

3 Holy Ghost! with joy divine,
Cheer this saddened heart of mine;
Bid my many woes depart,
Heal my wounded, bleeding heart.

4 Holy Spirit! all-divine,
Dwell within this heart of mine;
Cast down every idol-throne,
Reign supreme—and reign alone.

FULTON. 7s.

W. B. BRADBURY.

1. Gra - cious Spir - it, Love di - vine! Let thy light with - in me shine;

All my guilt - y fears re - move, Fill me with thy heavenly love.

200 *"Keep me, Lord!"* J. STOCKER.

GRACIOUS Spirit, Love divine!
Let thy light within me shine;
All my guilty fears remove,
Fill me with thy heavenly love.

2 Speak thy pardoning grace to me,
Set the burdened sinner free;
Lead me to the Lamb of God;
Wash me in his precious blood.

3 Life and peace to me impart,
Seal salvation on my heart;
Breathe thyself into my breast,—
Earnest of immortal rest.

4 Let me never from thee stray,
Keep me in the narrow way;
Fill my soul with joy divine,
Keep me, Lord! for ever thine.

HAYDN. S. M.   F. J. HAYDN.

1. Come, Ho-ly Spirit, come! Let thy bright beams arise; Dis-pel the sorrow from our minds, The darkness from our eyes.

201 *Giver of Grace.* J. HART.

Come, Holy Spirit, come!
  Let thy bright beams arise;
Dispel the sorrow from our minds,
  The darkness from our eyes.

2 Convince us of our sin;
  Then lead to Jesus' blood,
And to our wondering view reveal
  The mercies of our God.

3 Revive our drooping faith,
  Our doubts and fears remove,

And kindle in our breasts the flame
  Of never-dying love.

4 'Tis thine to cleanse the heart,
  To sanctify the soul,
To pour fresh life in every part,
  And new-create the whole.

5 Come, Holy Spirit, come;
  Our minds from bondage free;
Then shall we know, and praise, and love,
  The Father, Son, and thee.

MORNINGTON. S. M.   G. W. MORNINGTON.

1. Blest Com-fort-ter di-vine, Whose rays of heavenly love

A-mid our gloom and dark-ness shine, And point our souls a-bove;—

202 *"Still small voice."* L. H. H. SIGOURNEY.

Blest Comforter divine,
  Whose rays of heavenly love
Amid our gloom and darkness shine,
  And point our souls above;—

2 Thou, who with "still small voice,"
  Dost stop the sinner's way,
And bid the mourning saint rejoice,
  Though earthly joys decay;—

3 Thou, whose inspiring breath
  Can make the cloud of care,
And ev'n the gloomy vale of death,
  A smile of glory wear;—

4 Thou, who dost fill the heart
  With love to all our race;—
Blest Comforter, to us impart
  The blessings of thy grace.

WHITEFIELD. S. M.

EDWARD MILLER.

1. Come, Ho - ly Spir - it, come, With en - er - gy di - vine;

And on this poor be - night - ed soul, With beams of mer - cy shine.

203 *The heart melted.* ‘B. BEDDOME.

Come, Holy Spirit, come,
  With energy divine;
And on this poor benighted soul,
  With beams of mercy shine.

2 Oh, melt this frozen heart;
  This stubborn will subdue;
Each evil passion overcome,
  And form me all anew.

3 Mine will the profit be,
  But thine shall be the praise;
And unto thee will I devote
  The remnant of my days.

204 *Teaching Truth.* ANON.

Come, Spirit, source of light,
  Thy grace is unconfined;
Dispel the gloomy shades of night,
  The darkness of the mind.

2 Now to our eyes display
  The truth thy words reveal;
Cause us to run the heavenly way,
  Delighting in thy will.

3 Thy teachings make us know
  The mysteries of thy love,
The vanity of things below,
  The joy of things above.

4 While through this maze we stray,
  Oh, spread thy beams abroad;
Disclose the dangers of the way,
  And guide our steps to God.

205 *He works in us.* J. MONTGOMERY.

'Tis God the Spirit leads
  In paths before unknown;
The work to be performed is ours,
  The strength is all his own.

2 Supported by his grace
  We still pursue our way;
And hope at last to reach the prize,
  Secure in endless day.

3 'Tis he that works to will,
  'Tis he that works to do;
His is the power by which we act,
  His be the glory too.

OLNEY. S. M.

LOWELL MASON, arr.

1. Tis God the Spirit leads In paths before unknown; The work to be performed is ours, The strength is all his own.

SHAWMUT. S. M.   LOWELL MASON, arr.

1. Oh, where shall rest be found— Rest for the wea - ry soul?

'T were vain the o - cean depths to sound, Or pierce to eith - er pole.

206   *Deut.* 30 : 19.   J. MONTGOMERY.
OH, where shall rest be found—
Rest for the weary soul?
'T were vain the ocean depths to sound,
Or pierce to either pole.

2 The world can never give
The bliss for which we sigh:
'T is not the whole of life to live,
Nor all of death to die.

3 Beyond this vale of tears
There is a life above,
Unmeasured by the flight of years;
And all that life is love.

4 There is a death whose pang
Outlasts the fleeting breath:
Oh, what eternal horrors hang
Around the second death!

5 Lord God of truth and grace!
Teach us that death to shun;
Lest we be banished from thy face,
And evermore undone.

GORTON. S. M.   FROM BEETHOVEN.

1. Not all the blood of beasts On Jewish altars slain, Could give the guilty conscience peace, Or wash away the stain.

207   *"None other name."*   I. WATTS.
Nor all the blood of beasts
On Jewish altars slain,
Could give the guilty conscience peace,
Or wash away the stain.

2 But Christ the heavenly Lamb
Takes all our sins away,
A sacrifice of nobler name
And richer blood than they.

3 My faith would lay her hand
On that dear head of thine,
While like a penitent I stand,
And there confess my sin.

4 My soul looks back to see
The burdens thou didst bear,
When hanging on the cursèd tree,
And hopes her guilt was there.

5 Believing, we rejoice
To see the curse remove;
We bless the Lamb with cheerful voice,
And sing his dying love.

GANGES.² C. P. M.   S. CHANDLER.

·1. Awaked by Sinai's awful sound, My soul in bonds of guilt I found, And knew not where to go;

One solemn truth increased my pain, "The sinner must be born a-gain," Or sink to end-less woe.

208 *Regeneration needed.* s. OCCOM.

AWAKED by Sinai's awful sound,
My soul in bonds of guilt I found,
 And knew not where to go;
One solemn truth increased my pain,
"The sinner must be born again,"
 Or sink to endless woe.

2 I heard the law its thunders roll,
While guilt lay heavy on my soul—
 A·vast oppressive load;
All creature-aid I saw was vain;
"The sinner must be born again,"
 Or drink the wrath of God.

3 But while I thus in anguish lay,
The bleeding Saviour passed that way,
 My bondage to remove.
The sinner, once by justice slain,
Now by his grace is born again,
 And sings redeeming love.

209 *"In jeopardy."* C. WESLEY.

Lo! ON a narrow neck of land,
'Twixt two unbounded seas, I stand,
 Secure! insensible!
A point of time, a moment's space,
Removes me to you heavenly place,
 Or shuts me up in hell.

2 O God! my inmost soul convert,
And deeply on my thoughtful heart
 Eternal things impress:
Give me to feel their solemn weight,
And save me ere it be too late;
 Wake me to righteousness.

3 Before me place, in dread array,
The pomp of that tremendous day,
 When thou with clouds shalt come
To judge the nations at thy bar;
And tell me, Lord! shall I be there
 To meet a joyful doom!

MERIBAH. C. P. M.   LOWELL MASON.

1. Lo, on a nar-row neck of land, 'Twixt two unbounded seas I stand, Se-

cure! In-sen-si-ble! {A point of time, a moment's space, } Or shuts me up in hell.
{Removes me to yon heavenly place, }

WELLS. L. M.

ISRAEL HOLDROYD, *arr.*

1. Broad is the road that leads to death, And thousands walk to - geth - er there;

But wis - dom shows a nar - row path, With here and there a tra - vel - er.

210   *The narrow path.*   I. WATTS.

BROAD is the road that leads to death,
  And thousands walk together there;
But wisdom shows a narrow path,
  With here and there a traveler.

2 "Deny thyself and take thy cross,"—
  Is the Redeemer's great command:
Nature must count her gold but dross,
  If she would gain this heavenly land.

3 The fearful soul that tires and faints,
  And walks the ways of God no more,
Is but esteemed almost a saint, '
  And makes his own destruction sure.

4 Lord! let not all my hopes be vain:
  Create my heart entirely new;
Which hypocrites could ne'er attain,
  Which false apostates never knew.

REPENTANCE. L. M.

THEO. E. PERKINS.

1. Je - sus, en - grave it on my heart, That thou the one thing need - ful art;

I could from all things part - ed be, But nev - er, nev - er, Lord, from thee.

211   *"One thing needful."*   S. MEDLEY.

JESUS, engrave it on my heart,
  That thou the one thing needful art;
I could from all things parted be,
  But never, never, Lord, from thee.

2 Needful is thy most precious blood,
  To reconcile my soul to God;
Needful is thy indulgent care;
  Needful thy all-prevailing prayer.

3 Needful art thou, my guide, my stay,
Through all life's dark and weary way;
Nor less in death thou'lt needful be,
To bring my spirit home to thee.

4 Then needful still, my God, my King,
Thy name eternally I'll sing!
Glory and praise be ever his,—
The one thing needful Jesus is!

PRAYER. S. M.　　　　　　　　　　　　　　　　　　LEONARD MARSHALL.

1. Can sinners hope for heaven, Who love this world so well? Or dream of fu - ture hap - pi - ness, While on the road to hell?

212 *Pardon and Purity.*　　ANON.

CAN sinners hope for heaven,
　Who love this world so well?
Or dream of future happiness,
　While on the road to hell?

2 Shall they hosannas sing,
　With an unhallowed tongue?
Shall palms adorn the guilty hand
　Which does its neighbor wrong?

3 Thy grace, O God, alone,
　Good hope can e'er afford!
The pardoned and the pure shall see
　The glory of the Lord.

213　*"All downward."*　I. WATTS.

LIKE sheep we went astray,
　And broke the fold of God—
Each wandering in a different way,
　But all the downward road.

2 How dreadful was the hour,
　When God our wanderings laid,
And did at once his vengeance pour
　Upon the Shepherd's head!

3 How glorious was the grace,
　When Christ sustained the stroke!
His life and blood the Shepherd pays,
　A ransom for the flock.

4 But God shall raise his head,
　O'er all the sons of men,
And make him see a numerous seed,
　To recompense his pain.

214　*"Jesus only."*　H. BONAR.

NOT what these hands have done
　Can save this guilty soul;
Not what this toiling flesh has borne
　Can make my spirit whole.

2 Not what I feel or do
　Can give me peace with God;
Not all my prayers, and sighs, and tears,
　Can bear my awful load.

3 Thy work alone, O Christ,
　Can ease this weight of sin;
Thy blood alone, O Lamb of God,
　Can give me peace within.

IOWA. S. M.　　　　　　　　　　　　　　　　　　　A. CHAPIN.

1. A charge to keep I have, A God to glo-ri-fy, A nev-er-dy-ing soul to save, And fit it for the sky,

215　*Probation.*　C. WESLEY.

A CHARGE to keep I have,
　A God to glorify,
A never-dying soul to save,
　And fit it for the sky.

2 To serve the present age,
　My calling to fulfill;
Oh, may it all my powers engage
　To do my Master's will.

3 Arm me with jealous care,
　As in thy sight to live;
And oh, thy servant, Lord, prepare
　A strict account to give.

4 Help me to watch and pray,
　And on thyself rely,
Assured, if I my trust betray,
　I shall for ever die.

COWPER. C. M.   LOWELL MASON.

1. There is a foun-tain filled with blood, Drawn from Im-man-uel's veins; And

sinners, plunged beneath that flood, Lose all their guilt-y stains, Lose all their guilt-y stains.

216   *Zech.* 13: 1.   W. COWPER.

THERE is a fountain filled with blood,
  Drawn from Immanuel's veins;
And sinners, plunged beneath that flood,
  Lose all their guilty stains.

2 The dying thief rejoiced to see
  That fountain in his day;
And there may I, though vile as he,
  Wash all my sins away.

3 Dear dying Lamb, thy precious blood
  Shall never lose its power,
Till all the ransomed church of God
  Be saved to sin no more.

4 E'er since, by faith, I saw the stream
  Thy flowing wounds supply,
Redeeming love has been my theme,
  And shall be, till I die.

5 Then in a nobler, sweeter song,
  I'll sing thy power to save,
When this poor lisping, stammering tongue
  Lies silent in the grave.

217   *The Gospel.*   S. MEDLEY.

OH, what amazing words of grace
  Are in the gospel found,
Suited to every sinner's case
  Who hears the joyful sound!

2 Come, then, with all your wants and
  Your every burden bring; [wounds;
Here love, unchanging love, abounds,—
  A deep celestial spring.

3 This spring with living water flows,
  And heavenly joy imparts:
Come, thirsty souls! your wants disclose
  And drink, with thankful hearts.

FOUNTAIN. C. M.   WESTERN AIR.

1. There is a fountain filled with blood, Drawn from Immanuel's veins; And sinners plunged be-

FINE.   D. S.

neath that flood, Lose all their guilty stains, Lose all their guilty stains, Lose all their guilty stains.

ARLINGTON. C. M.

T. A. ARNE.

1. A - maz - ing grace! how sweet the sound That saved a wretch like me!

I once was lost, but now am found,— Was blind, but now I see.

218   *"Amazing grace."*   J. NEWTON.

AMAZING grace! how sweet the sound
  That saved a wretch like me!
I once was lost, but now am found—
  Was blind, but now I see.

2 'Twas grace that taught my heart to fear,
  And grace my fears relieved;
How precious did that grace appear,
  The hour I first believed!

3 Through many dangers, toils, and snares,
  I have already come;
'Tis grace hath brought me safe thus far,
  And grace will lead me home.

4 Yea—when this flesh and heart shall fail,
  And mortal life shall cease,
I shall possess, within the vail,
  A life of joy and peace.

5 The earth shall soon dissolve like snow,
  The sun forbear to shine;
But God, who called me here below,
  Will be for ever mine.

219   *"Salvation."*   I. WATTS.

SALVATION!—oh, the joyful sound!
  'Tis pleasure to our ears;
A sovereign balm for every wound,
  A cordial for our fears.

2 Buried in sorrow and in sin,
  At hell's dark door we lay;—
But we arise by grace divine,
  To see a heavenly day.

3 Salvation!—let the echo fly
  The spacious earth around;
While all the armies of the sky
  Conspire to raise the sound.

SIMPSON. C. M.

FROM LOUIS SPOHR.

1. Sal - va - tion!—oh, the joy - ful sound! 'Tis pleas - ure to our ears;

A sove - reign balm for ev - ery wound. A cor - dial for our fears.

SCOTLAND. 12s.
Small notes for hymn 477.
J. CLARK.

1. The voice of free grace cries, Escape to the mountain, For A - dam's lost race Christ hath

opened a fountain; { For sin and unclean-ness, and ev - ery transgression, His
{ Halle - lu - jah to the Lamb, who hath purchased our par - don, We'll

blood flows most freely in streams of salvation, His blood flows most freely in streams of sal-va-tion. }
praise him a - gain, when we pass over Jordan, We'll praise him a - gain, when we pass over Jordan. }

220
" Flee for life !"   R. BURDSALL.

The voice of free grace cries, Escape to
the mountain,
For Adam's lost race Christ hath opened
a fountain;
For sin and uncleanness, and every transgression,
His blood flows most freely in streams of
salvation.
    Hallelujah to the Lamb, etc.

2 Ye souls that are wounded! oh, flee to
the Saviour!
He calls you in mercy, 'tis infinite favor;
Your sins are increasing, escape to the
mountain—
His blood can remove them, it flows from
the fountain.
    Hallelujah to the Lamb, etc.

3 With joy shall we stand when escaped
to the shore;
With harps in our hands we will praise him
the more!
We'll range the sweet plains on the banks
of the river,
And sing of salvation for ever and ever!
    Hallelujah to the Lamb, etc.

LOVING-KINDNESS. L. M.
WESTERN MELODY.

1. Awake, my soul, to joyful lays, And sing thy great Redeemer's praise; He justly claims a song from me,

His loving-kindness, oh, how free! Loving kindness, loving-kindness, His loving-kindness, oh, how free!

THE NINETY AND NINE. P. M.

IRA D. SANKEY.

1. There were ninety and nine that safely lay In the shelter of the fold, But one was out on the hills a-way, Far off from the gates of gold— A-way on the moun-tains wild and bare, A-way from the ten-der Shepherd's care, A-way from the tender Shepherd's care.

221   *"To save the lost."*   E. C. CLEPHANE.

THERE were ninety and nine that safely lay
  In the shelter of the fold,
But one was out on the hills away,
  Far off from the gates of gold—
Away on the mountains wild and bare,
Away from the tender Shepherd's care.

2 "Lord, thou hast here thy ninety and nine:
  Are they not enough for thee?"
But the Shepherd made answer: "This of mine
  Has wandered away from me: [mine
And although the road be rough and steep
I go to the desert to find my sheep."

3 But none of the ransomed ever knew
  How deep were the waters crossed;
Nor how dark was the night that the Lord
    passed through
Ere he found his sheep that was lost;
Out in the desert he heard its cry—
'Twas helpless and sick, and ready to die.

4 But all through the mountains, thunder-
  And up from the rocky steep, [riven,
There rose a cry to the gate of heaven,
  "Rejoice! I have found my sheep!"
And the angels echoed around the throne,
"Rejoice, for the Lord brings back his own!'

---

222   L. M. *Loving-kindness.*   S. MEDLEY.

AWAKE, my soul, to joyful lays,
And sing thy great Redeemer's praise;
He justly claims a song from me:
His loving-kindness, oh, how free!

2 He saw me ruined in the fall,
Yet loved me, notwithstanding all;
He saved me from my lost estate:
His loving-kindness, oh, how great!

3 Though numerous hosts of mighty foes,
Though earth and hell my way oppose,
He safely leads my soul along:
His loving-kindness, oh, how strong!

4 When trouble, like a gloomy cloud,
Has gathered thick and thundered loud,
He near my soul has always stood:
His loving-kindness, oh, how good!

LENOX. H. M.   L. EDSON.

1. Arise, my soul, arise! Shake off thy guilty fears; The bleeding Sacrifice In my behalf appears;

Before the throne my Surety stands: Be -

Before the throne my Surety stands: My name is written on his hands.

fore the throne my Surety stands: Before the throne my Surety stands: My name is written on his hands.

223   *Our Surety.*   C. WESLEY.

ARISE, my soul, arise!
   Shake off thy guilty fears;
The bleeding Sacrifice
   In my behalf appears;
Before the throne my Surety stands:
My name is written on his hands.

2 He ever lives above,
   For me to intercede,
His all-redeeming love,
   His precious blood to plead;
His blood atoned for all our race,
And sprinkles now the throne of grace.

3 My God is reconciled;
   His pardoning voice I hear;
He owns me for his child;
   I can no longer fear;
With confidence I now draw nigh,
And Father, Abba, Father, cry.

224   *Year of Jubilee.*   C. WESLEY.

BLOW ye the trumpet, blow;—
   The gladly solemn sound;—
Let all the nations know,
   To earth's remotest bound,
The year of jubilee is come:
Return, ye ransomed sinners, home.

2 Jesus, our great High-Priest,
   Hath full atonement made;
Ye weary spirits, rest;
   Ye mournful souls, be glad:
The year of jubilee is come;
Return, ye ransomed sinners, home.

3 Extol the Lamb of God,
   The all-atoning Lamb;
Redemption in his blood
   Throughout the world proclaim:
The year of jubilee is come;
Return, ye ransomed sinners, home.

GLASGOW. C. M.   G. F. ROOT.

1. Great God, when I ap-proach thy throne, And all thy glo-ry see;

This is my stay, and this a-lone, That Je-sus died for me.

F. GIARDINI.

1. Awake, my heart, arise, my tongue, Prepare a tuneful voice; In God, the life of all my joys,
D. S.—Up-on a poor, pollut-ed worm,

A - loud will I re-joice. 'Tis he adorned my nak-ed soul, And made sal-va-tion mine;
He makes his graces shine.

225 *" The Seamless Robe."* I. WATTS.

AWAKE, my heart, arise, my tongue,
  Prepare a tuneful voice;
In God, the life of all my joys,
  Aloud will I rejoice.
'Tis he adorned my naked soul,
  And made salvation mine;
Upon a poor, polluted worm,
  He makes his graces shine.

2 And lest the shadow of a spot
  Should on my soul be found,
He took the robe the Saviour wrought,
  And cast it all around.

How far the heavenly robe exceeds
  What earthly princes wear!
These ornaments, how bright they shine!
  How white the garments are!

3 The Spirit wrought my faith and love,
  And hope and every grace;
But Jesus spent his life to work
  The robe of righteousness.
Strangely, my soul, art thou arrayed,
  By the great sacred Three;
In sweetest harmony of praise,
  Let all thy powers agree.

---

226 *"Jesus died for me."* ANON.

GREAT God, when I approach thy throne,
  And all thy glory see;
This is my stay, and this alone,
  That Jesus died for me.

2 How can a soul condemned to die,
  Escape the just decree?
Helpless, and full of sin am I,
  But Jesus died for me.

3 Burdened with sin's oppressive chain,
  Oh, how can I get free?
No peace can all my efforts gain,
  But Jesus died for me.

4 And Lord, when I behold thy face,
  This must be all my plea;
Save me by thy almighty grace,
  For Jesus died for me.

227 *Divine compassion.* A. STEELE

JESUS,—and didst thou leave the sky,
  To bear our griefs and woes?
And didst thou bleed, and groan and die,
  For thy rebellious foes?

2 Well might the heavens with wonder view
  A love so strange as thine!
No thought of angels ever knew
  Compassion so divine!

3 Is there a heart that will not bend
  To thy divine control?
Descend, O sovereign love, descend,
  And melt that stubborn soul.

4 Oh! may our willing hearts confess
  Thy sweet, thy gentle sway;
Glad captives of thy matchless grace,
  Thy righteous rule obey.

ALL TO CHRIST. P. M.

J. T. GRAPE.

1. I hear the Saviour say, Thy strength indeed is small; Child of weakness, watch and pray,

CHORUS.

Find in me thine all in all. Je-sus paid it all, All to him I owe;

Sin had left a crim-son stain; He washed it white as snow.

228   *The debt paid.*   E. M. HALL.

I HEAR the Saviour say,
  Thy strength indeed is small;
Child of weakness, watch and pray,
  Find in me thine all in all.

CHO.—Jesus paid it all,
    All to him I owe;
    Sin had left a crimson stain;
    He washed it white as snow.

2 Lord, now indeed I find
  Thy power, and thine alone,
Can change the leper's spots,
  And melt the heart of stone.—CHO.

3 For nothing good have I
  Whereby thy grace to claim—
I'll wash my garment white
  In the blood of Calvary's Lamb.—CHO.

4 When from my dying bed
  My ransomed soul shall rise,
Then "Jesus paid it all"
  Shall rend the vaulted skies.—CHO.

5 And when before the throne
  I stand in him complete,
I'll lay my trophies down,
  All down at Jesus' feet.—CHO.

SPANISH HYMN. 7s, 6l.

SPANISH MELODY.

FINE.   D.C.

1. From the cross uplifted high, Where the Saviour deigns to die, { What melodious sounds we hear, }
D. C. "Love's redeeming work is done—Come and welcome, sinner, come!" { Bursting on the ravished ear!— }

I AM COMING. P. M.   L. HARTSOUGH.

1. I hear thy wel-come voice, That calls me, Lord, to thee, For cleansing in thy
pre-cious blood, That flowed on Cal-va-ry. CHORUS. I am com-ing, Lord!
Com-ing now to thee! Wash me, cleanse me, in the blood That flowed on Cal-va-ry!

229   *"Atoning blood."*   L. HARTSOUGH.

I HEAR thy welcome voice,
  That calls me, Lord, to thee,
For cleansing in thy precious blood,
  That flowed on Calvary.

CHO.—I am coming, Lord !
    Coming now to thee;
  Wash me, cleanse me, in the blood
    That flowed on Calvary !

2 Though coming weak and vile,
  Thou dost my strength assure;

Thou dost my vileness fully cleanse,
  Till spotless all, and pure.—CHO.

3 'Tis Jesus calls me on
  To perfect faith and love,
To perfect hope, and peace, and trust,
  For earth and heaven above.—CHO.

4 All hail ! atoning blood !
  All hail ! redeeming grace !
All hail ! the gift of Christ, our Lord,
  Our Strength and Righteousness.—CHO.

230   7s, 6l. *"Come and welcome."*   T. HAWEIS.

FROM the cross uplifted high,
Where the Saviour deigns to die,
What melodious sounds we hear,
Bursting on the ravished ear !—
"Love's redeeming work is done—
Come and welcome, sinner, come !

2 "Sprinkled now with blood the throne—
Why beneath thy burdens groan?
On my pierced body laid,
Justice owns the ransom paid—
Bow the knee, and kiss the Son—
Come and welcome, sinner, come !

3 "Spread for thee, the festal board
See with richest bounty stored;
To thy Father's bosom pressed,
Thou shalt be a child confessed,
Never from his house to roam;
Come and welcome, sinner, come !

4 "Soon the days of life shall end—
Lo, I come—your Saviour, Friend !
Safe your spirit to convey
To the realms of endless day,
Up to my eternal home—
Come and welcome, sinner, come !"

7

TELL THE STORY. 7s, 6s. D.   W. G. FISCHER.

1. I love to tell the sto-ry Of unseen things above, Of Je-sus and his glory, Of Jesus and his love.

I love to tell the story, Because I know 'tis true; It satisfies my longings As nothing else can do.

CHORUS.

I love to tell the story, 'Twill be my theme in glory, To tell the old, old story Of Jesus and his love.

231   *The old, old story.*   K. HANKEY.

I LOVE to tell the story
  Of unseen things above,
Of Jesus and his glory,
  Of Jesus and his love.
I love to tell the story,
  Because I know 'tis true;
It satisfies my longings
  As nothing else can do.—CHO.

2 I love to tell the story:
  'Tis pleasant to repeat
What seems each time I tell it,
  More wonderfully sweet.
I love to tell the story:
  For some have never heard
The message of salvation,
  From God's own holy word.—CHO.

3 I love to tell the story;
  For those who know it best
Seem hungering and thirsting
  To hear it like the rest.
And when, in scenes of glory,
  I sing the NEW, NEW SONG,
'Twill be the OLD, OLD STORY
  That I have loved so long.—CHO.

232   *Jesus' Cross.*   ANON.

I SAW the cross of Jesus,
  When burdened with my sin;
I sought the cross of Jesus,
  To give me peace within;
I brought my soul to Jesus,
  He cleansed it in is blood;
And in the cross of Jesus
  I found my peace with God.

CHO.—No righteousness, no merit,
  No beauty can I plead;
Yet in the cross I glory,
  My title there I read.

2 Sweet is the cross of Jesus!
  There let my weary heart
Still rest in peace unshaken,
  Till with him, ne'er to part;
And then in strains of glory
  I'll sing his wondrous power,
Where sin can never enter,
  And death is known no more.

CHO.—I love the cross of Jesus,
  It tells me what I am;
A vile and guilty creature,
  Saved only through the Lamb.

RETURN. C. M. THOS. HASTINGS.

1. Re-turn, O wan-d'rer, to thy home, Thy Fa - ther calls for thee:

CODA.

No long-er now an ex - ile roam, In guilt and mis - e - ry. Re-turn, re-turn.

233 *The Prodigal Son.* T. HASTINGS.

RETURN, O wanderer, to thy home,
Thy Father calls for thee:
No longer now an exile roam
In guilt and misery.

2 Return, O wanderer, to thy home,
Thy Saviour calls for thee:

"The Spirit and the Bride say, Come;"
Oh, now for refuge flee!

3 Return, O wanderer, to thy home,
'Tis madness to delay:
There are no pardons in the tomb;
And brief is mercy's day!

BALERMA. C. M. HUGH WILSON.

1. Come, trem-bling sin - ner, in whose breast A thou-sand thoughts re - volve;

Come, with your guilt and fear op-pressed, And make this last re - solve.

234 *Esther 4: 16.* E. JONES.

COME, trembling sinner, in whose breast
A thousand thoughts revolve;
Come, with your guilt and fear oppressed,
And make this last resolve;—

2 "I'll go to Jesus, though my sins
Like mountains round me close;
I know his courts, I'll enter in,
Whatever may oppose.

3 "Prostrate I'll lie before his throne,
And there my guilt confess;

I'll tell him I'm a wretch undone,
Without his sovereign grace.

4 "Perhaps he will admit my plea,
Perhaps will hear my prayer;
But if I perish, I will pray,
And perish only there.

5 "I can but perish if I go;
I am resolved to try;
For if I stay away, I know
I must for ever die."

OWEN. S. M.   J. E. SWEETSER.

Sing rapidly.

1. Did Christ o'er sin - ners weep, And shall our cheeks be dry?

Let floods of pen - i - ten - tial grief Burst forth from ev - ery eye.

235 *Weeping for sinners.* B. BEDDOME.

Did Christ o'er sinners weep,
And shall our cheeks be dry?
Let floods of penitential grief
Burst forth from every eye.

2 The Son of God in tears
Angels with wonder see;
Be thou astonished, O my soul!
He shed those tears for thee.

3 He wept that we might weep;
Each sin demands a tear:
In heaven alone no sin is found,
And there's no weeping there.

236 *The call of love.* A. B. HYDE.

And canst thou, sinner! slight
The call of love divine?
Shall God, with tenderness, invite,
And gain no thought of thine?

2 Wilt thou not cease to grieve
The Spirit from thy breast,
Till he thy wretched soul shall leave
With all thy sins oppressed?

3 To-day, a pardoning God
Will hear the suppliant pray;
To-day, a Saviour's cleansing blood
Will wash thy guilt away.

DETROIT. S. M.   E. P. HASTINGS.

1. Now is th'ac-cepted time, Now is the day of grace; O sinners! come, with-out de - lay, And seek the Saviour's face.

237 *The accepted time.* J. DOBELL.

Now is the accepted time,
Now is the day of grace;
O sinners! come, without delay,
And seek the Saviour's face.

2 Now is the accepted time,
The Saviour calls to-day;
To-morrow it may be too late;—
Then why should you delay?

3 Now is the accepted time,
The gospel bids you come;
And every promise in his word
Declares there yet is room.

4 Lord, draw reluctant souls,
And feast them with thy love;
Then will the angels spread their wings,
And bear the news above.

EXPOSTULATION. 11s. J. HOPKINS.

1. Oh, turn ye, oh, turn ye, for why will ye die, When God in great mercy is coming so nigh?

Now Je-sus in-vites you, the Spir-it says, Come, And an-gels are wait-ing to welcome you home.

238 *"Why will ye die?"* J. HOPKINS.

Oh, turn ye, oh, turn ye, for why will ye die,
When God in great mercy is coming so nigh?
Now Jesus invites you, the Spirit says, Come,
And angels are waiting to welcome you home.

2 In riches, in pleasures, what can you obtain,
To soothe your affliction, or banish your pain?
To bear up your spirit when summoned to die,
Or waft you to mansions of glory on high?

3 And now Christ is ready your souls to receive,
Oh, how can you question, if you will believe?
If sin is your burden, why will you not come?
'Tis you he bids welcome; he bids you come home.

239 *"I made haste."* T. HASTINGS.

Delay not, delay not, O sinner, draw near,
The waters of life are now flowing for thee;
No price is demanded, the Saviour is here;
Redemption is purchased, salvation is free.

2 Delay not, delay not, O sinner, to come,
For Mercy still lingers and calls thee to-day:

Her voice is not heard in the vale of the tomb;
Her message unheeded will soon pass away.

3 Delay not, delay not, the Spirit of grace,
Long grieved and resisted, may take his sad flight,
And leave thee in darkness to finish thy race,
To sink in the gloom of eternity's night.

4 Delay not, delay not, the hour is at hand,
The earth shall dissolve and the heavens shall fade,
The dead, small and great, in the judgment shall stand;
What power then, O sinner, will lend thee its aid!

240 *"Acquaint thyself."* KNOX.

Acquaint thyself quickly, O sinner, with God,
And joy, like the sunshine, shall beam on thy road,
And peace, like the dewdrop, shall fall on thy head,
And sleep, like an angel, shall visit thy bed.

2 Acquaint thyself quickly, O sinner, with God,
And he shall be with thee when fears are abroad;
Thy Safeguard in danger that threatens thy path;
Thy Joy in the valley and shadow of death.

BERA. L. M.   J. E. GOULD.

1. Be - hold a Stran - ger at the door! He gent - ly knocks, has knocked be - fore,

Has wait - ed long, is wait - ing still; You treat no oth - er friend so ill.

241   *"At the door."*   J. GRIGG.

BEHOLD a Stranger at the door!
He gently knocks, has knocked before,
Has waited long, is waiting still;
You treat no other friend so ill.

2 Oh, lovely attitude! he stands
With melting heart and laden hands;
Oh, matchless kindness! and he shows
This matchless kindness to his foes.

3 But will he prove a friend indeed?
He will, the very friend you need—
The Friend of sinners; yes, 't is he,
With garments dyed on Calvary.

4 Rise, touched with gratitude divine,
Turn out his enemy and thine,
That soul-destroying monster sin,
And let the heavenly Stranger in.

INGHAM. L. M.   LOWELL MASON.

1. God call - ing yet! shall I not hear? Earth's pleasures shall I still hold dear?

Shall life's swift pass - ing years all fly, And still my soul in slumber lie?

242   *"God calling yet."*   J. BORTHWICK.

God calling yet! shall I not hear?
Earth's pleasures shall I still hold dear?
Shall life's swift passing years all fly,
And still my soul in slumber lie?

2 God calling yet! shall I not rise?
Can I his loving voice despise,
And basely his kind care repay?
He calls me still; can I delay?

3 God calling yet! and shall I give
No heed, but still in bondage live?
I wait, but he does not forsake;
He calls me still; my heart, awake!

4 God calling yet! I cannot stay;
My heart I yield without delay;
Vain world, farewell! from thee I part;
The voice of God hath reached my heart.

ASHWELL. L. M. LOWELL MASON.

1. Why will ye waste on trifling cares That life which God's compassion spares, While, in the various range of

thought, The one thing needful is for-got?

243 *One Thing needful.* P. DODDRIDGE.

WHY will ye waste on trifling cares
That life which God's compassion spares,
While, in the various range of thought,
The one thing needful is forgot?

2 Shall God invite you from above—
Shall Jesus urge his dying love—
Shall troubled conscience give you pain—
And all these pleas unite in vain?

3 Not so your eyes will always view
Those objects which you now pursue;
Not so will heaven and hell appear,
When death's decisive hour is near.

4 Almighty God! thy grace impart;
Fix deep conviction on each heart:
Nor let us waste on trifling cares
That life which thy compassion spares.

WHY NOT TO-NIGHT? L. M. WM. F. SHERWIN.

1. Oh, do not let the word de-part, And close thine eyes against the light; Poor sinner, harden

REFRAIN.

not thy heart; Thou wouldst be saved; why not to-night? Why not to-night? why not to-night?

Thou wouldst be saved—why not to-night?

244 *"Why not to-night?"* H. BONAR.

Oh, do not let the word depart,
And close thine eyes against the light;
Poor sinner, harden not thy heart:
Thou wouldst be saved; why not to-night?
REF.

2 To-morrow's sun may never rise
To bless thy long-deluded sight;
This is the time; oh, then be wise!
Thou wouldst be saved; why not to-night?
REF.

3 Our God in pity lingers still;
And wilt thou thus his love requite?
Renounce at length thy stubborn will;
Thou wouldst be saved; why not to-night?
REF.

4 Our blessèd Lord refuses none
Who would to him their souls unite;
Then be the work of grace begun:
Thou wouldst be saved; why not to-night?
REF.

THOS. HASTINGS.

1. Come to Calvary's ho - ly mountain, Sinners, ru - ined by the fall! Here a pure and

heal - ing foun - tain, Flows to you, to me, to all,— In a full, per-

pet - ual tide, Opened when our Sav - iour died, O - pened when our Saviour died.

245 *A fountain opened.* J. MONTGOMERY.

COME to Calvary's holy mountain,
Sinners, ruined by the fall!
Here a pure and healing fountain
Flows to you, to me, to all,—
In a full, perpetual tide,
Opened when our Saviour died.

2 Come, in sorrow and contrition,
Wounded, impotent, and blind!
Here the guilty, free remission,
Here the troubled, peace may find;
Health this fountain will restore,
He that drinks shall thirst no more—

3 He that drinks shall live for ever;
'Tis a soul-renewing flood:
God is faithful; God will never
Break his covenant in blood,
Signed when our Redeemer died,
Sealed when he was glorified.

GRACE. 8s, 7s, 4s.

C. C. CONVERSE, *arr.*

1. Come, ye sinners, poor and wretched, Weak and wounded, sick and sore, Jesus ready stands to save you,

D. S.—He is a - ble, He is a - ble,

FINE.

D. S.

Full of pit - y, love and power. He is a - ble, he is a - ble, He is willing, doubt no more.
He is willing, doubt no more.

COME, YE DISCONSOLATE. 11s, 10s.   S. WEBBE.

1. Come, ye dis-con-so-late, where'er ye lan-guish; Come to the mercy-seat, fer-vent-ly kneel;

Here bring your wounded hearts, here tell your anguish, Earth has no sorrow that heaven cannot heal.

246   *"Here speaks the Comforter."* T. MOORE.

COME, ye disconsolate, where'er ye languish:
  Come to the mercy-seat, fervently kneel;
Here bring your wounded hearts, here tell
    your anguish;
  Earth has no sorrow that heaven cannot
    heal.

2 Joy of the comfortless, light of the stray-
    ing,
  Hope of the penitent, fadeless and pure;

Here speaks the Comforter tenderly say-
    ing—
  Earth has no sorrow that heaven cannot
    cure.

3 Here see the Bread of Life; see waters
    flowing
  Forth from the throne of God, pure from
    above;
Come to the feast of love: come, ever knowing
  Earth has no sorrow but heaven can re-
    move.

247   *"Ho, ye needy!"*   J. HART.

COME, ye sinners, poor and wretched,
  Weak and wounded, sick and sore,
Jesus ready stands to save you,
  Full of pity, love and power.
      He is able,
  He is willing, doubt no more.

2 Ho, ye needy; come, and welcome;
    God's free bounty glorify!
True belief and true repentance,
  Every grace that brings us nigh,
      Without money,
  Come to Jesus Christ, and buy.

3 Let not conscience make you linger,
    Nor of fitness fondly dream;
All the fitness he requireth
  Is to feel your need of him;
      This he gives you;
  'Tis the Spirit's rising beam.

248   *"Mercy's Call."*   J. ALLEN.

SINNERS, will you scorn the message,
  Coming from the courts above?
Mercy beams in every passage;
  Every line is full of love;
      Oh! believe it,
  Every line is full of love.

2 Now the heralds of salvation
    Joyful news from heaven proclaim!
Sinners freed from condemnation,
  Through the all-atoning Lamb!
      Life receiving
  Through the all-atoning Lamb!

3 O ye angels, hovering round us,
    Waiting spirits, speed your way;
Haste ye to the court of heaven,
  Tidings bear without delay:
      Rebel sinners
  Glad the message will obey.

MARTYN. 7s. D.   S. B. MARSH.

1. { Sinners, turn, why will ye die? God, your Maker, asks you— Why? }
 { God, who did your be - ing give, Made you with him-self to live; }
 { He the fa - tal cause de - mands, }
 { Asks the work of his own hands,— }
D. C.—Why, ye thankless creatures, why Will ye cross his love, and die?

249   *Ezekiel* 33 : 11.   C. WESLEY.

SINNERS, turn, why will ye die?
God, your Maker, asks you—Why?
God, who did your being give,
Made you with himself to live;
He the fatal cause demands,
Asks the work of his own hands,—
Why, ye thankless creatures, why
Will ye cross his love, and die?

2 Sinners, turn, why will ye die?
God, your Saviour, asks you—Why?
He who did your your souls retrieve,
Died himself that ye might live.

Will ye let him die in vain?
Crucify your Lord again?
Why, ye ransomed sinners, why
Will ye slight his grace, and die?

3 Sinners, turn, why will ye die?
God, the Spirit, asks you—Why?
He, who all your lives hath strove,
Urged you to embrace his love:
Will ye not his grace receive?
Will ye still refuse to live?
Why, ye long-sought sinners! why,
Will ye grieve your God, and die?

HORTON. 7s.   XAVIER SCHNYDER VON WARTENSEE.

1. Come, said Je - sus' sa - cred voice, Come, and make my paths your choice;
I will guide you to your home, Wea - ry pil - grim, hith - er come!

250   *"Whosoever will."*   A. L. BARBAULD.

COME, said Jesus' sacred voice,
Come, and make my paths your choice;
I will guide you to your home,
Weary pilgrim, hither come!

2 Thou who, houseless, sole, forlorn,
Long hast borne the proud world's scorn,
Long hast roamed the barren waste,
Weary pilgrim, hither haste.

3 Ye who, tossed on beds of pain,
Seek for ease, but seek in vain;
Ye, by fiercer anguish torn,
In remorse for guilt who mourn;—

4 Hither come! for here is found
Balm that flows for every wound,
Peace that ever shall endure,
Rest eternal, sacred, sure.

WARNER. L. M.   GEO. KINGSLEY, *arr.*

1. With broken heart and contrite sigh, A trembling sinner, Lord, I cry; Thy pardoning grace is rich and free: O God, be mer-ci-ful to me!

2 I smite upon my troubled breast,
With deep and conscious guilt oppressed;
Christ and his cross my only plea:
O God, be merciful to me!

3 Nor alms, nor deeds that I have done,
Can for a single sin atone;
To Calvary alone I flee:
O God, be merciful to me!

4 And when, redeemed from sin and hell,
With all the ransomed throng I dwell,
My raptured song shall ever be,
God hath been merciful to me!

251   *"Be merciful, O God."*   C. ELVEN.

WITH broken heart and contrite sigh,
A trembling sinner, Lord, I cry:
Thy pardoning grace is rich and free:
O God, be merciful to me!

WOODWORTH. L. M.   W. B. BRADBURY.

1. Just as I am, with-out one plea, But that thy blood was shed for me,

And that thou bid'st me come to thee, O Lamb of God, I come! I come!

252   *"Lamb of God."*   C. ELLIOTT.

JUST as I am, without one plea,
But that thy blood was shed for me,
And that thou bid'st me come to thee,
  O Lamb of God, I come!

2 Just as I am, and waiting not
To rid my soul of one dark blot,
To thee whose blood can cleanse each spot,
  O Lamb of God, I come!

3 Just as I am, though tossed about
With many a conflict, many a doubt,

Fightings within, and fears without,
  O Lamb of God, I come!

4 Just as I am—thou wilt receive,
Wilt welcome, pardon, cleanse, relieve;
Because thy promise I believe.
  O Lamb of God, I come!

5 Just as I am—thy love unknown
Hath broken every barrier down;
Now, to be thine, yea, thine alone,
  O Lamb of God, I come!

LAODICEA. P. M.   WM. F. SHERWIN.

1. O Saviour, I am blind! Lead thou my way: Day to my filméd eye is dark—Ev'n night is only darker day, Oh! I am blind; Dear Saviour, I am blind!

253   *The Soul's Cry.*   S. S. CUTTING.

O SAVIOUR, I am blind!
   Lead thou my way;
Day to my filméd eye is dark—
Even night is only darker day;
   Oh! I am blind,
   Dear Saviour, I am blind!

2 O Saviour, I am deaf!
   Unstop my ear:
My heart would turn to thy dear voice,
The voice thy sheep alone will hear;
   Oh! I am deaf,
   Dear Saviour, I am deaf!

3 O Saviour, I am poor!
   Give me to eat:
My hungered heart loathes earthly food,
And heavenly manna craves for meat;
   Oh! I am poor,
   Dear Saviour, I am poor!

4 O Saviour, I believe,
   Blind, deaf and poor!
Sight give me; hearing; heavenly food;
Thou hast them in thy blesséd store.
   Now I believe,
   O Saviour, I believe!

AURELIA. 7s, 6s. D.   S. S. WESLEY.

1. I lay my sins on Jesus, The spotless Lamb of God; He bears them all, and frees us From the accursed load;

I bring my guilt to Jesus, To wash my crimson stains White in his blood most precious, Till not a stain remains.

254   *"None other name."*   H. BONAR.

I LAY my sins on Jesus,
   The spotless Lamb of God;
He bears them all, and frees us
   From the accurséd load;
I bring my guilt to Jesus,
   To wash my crimson stains
White in his blood most precious,
   Till not a stain remains.

2 I lay my wants on Jesus;
   All fullness dwells in him;
He healeth my diseases,
   He doth my soul redeem:

I lay my griefs on Jesus,
   My burdens and my cares;
He from them all releases,
   He all my sorrows shares.

3 I long to be like Jesus,
   Meek, loving, lowly, mild;
I long to be like Jesus,
   The Father's holy child:
I long to be with Jesus
   Amid the heavenly throng,
To sing with saints his praises,
   And learn the angels' song.

GAYLORD. 8s, 7s. D.   J. P. HOLBROOK, arr.

1. Take me, O my Father, take me! Take me, save me, thro' thy Son; That which thou wouldst have me, make me,
D. S.—Weary come I now, and praying—

FINE.   D. S.

Let thy will in me be done. Long from thee my footsteps straying, Thorny proved the way I trod;
Take me to thy love, my God.

255   " Take me."   RAY PALMER.

Take me, O my Father, take me!
  Take me, save me, through thy Son;
That which thou wouldst have me, make me,
  Let thy will in me be done.
Long from thee my footsteps straying,
  Thorny proved the way I trod;
Weary come I now, and praying—
  Take me to thy love, my God!

2 Fruitless years with grief recalling,
  Humbly I confess my sin;
At thy feet, O Father, falling,
  To thy household take me in.

Freely now to thee I proffer
  This relenting heart of mine;
Freely life and soul I offer—
  Gift unworthy love like thine.

3 Once the world's Redeemer, dying,
  Bare our sins upon the tree;
On that sacrifice relying,
  Now I look in hope to thee;
Father, take me! all forgiving,
  Fold me to thy loving breast;
In thy love for ever living,
  I must be for ever blest!

DEPENDENCE. P. M.   WM. F. SHERWIN.

1. I need thee, O my God, Thy all - sus-taining power; I need thy cleansing blood To

CHORUS.

save me every hour.   O Sav-iour! now behold me; Let thine arms enfold me; While at the cross I'm

kneeling, Oh, come, and bless me now!

256   "I need thee."   W. F. SHERWIN.

I need thee, O my God,
  Thy all-sustaining power;

I need thy cleansing blood
  To save me every hour.—Cho.

2 I need thy Spirit, Lord,
  My comfort day by day,
To guide my steps aright,
  And warn me when I stray.—Cho.

3 I need the sheltering Rock,
  Where, from the noon-tide heat,
My soul may rest awhile
  Beneath its calm retreat.—Cho.

THARAW. 7s. 61.   H. LAMSON, arr.

1. { Lord, be-fore thy throne we bend; Now to thee our prayers ascend: }
   { Servants to our Master true, Lo! we yield thee hom-age due: } Children, to thy

throne we fly, Abba, Fa-ther, hear our cry!

257   *Psalm 123.*   J. BOWDLER.

LORD, before thy throne we bend;
Now to thee our prayers ascend:
Servants to our Master true,
Lo! we yield thee homage due:
Children, to thy throne we fly,
Abba, Father, hear our cry!

2 Low before thee, Lord! we bow;
We are weak—but mighty thou:
Sore distressed, yet suppliant still,
Here we wait thy holy will;
Bound to earth, and rooted here,
Till our Saviour God appear.

3 Leave us not beneath the power
Of temptation's darkest hour:

Swift to seal their captives' doom,
See our foes exulting come!
Jesus, Saviour! yet be nigh,
Lord of life and victory.

258   *Backsliding confessed.*   J. NEWTON.

ONCE I thought my mountain strong,
   Firmly fixed no more to move;
Then my Saviour was my song,
   Then my soul was filled with love;
Those were happy, golden days,
Sweetly spent in prayer and praise.

2 Little then myself I knew,
   Little thought of Satan's power;
Now I feel my sins anew;
   Now I feel the stormy hour!
Sin has put my joys to flight;
Sin has turned my day to night.

3 Saviour, shine and cheer my soul,
   Bid my dying hopes revive;
Make my wounded spirit whole,
   Far away the tempter drive;
Speak the word and set me free,
Let me live alone to thee.

NUREMBURG. 7s. 61.   J. R. AHLE.

1. { Once I thought my moun-tain strong, Firm - ly fixed no more to move; }
   { Then my Sav - iour was my song, Then my soul was filled with love; }

Those were hap - py, gold - en days, Sweet - ly spent in prayer and praise.

AVON. C. M.   HUGH WILSON.

1. O thou, whose ten - der mercy hears Contrition's humble sigh; Whose hand indulgent wipes the

tears From sor - row's weep - ing eye;—

259   *"Return."*   A. STEELE.

O thou, whose tender mercy hears,
  Contrition's humble sigh;
Whose hand indulgent wipes the tears
  From sorrow's weeping eye;—

2 See, Lord, before thy throne of grace,
  A wretched wanderer mourn;
Hast thou not bid me seek thy face?
  Hast thou not said—"Return?"

3 And shall my guilty fears prevail
  To drive me from thy feet?
Oh, let not this dear refuge fail,
  This only safe retreat!

4 Oh, shine on this benighted heart,
  With beams of mercy shine!
And let thy healing voice impart
  The sense of joy divine.

COME, SINNER, COME. 7s, 4s.   WM. F. SHERWIN.

1. Hark! the Spirit whispers low, "Come, sinner, come; To the Saviour humbly bow, Come, sinner, come."

Lo! the Bride invites to-day Come, sinner, come; And let him that heareth say, Come, sinner, come.

260   *"Come, sinner, come."* WM. F. SHERWIN.

Hark! the Spirit whispers low,
  "Come, sinner, come;
To the Saviour humbly bow,
  Come, sinner, come."
Lo! the Bride invites to-day,
  Come, sinner, come;
And let him that heareth say,
  Come, sinner, come.

2 Haste, oh, haste! make no delay!
  Come, sinner, come;
Christ can wash thy sins away,
  Come, sinner, come.

To that fountain full and free,
  Come, sinner, come;
Flowing still for thee, for thee!
  Come, sinner, come.

3 Jesus waits, he lingers still;
  Come, sinner, come;
Only yield to him thy will,
  Come, sinner, come.
Will you not on him believe?
  Come, sinner, come;
Oh! do not the Spirit grieve;
  Come, sinner, come.

BETHANY. 6s, 4s.   LOWELL MASON.

1. { Near-er, my God, to thee! Nearer to thee, }
   { Ev'n though it be a cross (Omit)...... } That raiseth me; Still all my song shall be, Nearer, my God, to thee,
D. C.—Near-er, my God, to thee, (Omit)...... Near-er to thee.

261   *Genesis 23: 10–22.*   S. F. ADAMS.

Nearer, my God, to thee,
  Nearer to thee!
Ev'n though it be a cross
  That raiseth me!
Still all my song shall be,
Nearer, my God, to thee,
  Nearer to thee!

2 Though, like a wanderer,
    The sun gone down,
  Darkness be over me,
    My rest a stone,
  Yet in my dreams I'd be
  Nearer, my God, to thee
    Nearer to thee!

3 There let the way appear,
    Steps unto heaven;
  All that thou sendest me,
    In mercy given;
  Angels to beckon me
  Nearer, my God, to thee,
    Nearer to thee!

4 Then, with my waking thoughts
    Bright with thy praise,
  Out of my stony griefs
    Bethel I'll raise;
  So by my woes to be
  Nearer, my God, to thee,
    Nearer to thee!

MORE LOVE. 6s, 4s.   T. E. PERKINS.
                                                                          FINE.

1. More love to thee, O Christ! More love to thee! Hear thou the prayer I make, On bended knee;
D. S.—More love, O Christ, to thee, More love to thee!

This is my earnest plea,—More love, O Christ! to thee,

262   *"Lovest thou me?"*   E. P. PRENTISS.

More love to thee, O Christ!
  More love to thee!
Hear thou the prayer I make
  On bended knee;
This is my earnest plea,—
More love, O Christ, to thee,
  More love to thee!

2 Once earthly joy I craved,
    Sought peace and rest;
  Now thee alone I seek,
    Give what is best:
  This all my prayer shall be,—
  More love, O Christ, to thee,
    More love to thee!

3 Then shall my latest breath
    Whisper thy praise;
  This be the parting cry
    My heart shall raise,—
  This still its prayer shall be,—
  More love, O Christ, to thee,
    More love to thee!

REDEN. 6s, 4s. C. C. CONVERSE.

1. { Saviour! I follow on, Guided by thee, }
   { Seeing not yet the hand (*Omit.*) ...... } That leadeth me; Hushed be my heart and still, Fear I no further ill;
   D.C.—On-ly to meet thy will (*Omit.*) .... My will shall be.

263 *"A way they knew not."* C. S. ROBINSON.

SAVIOUR! I follow on,
  Guided by thee,
Seeing not yet the hand
  That leadeth me;
Hushed be my heart and still,
Fear I no further ill;
Only to meet thy will
  My will shall be.

2 Riven the rock for me
  Thirst to relieve,
Manna from heaven falls
  Fresh every eve;
Never a want severe
Causeth my eye a tear,
But thou dost whisper near,
  "Only believe!"

3 Often to Marah's brink
  Have I been brought;
Shrinking the cup to drink,
  Help I have sought;
And with the prayer's ascent,
Jesus the branch hath rent—
Quickly relief hath sent,
  Sweetening the draught.

4 Saviour! I long to walk
  Closer with thee;
Led by thy guiding hand,
  Ever to be;
Constantly near thy side,
Quickened and purified,
Living for him who died
  Freely for me!

MASON. 6s, 4s. WM. F. SHERWIN.

1. Saviour, who died for me, I give myself to thee; Thy love, so full—so free, Claims all my powers;

Be this my purpose high, To serve thee till I die, Whether my path shall lie 'Mid thorns or flow'rs.

264 *"Myself to Thee."* M. J. MASON.

SAVIOUR, who died for me,
I give myself to thee;
Thy love, so full—so free,
  Claims all my powers;
Be this my purpose high,
To serve thee till I die,
Whether my path shall lie
  'Mid thorns or flowers.

2 May it be joy for me
To follow only thee;—
Thy faithful servant be,
  Thine to the end.
For thee, I'll do and dare;
For thee the cross I'll bear;
To thee direct my prayer,
  On thee depend.

3 Saviour, with me abide;
Be ever near my side,
Support, defend and guide;
  I look to thee.
I lay my hand in thine,
And fleeting joys resign,
If I may call thee mine
  Eternally.

8

HERMON. C. M.   LOWELL MASON.

1. Oh, for a clos-er walk with God, A calm and heaven - - ly frame,—

A light to shine up - on the road That leads me to the Lamb!

265 *The closer walk.*   w. cowper.

Oh, for a closer walk with God,
 A calm and heavenly frame,—
A light to shine upon the road
 That leads me to the Lamb!

2 Where is the blessedness I knew
 When first I saw the Lord?
Where is the soul-refreshing view
 Of Jesus and his word?

3 What peaceful hours I once enjoyed!
 How sweet their memory still!
But they have left an aching void
 The world can never fill.

4 Return, O holy Dove, return,
 Sweet messenger of rest!
I hate the sins that made thee mourn,
 And drove thee from my breast.

5 The dearest idol I have known,
 Whate'er that idol be,
Help me to tear it from thy throne,
 And worship only thee.

6 So shall my walk be close with God,
 Calm and serene my frame;
So purer light shall mark the road
 That leads me to the Lamb.

266   *"What hourly dangers!"*   a. steele.

Alas! what hourly dangers rise!
 What snares beset my way!
To heaven, oh, let me lift mine eyes,
 And hourly watch and pray.

2 How oft my mournful thoughts complain,
 And melt in flowing tears!
My weak resistance, ah, how vain!
 How strong my foes and fears!

3 O gracious God! in whom I live,
 My feeble efforts aid;
Help me to watch, and pray, and strive,
 Though trembling and afraid.

4 Increase my faith, increase my hope,
 When foes and fears prevail;
And bear my fainting spirit up,
 Or soon my strength will fail.

5 Oh, keep me in thy heavenly way,
 And bid the tempter flee!
And let me never, never stray
 From happiness and thee.

267   *"Search me, O God."*   g. p. morris.

Searcher of hearts! from mine erase
 All thoughts that should not be,
And in its deep recesses trace
 My gratitude to thee!

2 Hearer of prayer! oh, guide aright
 Each word and deed of mine;
Life's battle teach me how to fight,
 And be the victory thine.

3 Father, and Son, and Holy Ghost!
 Thou glorious Three in One!
Thou knowest best what I need most,
 And let thy will be done.

COOLING. C. M.   A. J. ABBEY.

1. Sweet was the time when first I felt The Sav - iour's pardoning blood

Ap - plied to cleanse my soul from guilt, And bring me home to God.

268 *"Where is the blessedness?"* J. NEWTON.

SWEET was the time when first I felt
The Saviour's pardoning blood
Applied to cleanse my soul from guilt,
And bring me home to God.

2 Soon as the morn the light revealed,
His praises tuned my tongue;
And, when the evening shade prevailed,
His love was all my song.

3 In prayer, my soul drew near the Lord,
And saw his glory shine;
And when I read his holy word,
I called each promise mine.

4 Now, when the evening shade prevails,
My soul in darkness mourns;
And when the morn the light reveals,
No light to me returns.

5 Rise, Saviour! help me to prevail,
And make my soul thy care;

I know thy mercy cannot fail,
Let me that mercy share.

269 *"Nearer to thee."* B. CLEVELAND.

OH, could I find, from day to day,
A nearness to my God,
Then would my hours glide sweet away
While leaning on his word.

2 Lord, I desire with thee to live
Anew from day to day,
In joys the world can never give,
Nor ever take away.

3 Blest Jesus, come and rule my heart,
And make me wholly thine,
That I may never more depart,
Nor grieve thy love divine.

4 Thus, till my last, expiring breath,
Thy goodness I'll adore;
And when my frame dissolves in death,
My soul shall love thee more.

EVAN. C. M.   W. H. HAVERGAL, arr.

1. Oh, could I find, from day to day A nearness to my God, Then would my hours glide sweet away While leaning on his word.

1. I am coming to the cross; I am poor, and weak, and blind; I am counting all but dross; I shall full sal-va-tion find.
REF.—I am trusting, Lord, in thee, Dear Lamb of Cal-va-ry; Humbly at thy cross I bow; Save me, Je-sus, save me now.

270   *"Cleanseth from all sin."*   W. MC DONALD.

1 AM coming to the cross;
   I am poor and weak and blind;
I am counting all but dross;
   I shall full salvation find.

REF.— I am trusting, Lord, in thee,
   Dear Lamb of Calvary;
   Humbly at thy cross I bow;
   Save me, Jesus, save me now.

2 Long my heart has sighed for thee;
   Long has evil dwelt within ;
Jesus sweetly speaks to me,
   I will cleanse you from all sin.—REF.

3 Here I give my all to thee,—
   Friends and time and earthly store;
Soul and body thine to be—
   Wholly thine for evermore.—REF.

4 In the promises I trust;
   Now I feel the blood applied;
I am prostrate in the dust;
   I with Christ am crucified.—REF.

271   *Spiritual Songs, p. 192.*   C. WESLEY.

DEPTH of mercy !—can there be
Mercy still reserved for me?
Can my God his wrath forbear?
Me, the chief of sinners, spare?

2 I have long withstood his grace;
Long provoked him to his face;
Would not hearken to his calls;
Grieved him by a thousand falls.

3 Kindled his relentings are;
Me he now delights to spare;
Cries, how shall I give thee up ?—
Lets the lifted thunder drop.

4 There for me the Saviour stands;
Shows his wounds and spreads his hands !
God is love ! I know, I feel;
Jesus weeps, and loves me still.

272   *"Lovest thou Me."*   J. NEWTON.

'TIS a point I long to know,
   Oft it causes anxious thought;
Do I love the Lord, or no?
   Am I his, or am I not?

2 Could my heart so hard remain,
   Prayer a task and burden prove,
Every trifle give me pain,
   If I knew a Saviour's love?

3 Yet I mourn my stubborn will,
   Find my sin a grief and thrall;
Should I grieve for what I feel,
   If I did not love at all?

4 Could I joy with saints to meet,
   Choose the ways I once abhorred,
Find at times the promise sweet,
   If I did not love the Lord?

5 Lord, decide the doubtful case,
   Thou who art thy people's Sun;
Shine upon thy work of grace,
   If it be indeed begun.

273   *Spiritual Songs, p. 221.*   F. C. VAN ALSTYNE.

SAVIOUR, more than life to me,
I am clinging, clinging close to thee;
Let thy precious blood applied,
Keep me ever, ever near thy side.

REF.—Every day, every hour,
   Let me feel thy cleansing power:
   May thy tender love to me,
   Bind me closer, closer, Lord, to thee.

2 Through this changing world below,
Lead me gently, gently as I go;
Trusting thee, I cannot stray,
I can never, never lose my way,—REF.

3 Let me love thee more and more,
Till this fleeting, fleeting life is o'er;
Till my soul is lost in love,
In a brighter, brighter world above.—REF.

REFUGE. 7s. D. — J. P. HOLBROOK.
Choir.

1. Jesus! lov - er of my soul, Let me to thy bosom fly While the bil - lows near me roll, While the tem - pest still is high; Hide me, O my Saviour! hide, Till the storm of life is past; Safe in - to the ha - ven guide; Oh, receive my soul at last!

274 *Christ, our all.* C. WESLEY.

Jesus! lover of my soul,
  Let me to thy bosom fly
While the billows near me roll,
  While the tempest still is high;
Hide me, O my Saviour! hide,
  Till the storm of life is past;
Safe into the haven guide;
  Oh, receive my soul at last!

2 Other refuge have I none;
  Hangs my helpless soul on thee;
Leave, ah! leave me not alone,
  Still support and comfort me.
All my trust on thee is stayed;
  All my help from thee I bring;
Cover my defenceless head
  With the shadow of thy wing.

3 Thou, O Christ! art all I want;
  More than all in thee I find;
Raise the fallen, cheer the faint,
  Heal the sick, and lead the blind.
Just and holy is thy name,
  I am all unrighteousness;
Vile and full of sin I am,
  Thou art full of truth and grace.

4 Plenteous grace with thee is found,—
  Grace to pardon all my sin;
Let the healing streams abound,
  Make and keep me pure within;
Thou of life the fountain art,
  Freely let me take of thee;
Spring thou up within my heart,
  Rise to all eternity.

MARTYN. 7s. D. — S. B. MARSH.

1. {Je - sus! lover of my soul, Let me to thy bosom fly} {Hide me, O my Saviour! hide,
{While the billows near me roll, While the tempest still is high;} {Till the storm of life is past;}
D. C.—Safe in-to the haven guide; Oh, receive my soul at last.

ELLESDIE. 8s, 7s. D.   FROM J. C. W. A. MOZART.

1. Je-sus, I my cross have taken, All to leave and follow thee ; Naked, poor, despised, forsaken,
D. S.—Yet how rich is my condi - tion,

Thou, from hence, my all shalt be! Perish, ev-'ry fond am-bition, All I've sought, or hoped, or known,
God and heaven are still my own!

275   *Bearing the Cross.*   H. F. LYTE.

JESUS, I my cross have taken,
  All to leave, and follow thee;
Naked, poor, despised, forsaken,
  Thou, from hence, my all shalt be!
Perish, every fond ambition,
  All I've sought, or hoped, or known,
Yet how rich is my condition,
  God and heaven are still my own!

2 Let the world despise and leave me,
  They have left my Saviour, too;
Human hearts and looks deceive me—
  Thou art not, like them, untrue;
Oh, while thou dost smile upon me,
  God of wisdom, love, and might,
Foes may hate, and friends disown me,
  Show thy face, and all is bright.

3 Man may trouble and distress me,
  'T will but drive me to thy breast;
Life with trials hard may press me;
  Heaven will bring me sweeter rest!
Oh, 'tis not in grief to harm me,
  While thy love is left to me;
Oh, 't were not in joy to charm me,
  Were that joy unmixed with thee.

4 Go then, earthly fame and treasure!
  Come disaster, scorn, and pain!
In thy service pain is pleasure,
  With thy favor, loss is gain.
I have called thee—Abba, Father!
  I have stayed my heart on thee!
Storms may howl, and clouds may gather,
  All must work for good to me.

ESSEX. 8s, 7s.   THOMAS CLARK.

1. Soul, then know thy full salvation,   Joy, to find in every station Something still to do or bear.
Rise o'er sin, and fear, and care;   Something still to do or bear.

276   *The crown coming.*   H. F. LYTE.

SOUL, then know thy full salvation,
  Rise o'er sin, and fear, and care;
Joy, to find in every station
  Something still to do or bear.

2 Think what Spirit dwells within thee;
  Think what Father's smiles are thine;
Think that Jesus died to win thee!
  Child of heaven, canst thou repine?

3 Haste thee on from grace to glory,
  Armed by faith and winged by prayer!
Heaven's eternal day 's before thee,
  God's own hand shall guide thee there:

4 Soon shall close thy earthly mission,
  Soon shall pass thy pilgrim days,
Hope shall change to glad fruition,
  Faith to sight, and prayer to praise.

AUSTRIA. 8s, 7s. D.   F. J. HAYDN.

1. { Call Je-ho - vah thy sal-vation, Rest beneath th'Almighty's shade; }
   { In his se-cret hab - i - tation Dwell, and never be dismayed: } There no tumult can alarm thee,

Thou shalt dread no hidden snare; Guile nor violence can harm thee, In e - ter-nal safeguard there.

277   *Psalm 91.*   J. MONTGOMERY.

CALL Jehovah thy salvation,
  Rest beneath the Almighty's shade;
In his secret habitation
  Dwell, and never be dismayed:
There no tumult can alarm thee,
  Thou shalt dread no hidden snare;
Guile nor violence can harm thee,
  In eternal safeguard there.

2 From the sword, at noon-day wasting,
  From the noisome pestilence,
In the depth of midnight, blasting,
  God shall be thy sure defence:

Fear not thou the deadly quiver,
  When a thousand feel the blow;
Mercy shall thy soul deliver,
  Though ten thousand be laid low.

3 Since, with pure and firm affection,
  Thou on God hast set thy love,
With the wings of his protection,
  He will shield thee from above;
Thou shalt call on him in trouble,
  He will hearken, he will save;
Here, for grief reward thee double,
  Crown with life beyond the grave.

ALL THE DAYS. P. M.   WM. F. SHERWIN.

1. From thee, begetting sure conviction, Sound out, O ris - en Lord, always Those faithful words of

                              FINE.   REFRAIN.   D. S.

val - e - dic - tion, "Lo! I am with you all the days." All the days, All the days;
D.S.—Lo! I am with you all the days.

278   *"Always."—Matt. 28 : 20.*   A. COLES.

FROM thee, begetting sure conviction,
  Sound out, O risen Lord, always
Those faithful words of valediction,
  "Lo! I am with you all the days."—REF.

2 What things shall happen on the morrow
  Thou kindly hidest from our gaze;
But tellest us, in joy or sorrow,
  "Lo! I am with you all the days."—REF.

3 When round our head the tempest rages,
  And sink our feet in miry ways,
Thy voice comes floating down the ages—
  "Lo! I am with you all the days."—REF.

4 O thou who art our life and meetness!
  Not death shall daunt us or amaze,
Hearing those words of power and sweetness,
  "Lo! I am with you all the days."—REF.

WIMBORNE. L. M.   J. WHITAKER.

1. Stand up, my soul, shake off thy fears, And gird the gos - pel ar - mor on;

March to the gates of end - less joy, Where Je - sus, thy great Captain's gone.

279   *Ephesians 6 : 14.*   I. WATTS.

STAND up, my soul, shake off thy fears,
  And gird the gospel armor on;
March to the gates of endless joy,
  Where Jesus, thy great Captain's gone.

2 Hell and thy sins resist thy course,
  But hell and sin are vanquished foes;
Thy Saviour nailed them to the cross,
  And sung the triumph when he rose.

3 Then let my soul march boldly on,—
  Press forward to the heavenly gate;
There peace and joy eternal reign,
  And glittering robes for conquerors wait.

4 There shall I wear a starry crown,
  And triumph in almighty grace,
While all the armies of the skies
  Join in my glorious Leader's praise.

MISSIONARY CHANT. L. M.   C. ZEUNER.

1. Awake, our souls! away, our fears! Let every trembling thought be gone; Awake, and run the heavenly race, And put a cheerful courage on!

280   *Isaiah 40 : 28–31.*   I. WATTS.

AWAKE, our souls! away, our fears!
  Let every trembling thought be gone;
Awake, and run the heavenly race,
  And put a cheerful courage on!

2 True, 'tis a strait and thorny road,
  And mortal spirits tire and faint;
But they forget the mighty God,
  Who feeds the strength of every saint—

3 The mighty God, whose matchless power
  Is ever new and ever young,

And firm endures, while endless years
  Their everlasting circles run.

4 From thee, the overflowing spring,
  Our souls shall drink a fresh supply;
While such as trust their native strength
  Shall melt away, and droop, and die.

5 Swift as an eagle cuts the air,
  We'll mount aloft to thine abode;
On wings of love our souls shall fly,
  Nor tire amid the heavenly road!

PARK STREET. L. M.   F. M. A. VENUA.

1. Fountain of grace, rich, full, and free, What need I, that is not in thee? Full par-don,

strength to meet the day, And peace which none can take away, And peace which none can take away.

281   *"My springs in thee."*   J. EDMESTON.

FOUNTAIN of grace, rich, full, and free,
What need I, that is not in thee?
Full pardon, strength to meet the day,
And peace which none can take away.

2 Doth sickness fill my heart with fear,
'Tis sweet to know that thou art near;
Am I with dread of justice tried,
'Tis sweet to know that Christ hath died.

3 In life, thy promises of aid
Forbid my heart to be afraid;
In death, peace gently vails the eyes,—
Christ rose, and I shall surely rise.

282   *Jesus is forever mine.*   A. STEELE.

WHEN sins and fears, prevailing, rise,
And fainting hope almost expires,
To thee, O Lord, I lift my eyes;
To thee I breathe my soul's desires.

2 Art thou not mine, my living Lord?
And can my hope, my comfort die?
'Tis fixed on thine almighty word—
That word which built the earth and sky.

3 If my immortal Saviour lives,
Then my immortal life is sure;
His word a firm foundation gives;
Here may I build and rest secure.

4 Here, O my soul, thy trust repose;
If Jesus is for ever mine,
Not death itself—that last of foes—
Shall break a union so divine.

283   *"Complete in Him."*   G. W. HINSDALE.

MY soul complete in Jesus stands!
It fears no more the law's demands;
The smile of God is sweet within,
Where all before was guilt and sin.

2 My soul at rest in Jesus lives;
Accepts the peace his pardon gives;
Receives the grace his death secured,
And pleads the anguish he endured.

3 My soul its every foe defies,
And cries—'Tis God that justifies!
Who charges God's elect with sin?
Shall Christ, who died their peace to win?

4 A song of praise my soul shall sing,
To our eternal, glorious King!
Shall worship humbly at his feet,
In whom alone it stands complete.

284   2 Cor. 12: 9.   I. WATTS.

LET me but hear my Saviour say,
"Strength shall be equal to thy day;"
Then I rejoice in deep distress,
Leaning on all-sufficient grace.

2 I can do all things—or can bear
All suffering, if my Lord be there;
Sweet pleasures mingle with the pains,
While he my sinking head sustains.

3 I glory in infirmity,
That Christ's own power may rest on me;
When I am weak, then am I strong;
Grace is my shield, and Christ my song

ALEXANDER. S. M.   CHARLES ZEUNER.

1. Your harps, ye trembling saints, Down from the willows take; Loud to the praise of love di - vine   Bid every string a - wake.

285   *Our Salvation near.*   A. M. TOPLADY.

Your harps, ye trembling saints,
Down from the willows take:
Loud to the praise of love divine
Bid every string awake.

2 Though in a foreign land,
We are not far from home;
And nearer to our house above
We every moment come.

3 His grace will to the end
Stronger and brighter shine;
Nor present things, nor things to come,
Shall quench the spark divine.

4 When we in darkness walk,
Nor feel the heavenly flame,
Then is the time to trust our God,
And rest upon his name.

5 Soon shall our doubts and fears
Subside at his control;
His loving-kindness shall break through
The midnight of the soul.

6 Blest is the man, O God,
Who stays himself on thee;
Who waits for thy salvation, Lord,
Shall thy salvation see.

286   *"Be of good courage."*   J. WESLEY, *tr.*

Give to the winds thy fears;
Hope, and be undismayed;
God hears thy sighs and counts thy tears;
God shall lift up thy head.

2 Through waves, and clouds, and storms,
He gently clears thy way;
Wait thou his time; so shall this night
Soon end in joyous day.

3 What though thou rulest not!
Yet heaven, and earth, and hell
Proclaim, God sitteth on the throne,
And ruleth all things well.

4 Far, far above thy thought
His counsel shall appear,
When fully he the work has wrought,
That caused thy needless fear.

OLMUTZ. S. M.   LOWELL MASON, *arr.*

1. Your harps, ye trem - bling saints, Down from the wil - lows take:

Loud to the praise of love di - vine Bid ev - ery string a - wake.

ARCADIA. C. M.   THOS. HASTINGS.

1. In time of fear, when trou-ble's near, I look to thine a-bode; Though helpers
fail, and foes prevail, I'll put my trust in God, I'll put my trust.... in God.

287 *"What time I am afraid."* T. HASTINGS.
In time of fear, when trouble's near,
  I look to thine abode;
Though helpers fail, and foes prevail,
  I'll put my trust in God.

2 And what is life, 'mid toil and strife?
  What terror has the grave?
Thine arm of power, in peril's hour,
  The trembling soul will save.

3 In darkest skies, though storms arise,
  I will not be dismayed;
O God of light, and boundless might,
  My soul on thee is stayed!

288 *"I shall be with Him."* R. BAXTER.
Lord, it belongs not to my care
  Whether I die or live;
To love and serve thee is my share,
  And this thy grace must give.

2 If life be long, I will be glad
  That I may long obey;
If short, yet why should I be sad
  To soar to endless day?

3 Christ leads me through no darker rooms
  Than he went through before;
No one into his kingdom comes,
  But through his opened door.

4 Come, Lord, when grace has made me meet
  Thy blessèd face to see;
For if thy work on earth be sweet,
  What will thy glory be?

5 Then shall I end my sad complaints,
  And weary, sinful days,
And join with all triumphant saints
  Who sing Jehovah's praise.

6 My knowledge of that life is small;
  The eye of faith is dim;
But 'tis enough that Christ knows all,
  And I shall be with him.

289 *"If God be for us."* F. W. FABER.
God's glory is a wondrous thing,
  Most strange in all its ways,
And of all things on earth, least like
  What men agree to praise.

2 Oh, blest is he to whom is given
  The instinct that can tell
That God is on the field, when he
  Is most invisible!

3 And blest is he who can divine
  Where real right doth lie,
And dares to take the side that seems
  Wrong to man's blindfold eye!

4 Oh, learn to scorn the praise of men!
  Oh, learn to lose with God!
For Jesus won the world through shame,
  And beckons thee his road.

5 And right is right, since God is God;
  And right the day must win;
To doubt would be disloyalty,
  To falter would be sin!

CHRISTMAS. C. M.   G. F. HANDEL.

1. A - wake, my soul, stretch ev - ery nerve, And press with vig - or on; A heavenly

race demands thy zeal, And an im - mor - tal crown, And an im - mor - tal crown.

290   *The Race.*   P. DODDRIDGE.

AWAKE, my soul, stretch every nerve,
   And press with vigor on;
A heavenly race demands thy zeal,
   And an immortal crown.

2 A cloud of witnesses around
   Hold thee in full survey;
Forget the steps already trod,
   And onward urge thy way.

3 'Tis God's all-animating voice,
   That calls thee from on high,
'Tis his own hand presents the prize
   To thine aspiring eye.

4 Blest Saviour, introduced by thee
   Have I my race begun;
And, crowned with victory, at thy feet
   I'll lay my honors down.

291   *The Warfare.*   I. WATTS.

AM I a soldier of the cross,
   A follower of the Lamb?
And shall I fear to own his cause,
   Or blush to speak his name?

2 Must I be carried to the skies
   On flowery beds of ease?
While others fought to win the prize,
   And sailed through bloody seas?

3 Are there no foes for me to face?
   Must I not stem the flood?
Is this vile world a friend to grace,
   To help me on to God?

4 Sure I must fight, if I would reign;
   Increase my courage, Lord!
I'll bear the toil, endure the pain,
   Supported by thy word.

5 Thy saints, in all this glorious war,
   Shall conquer, though they die;
They view the triumph from afar,
   And seize it with their eye.

6 When that illustrious day shall rise,
   And all thine armies shine
In robes of victory through the skies,
   The glory shall be thine.

292   *"I'm not ashamed."*   I. WATTS.

I'M NOT ashamed to own my Lord,
   Or to defend his cause;
Maintain the honor of his word,
   The glory of his cross.

2 Jesus, my God!—I know his name—
   His name is all my trust;
Nor will he put my soul to shame,
   Nor let my hope be lost.

3 Firm as his throne his promise stands,
   And he can well secure
What I've committed to his hands,
   Till the decisive hour.

4 Then will he own my worthless name
   Before his Father's face,
And in the new Jerusalem
   Appoint my soul a place.

ROGERS. C. M.
FROM CANTICA LAUDIS.

1. Sing, all ye ran-somed of the Lord, Your great De-liv-'rer sing;

Ye pil-grims, now for Zi - on bound, Be joy - ful in.... your King.
Be joyful in your King.

293 *Isaiah 35: 8-10.* P. DODDRIDGE.

SING, all ye ransomed of the Lord,
 Your great Deliverer sing;
Ye pilgrims, now for Zion bound,
 Be joyful in your King.

2 His hand divine shall lead you on,
 Through all the blissful road;
Till to the sacred mount you rise,
 And see your gracious God.

3 Bright garlands of immortal joy
 Shall bloom on every head;
While sorrow, sighing, and distress,
 Like shadows, all are fled.

4 March on in your Redeemer's strength;
 Pursue his footsteps still;
And let the prospect cheer your eye
 While laboring up the hill.

MAITLAND. C. M.
G. N. ALLEN.

1. Must Jesus bear the cross alone, And all the world go free? No, there's a cross for ev'ry one, And there's a cross for me.

294 *No cross, no crown.* T. SHEPHERD, *alt.*

MUST Jesus bear the cross alone,
 And all the world go free?
No, there's a cross for every one,
 And there's a cross for me.

2 How happy are the saints above,
 Who once went sorrowing here!
But now they taste unmingled love,
 And joy without a tear.

3 The consecrated cross I'll bear,
 Till death shall set me free;
And then go home my crown to wear,
 For there's a crown for me.

4 Upon the crystal pavement, down
 At Jesus' piercéd feet,
Joyful, I'll cast my golden crown,
 And his dear name repeat.

5 And palms shall wave, and harps shall ring,
 Beneath heaven's arches high;
The Lord that lives, the ransomed sing,
 That lives no more to die.

6 Oh, precious cross! oh, glorious crown!
 Oh, resurrection day!
Ye angels, from the stars come down,
 And bear my soul away.

RENOVATION. S. M.   J. N. HUMMEL.

1. The people of the Lord Are on their way to heaven; There they obtain their great reward; The prize will there be given.

295   *Christian Pilgrims.*   T. KELLY.

THE people of the Lord
  Are on their way to heaven;
There they obtain their great reward;
  The prize will there be given.

2 'Tis conflict here below;
  'Tis triumph there, and peace:
On earth we wrestle with the foe;
  In heaven our conflicts cease.

3 'Tis gloom and darkness here;
  'Tis light and joy above;
There all is pure, and all is clear;
  There all is peace and love.

4 There rest shall follow toil,
  And ease succeed to care:
The victors there divide the spoil;
  They sing and triumph there.

5 Then let us joyful sing:
  The conflict is not long:
We hope in heaven to praise our King
  In one eternal song.

296   *"Jehovah Jireh."*   J. SWAIN.

I STAND on Zion's mount,
  And view my starry crown;
No power on earth my hope can shake,
  Nor hell can thrust me down.

2 The lofty hills and towers,
  That lift their heads on high,
Shall all be leveled low in dust—
  Their very names shall die.

3 The vaulted heavens shall fall,
  Built by Jehovah's hands;
But firmer than the heavens, the Rock
  Of my salvation stands!

297   *"Goeth forth weeping."*   G. BURGESS.

THE harvest dawn is near,
  The year delays not long;
And he who sows with many a tear,
  Shall reap with many a song.

2 Sad to his toil he goes,
  His seed with weeping leaves;
But he shall come, at twilight's close,
  And bring his golden sheaves.

LABAN. S. M.   LOWELL MASON.

1. My soul, be on thy guard! Ten thousand foes a-rise; And hosts of sin are pressing hard To draw thee from the skies.

298   *"Watch."*   G. HEATH.

MY soul, be on thy guard,
  Ten thousand foes arise;
And hosts of sin are pressing hard
  To draw thee from the skies.

2 Oh, watch, and fight, and pray!
  The battle ne'er give o'er;
Renew it boldly every day,
  And help divine implore.

3 Ne'er think the victory won,
  Nor lay thine armor down;
Thine arduous work will not be done,
  Till thou obtain thy crown.

4 Fight on, my soul, till death
  Shall bring thee to thy God!
He'll take thee at thy parting breath,
  Up to his blest abode.

CLAPTON. S. M. WILLIAM JONES.

1. My soul, weigh not thy life A - -gainst thy heaven - ly crown;

Nor suf - fer Sa - tan's dead - liest strife To beat thy_ cour - age down.

299 *"Weigh not thy life."* ANON.

My soul, weigh not thy life
Against thy heavenly crown;
Nor suffer Satan's deadliest strife
To beat thy courage down.

2 With prayer and crying strong,
Hold on the fearful fight,
And let the breaking day prolong
The wrestling of the night.

3 The battle soon will yield,
If thou thy part fulfill;
For strong as is the hostile shield,
Thy sword is stronger still.

4 Thine armor is divine,
Thy feet with victory shod;
And on thy head shall quickly shine
The diadem of God.

DENNIS. S. M. LOWELL MASON, arr.

1. How gen - tle God's commands! How kind his pre - cepts are!

Come, cast your bur - dens on the Lord, And trust his con - stant care.

300 *"He careth."* P. DODDRIDGE.

How GENTLE God's commands!
How kind his precepts are!
Come, cast your burdens on the Lord,
And trust his constant care.

2 Beneath his watchful eye
His saints securely dwell;
That hand which bears creation up
Shall guard his children well.

3 Why should this anxious load
Press down your weary mind?
Haste to your heavenly Father's throne,
And sweet refreshment find.

4 His goodness stands approved,
Unchanged from day to day;
I'll drop my burden at his feet,
And bear a song away.

OASKEY. 7s, 6s. D.   T. E. PERKINS.

1. Sometimes a light sur-pris - es   The Christian while he sings;   It   is the Lord who ris - es
D. S.—A   sea-son of clear shin-ing,

With heal-ing in his wings: When comforts are de - clin-ing,   He grants the soul a - gain
To cheer it af - ter rain.

301   *Matthew 6 : 25-34.*   W. COWPER.

SOMETIMES a light surprises
   The Christian while he sings;
It is the Lord who rises
   With healing in his wings:
When comforts are declining,
   He grants the soul again
A season of clear shining,
   To cheer it after rain.

2 In holy contemplation,
   We sweetly then pursue
The theme of God's salvation,
   And find it ever new:
Set free from present sorrow,
   We cheerfully can say,
Let the unknown to-morrow
   Bring with it what it may.

3 It can bring with it nothing,
   But he will bring us through;
Who gives the lilies clothing,
   Will clothe his people too:
Beneath the spreading heavens,
   No creature but is fed;
And he who feeds the ravens,
   Will give his children bread.

4 Though vine nor fig-tree neither,
   Their wonted fruit should bear,
Though all the fields should wither,
   Nor flocks, nor herds be there;

Yet God the same abiding,
   His praise shall tune my voice,
For while in him confiding,
   I cannot but rejoice.

302   *Perfect peace.*   A. E. WARING.

IN heavenly love abiding,
   No change my heart shall fear,
And safe is such confiding,
   For nothing changes here:
The storm may roar without me,
   My heart may low be laid,
But God is round about me,
   And can I be dismayed?

2 Wherever he may guide me,
   No want shall turn me back;
My Shepherd is beside me,
   And nothing can I lack:
His wisdom ever waketh,
   His sight is never dim:
He knows the way he taketh,
   And I will walk with him.

3 Green pastures are before me,
   Which yet I have not seen;
Bright skies will soon be o'er me,
   Where darkest clouds have been:
My hope I cannot measure;
   My path to life is free;
My Saviour has my treasure,
   And he will walk with me.

YARMOUTH. 7s, 6s. D. LOWELL MASON, *arr.*

1. Stand up! stand up for Jesus! Ye soldiers of the cross;
Lift high his royal banner, (*Omit*) .... It must not suffer loss: From vict'ry unto vict'ry His army shall he

lead, Till every foe is vanquished, Till every foe is vanquished, Till every foe is vanquished, And Christ is Lord in-deed.

303 *"Having done all, stand."* G. DUFFIELD.

STAND up!—stand up for Jesus!
Ye soldiers of the cross;
Lift high his royal banner,
It must not suffer loss:
From victory unto victory
His army shall he lead,
Till every foe is vanquished,
And Christ is Lord indeed.

2 Stand up!—stand up for Jesus!
The trumpet call obey;
Forth to the mighty conflict,
In this his glorious day:
"Ye that are men, now serve him,"
Against unnumbered foes;
Let courage rise with danger,
And strength to strength oppose.

3 Stand up!—stand up for Jesus!
Stand in his strength alone;
The arm of flesh will fail you—
Ye dare not trust your own:
Put on the gospel armor,
And, watching unto prayer,
Where duty calls, or danger,
Be never wanting there.

4 Stand up!—stand up for Jesus!
The strife will not be long;
This day, the noise of battle,
The next, the victor's song:
To him that overcometh,
A crown of life shall be;
He with the King of glory
Shall reign eternally!

WEBB. 7s, 6s. D. G. J. WEBB.

1. In heavenly love a-bid-ing, No change my heart can fear; And safe is such con-fid-ing,
D. S.—But God is round a-bout me,

For nothing changes here. The storm may roar without me, My heart may low be laid,
And can I be dismayed?

9

WILLOUGHBY. C. P. M.   CRANE.

1. Come on, my partners in dis-tress, My comrades through the wilderness, Who still your bodies feel:

A-while forget your griefs and fears, And look beyond this vale of tears, To that ce-les-tial hill.

304   *"Bliss-inspiring hope."*   C. WESLEY.

COME on, my partners in distress,
My comrades through the wilderness,
  Who still your bodies feel:
Awhile forget your griefs and fears,
And look beyond this vale of tears,
  To that celestial hill.

2 Beyond the bounds of time and space,
Look forward to that heavenly place,
  The saints' secure abode;
On faith's strong eagle-pinions rise,
And force your passage to the skies,
  And scale the mount of God.

3 Who suffer with our Master here,
We shall before his face appear,
  And by his side sit down;
To patient faith the prize is sure;
And all that to the end endure
  The cross, shall wear the crown.

305   *"Complete in him."*   ANON.

COME join, ye saints, with heart and voice,
Alone in Jesus to rejoice,
  And worship at his feet;
Come, take his praises on your tongues,
And raise to him your thankful songs,
  "In him ye are complete!"

2 In him, who all our praise excels,
The fullness of the Godhead dwells,
  And all perfections meet:
The head of all celestial powers,
Divinely theirs, divinely ours;—
  "In him ye are complete!"

3 Still onward urge your heavenly way,
Dependent on him day by day,
  His presence still entreat;
His precious name for ever bless,
Your glory, strength, and righteousness,--
  "In him ye are complete!"

FATHERLAND. P. M.   WESTERN MELODY.

1. Je-sus, still lead on, Till our rest be won; And although the way be cheerless, We will follow,

calm and fearless: Guide us by thy hand To our Fa-ther-land, To our Fa-ther-land.

BREMEN. C. P. M. THOS. HASTINGS.

1. Fear not, O lit - tle flock, the foe Who mad - ly seeks your o - ver-throw; Dread

not his rage and power; { What tho' your courage sometimes faints, / His seeming triumph o'er God's saints } Lasts but a lit - tle hour.

306 *"Fear not, little flock."* C. WINKWORTH, tr.

FEAR not, O little flock, the foe
Who madly seeks your overthrow;
  Dread not his rage and power;
What tho' your courage sometimes faints,
His seeming triumph o'er God's saints
  Lasts but a little hour.

2 Be of good cheer; your cause belongs
To him who can avenge your wrongs;
  Leave it to him, our Lord!
Though hidden yet from mortal eyes,
He sees the Gideon that shall rise
  To save us, and his word.

3 As true as God's own word is true,
Not earth nor hell with all their crew
  Against us shall prevail;
A jest and by-word are they grown;
God is with us, we are his own,
  Our victory cannot fail!

4 Amen, Lord Jesus, grant our prayer!
Great Captain, now thine arm make bare,
  Fight for us once again!
So shall thy saints and martyrs raise
A mighty chorus to thy praise,
  . World without end: Amen!

307 *"Casting all care on God."* J. ANSTICE.

O LORD! how happy should we be,
If we could cast our care on thee,
  If we from self could rest;
And feel, at heart, that One above,
In perfect wisdom, perfect love,
  Is working for the best!

2 How far from this our daily life,
Ever disturbed by anxious strife,
  By sudden, wild alarms!
Oh, could we but relinquish all
Our earthly props, and simply fall
  On thine almighty arms!

308 P. M. *"Lead on."* ZINZENDORF.

JESUS still lead on,
  Till our rest be won;
And although the way be cheerless,
We will follow, calm and fearless;
  Guide us by thy hand
  To our Fatherland.

2 If the way be drear,
  If the foe be near,
Let not faithless fears o'ertake us,
Let not faith and hope forsake us;
  For, through many a foe,
  To our home we go.

3 When we seek relief
  From a long-felt grief,
When temptations come, alluring,
Make us patient and enduring;
  Show us that bright shore
  Where we weep no more.

4 Jesus, still lead on,
  Till our rest be won;
Heavenly Leader, still direct us,
Still support, console, protect us,
  . Till we safely stand
  In our Fatherland.

PORTUGUESE HYMN. 11s.　　　　　J. READING.

1. How firm a foundation, ye saints of the Lord! Is laid for your faith in his excellent word! What more can he

say, than to you he hath said,—To you, who for refuge to Jesus hath fled, To you, who for refuge to Jesus have fled?

309　　　"Fear Not."　　G. KEITH.

How FIRM a foundation, ye saints of the
　　Lord!
Is laid for your faith in his excellent word!
What more can he say, than' to you he
　　hath said,—
To you, who for refuge to Jesus have fled?

2 "Fear not, I am with thee, oh, be not
　　dismayed,
For I am thy God, I will still give thee
　　aid;
I'll strengthen thee, help thee, and cause
　　thee to stand,
Upheld by my gracious, omnipotent hand.

3 "When through the deep waters I call
　　thee to go,
The rivers of sorrow shall not overflow;
For I will be with thee thy trouble to bless,
And sanctify to thee thy deepest distress.

4 "When through fiery trials thy pathway
　　shall lie,
My grace, all-sufficient, shall be thy supply;
The flame shall not hurt thee; I only design
Thy dross to consume, and thy gold to refine.

5 "Ev'n down to old age all my people
　　shall prove
My sovereign, eternal, unchangeable love;
And then, when gray hairs shall their tem-
　　ples adorn,
Like lambs they shall still in my bosom be
　　borne.

6 "The soul that on Jesus hath leaned for
　　repose,
I will not—I will not desert to his foes;
That soul—though all hell should endeavor
　　to shake,
I'll never—no never—no never forsake!"

CANA. 11s.　　　　　GEO. KINGSLEY.

1. { The Lord is my Shepherd, no want shall I know; }
　 { I feed in green pastures, safe-fold-ed I rest; } He lead-eth my soul where the still-waters flow,
D. C.—Re-stores me when wand'ring, redeems when op-pressed.

GOSHEN. 11s.   THOS. HASTINGS, arr.

1. The Lord is my Shep-herd, no want shall I know; I feed in green
D. S. Re - stores me when

pas-tures, safe-fold-ed I rest; He lead-eth my soul where the still waters flow,
wand'ring, re-deems when oppressed.

310 Psalm 23. J. MONTGOMERY.

THE Lord is my Shepherd, no want shall
  I know;
I feed in green pastures, safe-folded I rest;
He leadeth my soul where the still waters flow,
  Restores me when wandering, redeems
    when oppressed.

2 Through the valley and shadow of death
    though I stray,
  Since thou art my Guardian, no evil I fear;
Thy rod shall defend me, thy staff be my stay;
  No harm can befall, with my Comforter near.

3 In the midst of affliction, my table is spread;
  With blessings unmeasured my cup run-
    neth o'er;
With perfume and oil thou anointest my head;
  Oh, what shall I ask of thy providence
    more?

4 Let goodness and mercy, my bountiful God!
  Still follow my steps till I meet thee above;
I seek, by the path which my forefathers trod
  Through the land of their sojourn, thy
    kingdom of love.

311 "Faint, yet pursuing." ANON.

THOUGH faint, yet pursuing, we go on our way;
The Lord is our Leader, his word is our stay;
Tho' suffering, and sorrow, and trial be near,
The Lord is our Refuge, and whom can we fear?

2 He raiseth the fallen, he cheereth the faint;
  The weak, and oppressed—he will hear
    their complaint;
The way may be weary, and thorny the road,
  But how can we falter?—our help is in God!

3 And to his green pastures our footsteps
    he leads;
  His flock in the desert how kindly he feeds!
The lambs in his bosom he tenderly bears,
  And brings back the wanderers all safe from
    the snares.

4 Though clouds may surround us, our God
    is our light;
  Though storms rage around us, our God is
    our might;
So, faint yet pursuing, still onward we come:
  The Lord is our Leader, and heaven is our
    home!

STEPHANOS. P. M.   W. H. MONK.

1. Art thou weary, art thou languid, Art thou sore distressed? "Come to me," saith One, "and coming, Be at rest!"

312   *Our Master.*   J. M. NEALE, *tr.*

ART thou weary, art thou languid,
   Art thou sore distressed?
"Come to me," saith One, "and coming,
   Be at rest."

2 Hath he marks to lead me to him,
   If he be my Guide?—
"In his feet and hands are wound-prints,
   And his side."

3 Is there diadem, as Monarch,
   That his brow adorns?—
"Yea, a crown, in very surety;
   But of thorns."

4 If I find him, if I follow,
   What his guerdon here?—
"Many a sorrow, many a labor,
   Many a tear."

5 If I still hold closely to him,
   What hath he at last?—
"Sorrow vanquished, labor ended,
   Jordan passed."

6 If I ask him to receive me,
   Will he say me nay?—
"Not till earth, and not till heaven
   Pass away."

7 Finding, following, keeping, struggling,
   Is he sure to bless?—
"Saints, apostles, prophets, martyrs,
   Answer, Yes."

RIALTO. S. M.   GEO. F. ROOT.

1. For me to live is Christ, To die is end-less gain; For him I glad-ly bear the cross, And welcome grief and pain.

313   *"To live is Christ."*   ANON.

FOR me to live is Christ,
   To die is endless gain;
For him I gladly bear the cross,
   And welcome grief and pain.

2 A pilgrimage my lot,
   My home is in the skies;
I nightly pitch my tent below,
   And daily higher rise.

3 I fare with Christ my Lord;
   His path the path I choose;
They joy who suffer most with him—
   They win who with him lose.

4 The dawn on distant hills
   Shines o'er the vales below;
The shadows of this world are lost
   In light to which I go.

5 My journey soon will end,
   My scrip and staff laid down:
Oh, tempt me not with earthly toys—
   I go to wear a crown.

6 Faithful may I endure,
   And hear my Saviour say,
Thrice welcome home, belovéd child,
   Inherit endless day!

PALESTRINA. C. M.　　　　　　　　　　　C. P. A. PALESTRINA.

1. Un-shak-en as the sa-cred hill, And fixed as mountains be,

Firm as a rock the soul shall rest, That leans, O Lord, on thee!

314　　*Psalm 125.*　　I. WATTS.

Unshaken as the sacred hill,
　And fixed as mountains be,
Firm as a rock the soul shall rest,
　That leans, O Lord, on thee !

2 Not walls nor hills could guard so well
Old Salem's happy ground,

As those eternal arms of love,
　That every saint surround.

3 Deal gently, Lord, with souls sincere,
　And lead them safely on
To the bright gates of Paradise,
　Where Christ, their Lord, is gone.

TOPAZ. P. M.　　　　　　　　　　　　　C. BEECHER.

1. A-long the mountain track of life, A-long the wea-ry lea, In rocks, in storms, in

joy, in strife, Let this my heart-cry be,— "Nearer to thee— near-er to thee."

315　　*"Nearer to thee."*　　CAREY.

Along the mountain track of life,
　Along the weary lea,
In rocks, in storms, in joy, in strife,
　Let this my heart-cry be,—
　　"Nearer to thee—nearer to thee."

2 This pilgrim-path by thee was trod,
　Jesus,—my King, by thee,
Traced by thy tears, thy feet, thy blood,
　In love, in death, for me:
　　Oh, bring my soul nearer to thee.

3 Let every step, let every thought
　Sweet memories bear of thee;
And hear the soul thy love hath bought,
　Whose every cry shall be—
　　"Nearer to thee—nearer to thee."

4 Thou wilt ! thou dost !—a still small voice
　Whispers of faith in thee,
Of hope that might in grief rejoice,
　If still the way-cry be,—
　　"Nearer to thee—nearer to thee."

LEAD ME ON. P. M.

C. C. CONVERSE.

1. Trav'ling to the bet-ter land, O'er the desert's scorching sand, Father! let me grasp thy hand; Lead me on, lead me on!

316 *"Lead me on."* ANON.

TRAVELING to the better land,
O'er the desert's scorching sand,
Father! let me grasp thy hand;
   Lead me on, lead me on!

2 When at Marah, parched with heat,
I the sparkling fountain greet,
Make the bitter water sweet;
   Lead me on!

3 When the wilderness is drear,
Show me Elim's palm-grove near,
And her wells, as crystal clear:
   Lead me on!

4 Through the water, through the fire,
Never let me fall or tire,
Every step brings Canaan nigher:
   Lead me on!

5 Bid me stand on Nebo's height,
Gaze upon the land of light,
Then, transported with the sight,
   Lead me on!

6 When I stand on Jordan's brink,
Never let me fear or shrink;
Hold me, Father, lest I sink:
   Lead me on!

7 When the victory is won,
And eternal life begun,
Up to glory lead me on!
   Lead me on, lead me on!

HOUGHTON. 10s, 11s.

WM. GARDINER.

1. Though troubles as-sail, and dangers af-fright, Though friends should all fail, and foes all unite,

Yet one thing secures us, whatev-er be-tide, The promise as-sures us, "The Lord will provide."

317 *The Lord will provide.* J. NEWTON.

THOUGH troubles assail, and dangers affright,
Though friends should all fail, and foes all unite,
Yet one thing secures us, whatever betide,
The promise assures us, "The Lord will provide."

2 The birds, without barn or store-house, are fed;
From them let us learn to trust for our bread:
His saints what is fitting shall ne'er be denied,
So long as 'tis written, "The Lord will provide."

3 When life sinks apace, and death is in view,
The word of his grace shall comfort us through:
Not fearing or doubting, with Christ on our side,
We hope to die shouting, "The Lord will provide."

STAR OF BETHLEHEM. L. M. D.   SCOTCH MELODY.

1. When, marshaled on the night-ly plain, The glittering host be-stud the sky,

One star a-lone, of all the train, Can fix the sin-ner's wandering eye.
D. 8.—But one a-lone the Sav-iour speaks,—It is the Star of Beth-le-hem.

Hark! hark! to God the cho-rus breaks From ev-ery host, from ev-ery gem;

318 *"They saw the Star."* H. K. WHITE.

WHEN, marshaled on the nightly plain,
  The glittering host bestud the sky,
One star alone, of all the train,
  Can fix the sinner's wandering eye.
Hark! hark! to God the chorus breaks
  From every host, from every gem;
But one alone the Saviour speaks,—
  It is the Star of Bethlehem.

2 Once on the raging seas I rode,
  The storm was loud the night was dark,
The ocean yawned, and rudely blowed
  The wind that tossed my foundering bark.
Deep horror then my vitals froze;
  Death-struck, I ceased the tide to stem;
When suddenly a star arose,—
  It was the Star of Bethlehem!

3 It was my guide, my light, my all;
  It bade my dark forebodings cease,
And through the storm and danger's thrall
  It led me to the port of peace.
Now safely moored, my perils o'er,
  I'll sing, first in night's diadem,
For ever and for evermore,
  The Star, the Star of Bethlehem!

319 *Spiritual Songs*, p. 283. J. H. GILMORE.

HE leadeth me! oh, blesséd thought,
Oh, words with heavenly comfort fraught!
Whate'er I do, where'er I be,
Still 'tis God's hand that leadeth me.
  REFRAIN.
    He leadeth me! he leadeth me!
    By his own hand he leadeth me;
    His faithful follower I would be,
    For by his hand he leadeth me!

2 Sometimes 'mid scenes of deepest gloom,
Sometimes where Eden's bowers bloom,
By waters still, o'er troubled sea,—
Still 'tis his hand that leadeth me!—REF.

3 Lord! I would clasp thy hand in mine,
Nor ever murmur nor repine;
Content whatever lot I see,
Since 'tis my God that leadeth me.—REF.

4 And when my task on earth is done,
When by thy grace the victory's won,
Ev'n death's cold wave I will not flee,
Since God through Jordan leadeth me.—
                                    REF

BARTIMEUS. 8s, 7s.   STEPHEN JENKS.

1. One there is, a - bove all oth - ers, Well de-serves the name of Friend;

His is love be - yond a broth-er's, Cost - ly, free, and knows no end.

320   *"Closer than a brother."*   J. NEWTON.

ONE there is, above all others,
  Well deserves the name of Friend;
His is love beyond a brother's,
  Costly, free, and knows no end.

2 Which of all our friends, to save us,
  Could or would have shed his blood?
But our Jesus died to have us
  Reconciled in him to God.

3 When he lived on earth abaséd,
  Friend of sinners was his name;
Now above all glory raiséd,
  He rejoices in the same.

4 Oh, for grace our hearts to soften!
  Teach us, Lord, at length, to love;
We, alas! forget too often
  What a friend we have above.

321   *"Jesus only."*   E. NASON.

JESUS only, when the morning
  Beams upon the path I tread;
Jesus only, when the darkness
  Gathers round my weary head.

2 Jesus only, when the billows
  Cold and sullen o'er me roll;
Jesus only, when the trumpet
  Rends the tomb and wakes the soul.

3 Jesus only, when, adoring,
  Saints their crowns before him bring;
Jesus only, I will, joyous,
  Through eternal ages sing.

322   *None but Jesus.*   A. R. COUSIN.

NONE but Christ: his merit hides me,
  He was faultless—I am fair;
None but Christ, his wisdom guides me,
  He was out-cast—I'm his care.

2 None but Christ: his Spirit seals me,
  Gives me freedom with control;
None but Christ, his bruising heals me,
  And his sorrow soothes my soul.

3 None but Christ: his life sustains me,
  Strength and song to me he is;
None but Christ, his love constrains me,
  He is mine and I am his.

323   *"With you always."*   E. H. NEVIN.

ALWAYS with us, always with us—
  Words of cheer and words of love;
Thus the risen Saviour whispers,
  From his dwelling-place above.

2 With us when we toil in sadness,
  Sowing much and reaping none;
Telling us that in the future
  Golden harvests shall be won.

3 With us when the storm is sweeping
  O'er our pathway dark and drear;
Waking hope within our bosoms,
  Stilling every anxious fear.

4 With us in the lonely valley,
  When we cross the chilling stream—
Lighting up the steps to glory
  With salvation's radiant beam.

GREENWOOD. S. M.   J. E. SWEETSER.

1. Since Je - sus is my friend, And I to him be - long,

It mat - ters not what foes in - tend, How - ev - er fierce and strong.

324 *"Jesus is my friend."* C. WINKWORTH, *tr.*

SINCE Jesus is my friend,
  And I to him belong,
It matters not what foes intend,   •
  However fierce and strong.

2 He whispers in my breast
  Sweet words of holy cheer,
How they who seek in God their rest
  Shall ever find him near;—

3 How God hath built above
  A city fair and new,
Where eye and heart shall see and prove
  What faith has counted true.

4 My heart for gladness springs;
  It cannot more be sad;
For very joy it smiles and sings,—
  Sees naught but sunshine glad.

5 The sun that lights mine eyes
  Is Christ, the Lord I love;
I sing for joy of that which lies
  Stored up for me above.

325   *Psalm 23.*   I. WATTS.

THE Lord my Shepherd is,
  I shall be well supplied;
Since he is mine, and I am his,
  What can I want beside?

2 He leads me to the place
  Where heavenly pasture grows,
Where living waters gently pass,
  And full salvation flows.

3 If e'er I go astray,
  He doth my soul reclaim;
And guide me in his own right way,
  For his most holy name.

4 While he affords his aid,
  I cannot yield to fear;
Tho' I should walk thro' death's dark shade,
  My Shepherd's with me there.

5 In spite of all my foes,
  Thou dost my table spread;
My cup with blessings overflows,
  And joy exalts my head.

6 The bounties of thy love
  Shall crown my future days;
Nor from thy house will I remove,
  Nor cease to speak thy praise.

326   *Unseen, we love.*   I. WATTS.

NOT with our mortal eyes
  Have we beheld the Lord;
Yet we rejoice to hear his name;
  And love him in his word.

2 On earth we want the sight
  Of our Redeemer's face;
Yet, Lord, our inmost thoughts delight
  To dwell upon thy grace.

3 And when we taste thy love,
  Our joys divinely grow
Unspeakable, like those above,
  And heaven begins below.

FEDERAL STREET. L. M.   H. K. OLIVER.

1. Je - sus! and shall it ev - er be, A mor - tal man a - shamed of thee?

A - shamed of thee, whom an - gels praise, Whose glo - ries shine through end - less days?

327   *"Ashamed of me."*   J. GRIGG.

JESUS! and shall it ever be,
A mortal man ashamed of thee?
Ashamed of thee, whom angels praise,
Whose glories shine through endless days?

2 Ashamed of Jesus! sooner far
Let evening blush to own a star;
He sheds the beams of light divine
O'er this benighted soul of mine.

3 Ashamed of Jesus! that dear Friend
On whom my hopes of heaven depend!
No; when I blush, be this my shame,
That I no more revere his name.

4 Ashamed of Jesus! yes, I may,
When I've no guilt to wash away;
No tear to wipe, no good to crave,
No fears to quell, no soul to save.

5 Till then—nor is my boasting vain—
Till then, I boast a Saviour slain!
And, oh, may this my glory be
That Christ is not ashamed of me!

328   *Jesus all in all.*   RAY PALMER, tr.

JESUS, thou Joy of loving hearts,
  Thou Fount of life! thou Light of men!
From the best bliss that earth imparts,
  We turn unfilled to thee again.

2 Thy truth unchanged hath ever stood;
  Thou savest those that on thee call;
To them that seek thee thou art good,
  To them that find thee, All in All.

3 We taste thee, O thou Living Bread,
  And long to feast upon thee still;
We drink of thee, the Fountain Head,
  And thirst our souls from thee to fill!

4 Our restless spirits yearn for thee,
  Where'er our changeful lot is cast;
Glad, when thy gracious smile we see,
  Blest, when our faith can hold thee fast.

5 O Jesus, ever with us stay;
  Make all our moments calm and bright;
Chase the dark night of sin away,
  Shed o'er the world thy holy light!

329   *"Not your own."*   S. F. SMITH.

OH, not my own these verdant hills,
  And fruits, and flowers, and stream, and
    wood;
But his who all with glory fills,
  Who bought me with his precious blood.

2 Oh, not my own this wondrous frame,
  Its curious work, its living soul;
But his who for my ransom came;
  Slain for my sake, he claims the whole.

3 Oh, not my own the grace that keeps
  My feet from fierce temptations free;
Oh, not my own the thought that leaps,
  Adoring, blessèd Lord, to thee.

4 Oh, not my own; I'll soar and sing,
  When life, with all its toils, is o'er,
And thou thy trembling lamb shalt bring
  Safe home, to wander nevermore.

HURSLEY. L. M. W. H. MONK, *arr.*

1. Oh, sweetly breathe the lyres a - bove, When an - gels touch the quivering string;

And wake, to chant Im - man - uel's love, Such strains as an - gel - lips can sing.

330   *Immanuel.*   RAY PALMER.

Oh, sweetly breathe the lyres above,
  When angel's touch the quivering string,
And wake, to chant Immanuel's love,
  Such strains as angel-lips can sing!

2 And sweet, on earth, the choral swell,
  From mortal tongues, of gladsome lays;
When pardoned souls their raptures tell,
  And, grateful, hymn Immanuel's praise.

3 Jesus, thy name our souls adore;
  We own the bond that makes us thine;
And carnal joys that charmed before,
  For thy dear sake we now resign.

4 Our hearts, by dying love subdued,
  Accept thine offered grace to-day;
Beneath the cross, with blood bedewed,
  We bow, and give ourselves away.

5 In thee we trust,—on thee rely;
  Though we are feeble, thou art strong;
Oh, keep us till our spirits fly
  To join the bright, immortal throng!

331   *Robe of Righteousness.*   J. WESLEY, *tr.*

Jesus, thy Blood and Righteousness
My beauty are, my glorious dress;
'Midst flaming worlds, in these arrayed,
With joy shall I lift up my head.

2 Lord, I believe thy precious blood,—
Which, at the mercy-seat of God,
For ever doth for sinners plead,—
For me, ev'n for my soul, was shed.

3 When from the dust of death I rise
To claim my mansion in the skies—
Ev'n then, this shall be all my plea:
Jesus hath lived, hath died for me.

4 This spotless robe the same appears,
When ruined nature sinks in years;
No age can change its glorious hue,
The robe of Christ is ever new.

5 Oh, let the dead now hear thy voice:
Bid, Lord, thy mourning ones rejoice;
Their beauty this, their glorious dress,
Jesus, the Lord our Righteousness.

GRACE CHURCH. L. M. I. PLEYEL.

1. Jesus, thy Blood and Righteousness My beauty are, my glorious dress; 'Midst flaming worlds, in these arrayed, With joy shall I lift up my head.

LIGHT OF THE WORLD. P. M.   P. P. BLISS.

1. { The whole world was lost in the darkness of sin; The Light of the world is Je - sus;}
   { Like sunshine at noonday his glo-ry shone in,   The Light of the world is (Omit.......}

Je - sus.   Come to the Light, 'tis shin-ing for thee;   Sweet-ly   the   Light has

dawned upon me;   Once I was blind, but now I can see: The Light of the world is Je - sus.

332   *"I am the Light."*   ANON.

THE whole world was lost in the darkness
      of sin;
   The Light of the world is Jesus;
Like sunshine at noonday his glory shone in,
   The Light of the world is Jesus.—REF.

2 No darkness have we who in Jesus abide,
   The Light of the world is Jesus;

We walk in the light when we follow our
      Guide,
   The Light of the world is Jesus.—REF.

3 No need of the sunlight in heaven, we're
      told,
   The Light of the world is Jesus;
The Lamb is the light in the City of Gold,
   The Light of the world is Jesus.—REF.

---

333   *Spiritual Songs*, p. 187.   S. D. PHELPS.

SAVIOUR, thy dying love
   Thou gavest me:
Nor should I aught withhold,
   Dear Lord, from thee:
In love my soul would bow,
   My heart fulfill its vow,
Some offering bring thee now,
   Something for thee.

2 O'er the blest mercy-seat,
   Pleading for me,
My feeble faith looks up,
   Jesus, to thee:

Help me the cross to bear,
Thy wondrous love declare,
Some song to raise, or prayer,
   Something for thee.

3 Give me a faithful heart—
   Likeness to thee,
That each departing day
   Henceforth may see
Some work of love begun,
Some deed of kindness done,
Some wanderer sought and won,
   Something for thee.

OLIVET. 6s, 4s. LOWELL MASON.

1. My faith looks up to thee, Thou Lamb of Calvary, Saviour divine! { Now hear me while I pray, Take all my guilt away, } Oh, let me from this day Be wholly thine!

334 *"Look unto Me."* RAY PALMER.

My faith looks up to thee,
Thou Lamb of Calvary,
  Saviour divine!
Now hear me while I pray,
Take all my guilt away,
Oh, let me from this day
  Be wholly thine!

2 May thy rich grace impart
Strength to my fainting heart,
  My zeal inspire;
As thou hast died for me,
Oh, may my love to thee
Pure, warm, and changeless be,
  A living fire!

3 While life's dark maze I tread,
And griefs around me spread,
  Be thou my guide;
Bid darkness turn to day,
Wipe sorrow's tears away,
Nor let me ever stray
  From thee aside.

4 When ends life's transient dream,
When death's cold, sullen stream
  Shall o'er me roll,
Blest Saviour! then, in love,
Fear and distrust remove;
Oh, bear me safe above,
  A ransomed soul!

LYTE. 6s, 4s. J. P. HOLBROOK.

1. Je-sus, thy name I love, All oth-er names above, Je-sus, my Lord! { Oh, thou art all to me! Nothing to please I see,

Nothing a-part from thee, Jesus, my Lord!

Oh, how great is thy love,
All other loves above,
Love that I daily prove,
  Jesus, my Lord!

3 When unto thee I flee,
Thou wilt my refuge be,
  Jesus, my Lord!
What need I now to fear?
What earthly grief or care,
Since thou art ever near?
  Jesus, my Lord!

335 *"Jesus my Lord!"* J. G. DECK.

JESUS, thy name I love,
All other names above,
  Jesus, my Lord!
Oh, thou art all to me!
Nothing to please I see,
Nothing apart from thee,
  Jesus, my Lord!

2 Thou, blesséd Son of God,
Hast bought me with thy blood,
  Jesus, my Lord!

4 Soon thou wilt come again!
I shall be happy then,
  Jesus, my Lord!
Then thine own face I'll see,
Then I shall like thee be,
Then evermore with thee,
  Jesus, my Lord!

DEDHAM. C. M.   WM. GARDINER.

1. Oh, for a thou-sand tongues to sing My dear Re-deem-er's praise!

The glo-ries of my God and King, The tri-umphs of his grace!

336   *Thanks for victory.*   C. WESLEY.

Oh, for a thousand tongues to sing
My dear Redeemer's praise!
The glories of my God and King,
The triumphs of his grace!

2 My gracious Master and my God!
Assist me to proclaim,
To spread, through all the earth abroad,
The honors of thy name.

3 Jesus—the name that calms my fears,
That bids my sorrows cease;
'T is music to my ravished ears;
'T is life, and health, and peace.

4 He breaks the power of canceled sin,
He sets the prisoner free;
His blood can make the foulest clean;
His blood availed for me.

5 Let us obey, we then shall know,
Shall feel our sins forgiven;
Anticipate our heaven below,
And own that love is heaven.

337   *"Remember me."*   T. HAWEIS.

O thou, from whom all goodness flows,
I lift my soul to thee;
In all my sorrows, conflicts, woes,
O Lord, remember me!

2 When on my aching, burdened heart
My sins lie heavily,
Thy pardon grant, new peace impart;
Thus, Lord, remember me!

3 When trials sore obstruct my way,
And ills I cannot flee,
Oh, let my strength be as my day—
Dear Lord, remember me!

4 When in the solemn hour of death
I wait thy just decree,
Be this the prayer of my last breath:
Now, Lord, remember me!

338   *"A clean heart."*   C. WESLEY.

Oh, for a heart to praise my God,
A heart from sin set free;
A heart that always feels thy blood
So freely shed for me!

2 A heart resigned, submissive, meek,
My dear Redeemer's throne;
Where only Christ is heard to speak,
Where Jesus reigns alone!

3 Oh, for a lowly, contrite heart,
Believing, true, and clean!
Which neither life nor death can part
From him that dwells within.

4 A heart in every thought renewed,
And filled with love divine;
Perfect, and right, and pure, and good;
An image, Lord! of thine.

5 Thy nature, gracious Lord, impart;
Come quickly from above;
Write thy new name upon my heart,—
Thy new, best name of Love.

LOVE, AND COMMUNION WITH CHRIST.

SOUTHPORT. C. M. — GEORGE KINGSLEY.

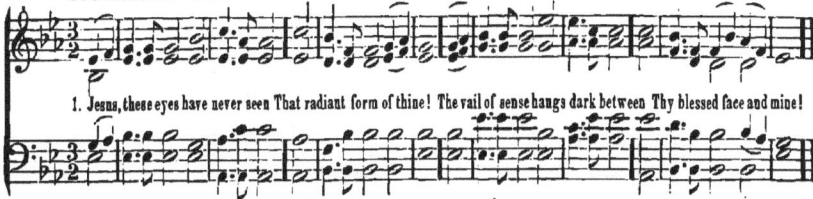

1. Jesus, these eyes have never seen That radiant form of thine! The vail of sense hangs dark between Thy blessed face and mine!

339 *"Whom unseen, we love."* RAY PALMER.

JESUS, these eyes have never seen
  That radiant form of thine!
The vail of sense hangs dark between
  Thy blessèd face and mine!

2 I see thee not, I hear thee not,
  Yet art thou oft with me;
And earth hath ne'er so dear a spot,
  As where I meet with thee.

3 Like some bright dream that comes un-
  When slumbers o'er me roll, [sought,
Thine image ever fills my thought,
  And charms my ravished soul.

4 Yet though I have not seen, and still
  Must rest in faith alone;
I love thee, dearest Lord!—and will,
  Unseen, but not unknown.

5 When death these mortal eyes shall seal,
  And still this throbbing heart,
The rending vail shall thee reveal,
  All glorious as thou art!

340 *Strength, Fortress, Refuge.* A. STEELE.

DEAR Refuge of my weary soul,
  On thee, when sorrows rise,
On thee, when waves of trouble roll,
  My fainting hope relies.

2 To thee I tell each rising grief,
  For thou alone canst heal;
Thy word can bring a sweet relief
  For every pain I feel.

3 But oh, when gloomy doubts prevail,
  I fear to call thee mine;
The springs of comfort seem to fail,
  And all my hopes decline.

4 Yet, gracious God, where shall I flee?
  Thou art my only trust;
And still my soul would cleave to thee,
  Though prostrate in the dust.

5 Thy mercy-seat is open still,
  Here let my soul retreat,
With humble hope attend thy will,
  And wait beneath thy feet.

GEER. C. M. — H. W. GREATOREX.

1. Dear Ref- uge of my wea - ry soul, On thee, when sor - rows rise,

On thee, when waves of troub - le roll, My faint - ing hope re - lies.

10

PENIEL. C. M.   THOS. HASTINGS.

1. My God! the spring of all my joys, The life of my de-lights,

The glo-ry of my bright-est days, And com-fort of my nights!

341   *"Altogether Lovely."*   I. WATTS.

My God! the spring of all my joys,
    The life of my delights,
The glory of my brightest days,
    And comfort of my nights!

2 In darkest shades if he appear,
    My dawning is begun:
He is my soul's sweet morning star,
    And he my rising sun.

3 The opening heavens around me shine
    With beams of sacred bliss,
While Jesus shows his heart is mine,
    And whispers, I am his!

4 My soul would leave this heavy clay,
    At that transporting word;
Run up with joy the shining way,
    To embrace my dearest Lord!

MELODY. C. M.   A. CHAPIN.

1. Je-sus, who on his glo-rious throne Rules heaven, and earth, and sea,

Is pleased to claim me for his own And give him-self to me.

342   *"To live is Christ."*   J. NEWTON.

JESUS, who on his glorious throne
    Rules heaven, and earth, and sea;
Is pleased to claim me for his own
    And give himself to me.

2 His person fixes all my love,
    His blood removes my fear;
And while he pleads for me above,
    His arm preserves me here.

3 His word of promise is my food,
    His Spirit is my guide;
Thus daily is my strength renewed,
    And all my wants supplied.

4 For him I count as gain each loss,
    Disgrace for him renown;
Well may I glory in my cross,
    While he prepares my crown

LOVE, AND COMMUNION WITH CHRIST.

HOLY CROSS. C. M.

FROM MENDELSSOHN.

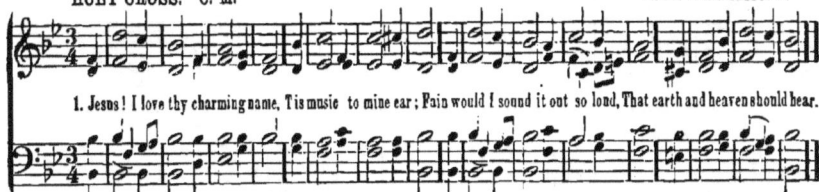

1. Jesus! I love thy charming name, Tis music to mine ear; Fain would I sound it out so loud, That earth and heaven should hear.

343   *"His name Jesus."*   P. DODDRIDGE.

JESUS! I love thy charming name,
  'Tis music to mine ear;
Fain would I sound it out so loud,
  That earth and heaven should hear.

2 Yes!—thou art precious to my soul,
  My transport and my trust;
Jewels, to thee, are gaudy toys,
  And gold is sordid dust

3 All my capacious powers can wish,
  In thee doth richly meet;
Not to mine eyes is light so dear,
  Nor friendship half so sweet.

4 Thy grace still dwells upon my heart,
  And sheds its fragrance there;—
The noblest balm of all its wounds,
  The cordial of its care.

HEBER. C. M.

GEO. KINGSLEY.

1. How sweet the name of Jesus sounds In a be-liev-er's ear! It soothes his sorrows, heals his wounds, And drives away his fear.

344   *"He is precious."*   J NEWTON.

How SWEET the name of Jesus sounds
  In a believer's ear!
It soothes his sorrows, heals his wounds,
  And drives away his fear.

2 It makes the wounded spirit whole,
  And calms the troubled breast;
'Tis manna to the hungry soul,
  And to the weary, rest.

3 Jesus! my Shepherd, Guardian, Friend,
  My Prophet, Priest, and King;
My Lord, my Life, my Way, my End,
  Accept the praise I bring.

4 Weak is the effort of my heart,
  And cold my warmest thought;
But when I see thee as thou art,
  I'll praise thee as I ought.

5 Till then I would thy love proclaim,
  With every fleeting breath;
And may the music of thy name,
  Refresh my soul in death.

345   *"Jesus only."*   E. CASWALL, tr

JESUS, the very thought of thee,
  With sweetness fills my breast;
But sweeter far thy face to see
  And in thy presence rest.

2 Nor voice can sing, nor heart can frame,
  Nor can the memory find
A sweeter sound than thy blest name,
  O Saviour of mankind!

3 O Hope of every contrite heart!
  O Joy of all the meek!
To those who fall, how kind thou art!
  How good to those who seek!

4 But what to those who find? Ah! this,
  Nor tongue nor pen can show;
The love of Jesus, what it is,
  None but his loved ones know.

5 Jesus, our only joy be thou,
  As thou our prize wilt be;
Jesus, be thou our glory now,
  And through eternity.

STILL WATER. 10s, 11s.   THOS. HASTINGS.

1. Oh, tell me, thou life and de-light of my soul, Where the flock of thy pasture are feed -

ing, I seek thy pro-tection, I need thy con-trol, I would go where my Shepherd is leading.

346   *Cant.* 1: 7, 8.   THOS. HASTINGS.

Oh, tell me, thou life and delight of my soul,
  Where the flock of thy pasture are feed-
    ing;
I seek thy protection, I need thy control,
  I would go where my Shepherd is leading.

2 Oh, tell me the place where thy flock are
    at rest,
  Where the noontide will find them re-
    posing;
The tempest now rages, my soul is dis-
    tressed,
  And the pathway of peace I am losing.

3 And why should I stray with the flocks
    of thy foes,
  In the desert where now they are rov-
    ing,

Where hunger and thirst, where affliction
    and woes,
  And temptations their ruin are proving?

4 Ah, when shall my woes and my wander-
    ings cease,
  And the follies that fill me with weeping?
Thou Shepherd of Israel, restore me that
    peace,
  Thou dost give to the flock thou art
    keeping.

5 A voice from the Shepherd now bids
    me return
By the way where the footprints are
    lying;
No longer to wander, no longer to mourn:
  And homeward my spirit is flying.

SPANISH HYMN. 7s. 6L   SPANISH MELODY.

1. Blessed Saviour, thee I love, All my other joys a-bove; } { All my hopes in thee a-bide,
D.C.—Ev - er let my glo-ry be On-ly, on-ly, on-ly thee. } { Thou my hope, and naught beside; }

ARIEL. C. P. M. LOWELL MASON, arr.

1. Oh, could I speak the matchless worth, Oh, could I sound the glories forth, Which in my Saviour shine!

{ I'd soar, and touch the heavenly strings, And vie with Gabriel while he sings } In notes almost di-vine, In notes almost di-vine.

347 *"He is precious."* S. MEDLEY.

Oh, could I speak the matchless worth,
Oh, could I sound the glories forth,
  Which in my Saviour shine!
I'd soar, and touch the heavenly strings,
And vie with Gabriel while he sings
  In notes almost divine.

2 I'd sing the precious blood he spilt,
My ransom from the dreadful guilt,
  Of sin and wrath divine!
I'd sing his glorious righteousness,
In which all-perfect heavenly dress
  My soul shall ever shine.

3 I'd sing the characters he bears,
And all the forms of love he wears,
  Exalted on his throne:
In loftiest songs of sweetest praise,
I would to everlasting days.
  Make all his glories known.

4 Well—the delightful day will come,
When my dear Lord will bring me home,
  And I shall see his face:
Then with my Saviour, Brother, Friend,
A blest eternity I'll spend,
  Triumphant in his grace.

348 7s, 6l. *"Only thee."* G. DUFFIELD.

Blessed Saviour! thee I love,
All my other joys above;
All my hopes in thee abide,
Thou my hope, and naught beside:
Ever let my glory be,
Only, only, only thee.

2 Once again beside the cross,
All my gain I count but loss;
Earthly pleasures fade away,—
Clouds they are that hide my day:
Hence, vain shadows! let me see
Jesus, crucified for me.

3 Blessèd Saviour, thine am I,
Thine to live, and thine to die;
Height, or depth, or earthly power,
Ne'er shall hide my Saviour more:
Ever shall my glory be
Only, only, only thee!

349 7s, 6l. *"I am thine."* F. R. HAVERGAL.

Jesus, Master, whose I am,
Purchased thine alone to be,
By thy blood, O spotless Lamb,
  Shed so willingly for me;
Let my heart be all thine own,
Let me live to thee alone.

2 Other lords have long held sway;
  Now thy name alone to bear,
Thy dear voice alone obey,
  Is my daily, hourly prayer.
Whom have I in heaven but thee?
Nothing else my joy can be.

3 Jesus, Master, I am thine;
  Keep me faithful, keep me near;
Let thy presence in me shine
  All my homeward way to cheer.
Jesus, at thy feet I fall,
Oh, be thou my All in all.

PAULINA. 11s.   L. W. BACON, arr.

1. I once was a stranger to grace and to God; I knew not my danger, and felt not my load;

Though friends spoke in rapture of Christ on the tree, Je - hovah, my Saviour, seemed nothing to me.

350   *Love and assurance.*   R. M. MC CHEYNE.

I once was a stranger to grace and to God;
I knew not my danger, and felt not my load;
Though friends spoke in rapture of Christ
    on the tree,
Jehovah, my Saviour, seemed nothing to me.

2 When free grace awoke me by light from
    on high,
Then legal fears shook me: I trembled to die:
No refuge, no safety, in self could I see:
Jehovah, thou only my Saviour must be!

3 My terrors all vanished before his sweet
    name;
My guilty fears banished, with boldness I
    came
To drink at the fountain, so copious and free:
Jehovah, my Saviour, is all things to me.

4 Jehovah, the Lord, is my treasure and
    boast;
Jehovah, my Saviour, I ne'er can be lost;
In thee I shall conquer, by flood and by
    field,
Jehovah my anchor, Jehovah my shield!

351   *"Looking unto Jesus."*   ANON.

O eyes that are weary, and hearts that
    are sore!
Look off unto Jesus, now sorrow no more!
The light of his countenance shineth so
    bright,
That here, as in heaven, there need be no
    night.

2 While looking to Jesus, my heart can-
    not fear;
I tremble no more when I see Jesus near;
I know that his presence my safeguard
    will be,
For, "Why are you troubled?" he saith
    unto me.

3 Still looking to Jesus, oh, may I be found,
When Jordan's dark waters encompass me
    round:
They bear me away in his presence to be:
I see him still nearer whom always I see.

4 Then, then shall I know the full beauty
    and grace
Of Jesus, my Lord, when I stand face to face;
Shall know how his love went before me
    each day,
And wonder that ever my eyes turned away.

MAGILL. 11s.   T. E. PERKINS.

1. Come, Je-sus, Redeemer, abide thou with me; Come, gladden my spirit, that waiteth for thee;

Thy smile every shadow shall chase from my heart, And soothe every sorrow though keen be the smart.

352   *"I will come to you."*   RAY PALMER.

COME, Jesus, Redeemer, abide thou with me;
Come, gladden my spirit that waiteth for thee;
Thy smile every shadow shall chase from my heart,
And soothe every sorrow though keen be the smart.

2 Without thee but weakness, with thee I am strong;
By day thou shalt lead me, by night be my song;
Though dangers surround me, I still every fear,
Since thou, the Most Mighty, my Helper, art near.

3 Thy love, oh, how faithful! so tender, so pure!
Thy promise, faith's anchor, how steadfast and sure!
That love, like sweet sunshine, my cold heart can warm,
That promise make steady my soul in the storm.

4 Breathe, breathe on my spirit, oft ruffled, thy peace:
From restless, vain wishes, bid thou my heart cease;
In thee all its longings henceforward shall end,
Till, glad, to thy presence my soul shall ascend.

5 Oh, then, blesséd Jesus, who once for me died,
Made clean in the fountain that gushed from thy side,
I shall see thy full glory, thy face shall behold,
And praise thee with raptures for ever untold!

353   *"Distresses for Christ's sake."*   C. FRY.

FOR what shall I praise thee, my God and my King,
For what blessings the tribute of gratitude bring?
Shall I praise thee for pleasure, for health, or for ease,
For the sunshine of youth, for the garden of peace?

2 For this I should praise; but if only for this,
I should leave half untold the donation of bliss!
I thank thee for sickness, for sorrow, and care,
For the thorns I have gathered, the anguish I bear;—

3 For nights of anxiety, watching, and tears,
A present of pain, a prospective of fears;
I praise thee, I bless thee, my Lord and my God,
For the good and the evil thy hand hath bestowed!

CHRISTIAN EXPERIENCE AND GRACES.

ROSEFIELD. 7s. 6l. — C. R. A. MALAN

1. { Bless-ed are the sons of God, They are bought with Christ's own blood; }
{ They are ransomed from the grave; Life e - ter - nal they shall have: } With them numbered may we be, Here, and in e - ter - ni - ty.

One with God, with Jesus one:
Glory is in them begun:
With them numbered may we be,
Here, and in eternity.

354 *Brotherly Love.* J. HUMPHREYS.

BLESSED are the sons of God,
They are bought with Christ's own blood;
They are ransomed from the grave;
Life eternal they shall have:
With them numbered may we be,
Here, and in eternity.

2 They are justified by grace,
They enjoy the Saviour's peace;
All their sins are washed away;
They shall stand in God's great day:
With them numbered may we be,
Here, and in eternity.

3 They are lights upon the earth,
Children of a heavenly birth,—

355 *Charity.* C. WINKWORTH, tr.

THOUGH I speak with angel tongues
Bravest words of strength and fire,
They are but as idle songs,
If no love my heart inspire;
All the eloquence shall pass
As the noise of sounding brass.

2 Though I lavish all I have
On the poor in charity,
Though I shrink not from the grave,
Or unmoved the stake can see,—
Till by love the work be crowned,
All shall profitless be found.

3 Come, thou Spirit of pure love,
Who didst forth from God proceed,
Never from my heart remove;
Let me all thy impulse heed;
Let my heart henceforward be
Moved, controlled, inspired by thee.

GUIDE. 7s. 6l. — M. M. WELLS.

FINE.

1. Qui - et, Lord, my fro - ward heart; Make me teach - a - ble and mild,
D. C.—From dis - trust and en - vy free, Pleased with all that pleas - es thee.

Up - right, sim - ple, free from art; Make me as a wean - ed child;

D. C.

REPOSE. 7s. 6 l.   J. P. HOLBROOK, *arr.*

1. Qui - et, Lord, my froward heart, Make me teach-a-ble and mild, Upright, simple, free from art,

Make me as a weaned child: From distrust and en - vy free, Pleased with all that pleases thee.

356   *Psalm* 131.   J. NEWTON.

QUIET, Lord, my froward heart,
  Make me teachable and mild,
Upright, simple, free from art,
  Make me as a weanéd child:
From distrust and envy free,
Pleased with all that pleases thee.

2 What thou shalt to-day provide,
  Let me as a child receive;
What to-morrow may betide,
  Calmly to thy wisdom leave:
'Tis enough that thou wilt care;
Why should I the burden bear?

3 As a little child relies
  On a care beyond his own,
Knows he's neither strong nor wise,
  Fears to stir a step alone;—
Let me thus with thee abide,
As my Father, Guard, and Guide.

357   *Trust.*   E. H. NEVIN

SAVIOUR, happy would I be,
  If I could but trust in thee;
Trust thy wisdom me to guide;
Trust thy goodness to provide;
Trust thy saving love and power;
Trust thee every day and hour:—

2 Trust thee as the only light
  In the darkest hour of night;
Trust in sickness, trust in health;
Trust in poverty and wealth;
Trust in joy and trust in grief;
Trust thy promise for relief:—

3 Trust thy blood to cleanse my soul;
  Trust thy grace to make me whole;
Trust thee living, dying too;
Trust thee all my journey through;
Trust thee till my feet shall be
Planted on the crystal sea.

HALLE. 7s, 6 l.   F. J. HAYDN.

1. { Ab-ba, Father, hear thy child, Late in Je - sus re - conciled; }
   { Hear, and all the graces shower, All the joy, and peace, and power; } All my Saviour asks above, All the life and heaven of love.

358   *Spirituality.*   C. WESLEY.

ABBA, Father, hear thy child,
Late in Jesus reconciled;
Hear, and all the graces shower,
All the joy, and peace, and power;
All my Saviour asks above,
All the life and heaven of love.

2 Holy Ghost, no more delay;
Come, and in thy temple stay:
Now, thine inward witness bear,
Strong, and permanent, and clear:
Spring of life, thyself impart;
Rise eternal in my heart.

MOUNT AUBURN. C. M. — GEO. KINGSLEY.

1. Lord, I be-lieve; thy power I own; Thy word I would o-bey;
I wan-der com-fort-less and lone, When from thy truth I stray.

359   *Faith.*   J. R. WREFORD.

Lord, I believe; thy power I own;
   Thy word I would obey;
I wander comfortless and lone,
   When from thy truth I stray.

2 Lord, I believe; but gloomy fears
   Sometimes bedim my sight;
I look to thee with prayers and tears,
   And cry for strength and light.

3 Lord, I believe; but oft, I know,
   My faith is cold and weak:
My weakness strengthen, and bestow
   The confidence I seek.

4 Yes! I believe; and only thou
   Canst give my soul relief:
Lord, to thy truth my spirit bow;
   "Help thou mine unbelief!"

360   *Meekness.*   T. H. GILL.

Lord! when I all things would possess,
   I crave but to be thine;
Oh, lowly is the loftiness
   Of these desires divine.

2 Each gift but helps my soul to learn
   How boundless is thy store;
I go from strength to strength, and yearn
   For thee, my Helper, more.

3 How can my soul divinely soar,
   How keep the shining way,
And not more tremblingly adore,
   And not more humbly pray!

4 The more I triumph in thy gifts,
   The more I wait on thee;
The grace that mightily uplifts
   Most sweetly humbleth me.

5 The heaven where I would stand complete
   My lowly love shall see,
And stronger grow the yearning sweet,
   My holy One! for thee.

361   *Calmness.*   H. BONAR.

Calm me, my God, and keep me calm;
   Let thine outstretchéd wing
Be like the shade of Elim's palm,
   Beside her desert spring.

2 Yes, keep me calm, though loud and rude
   The sounds my ear that greet,—
Calm in the closet's solitude,
   Calm in the bustling street,—

3 Calm in the hour of buoyant health,
   Calm in my hour of pain,
Calm in my poverty or wealth,
   Calm in my loss or gain,—

4 Calm in the sufferance of wrong,
   Like him who bore my shame,
Calm 'mid the threatening, taunting throng,
   Who hate thy holy name.

5 Calm me, my God, and keep me calm,
   Soft resting on thy breast;
Soothe me with holy hymn and psalm,
   And bid my spirit rest.

CORINTH. C. M.

LOWELL MASON.

1. My God, how won - der - ful thou art, Thy ma - jes - ty how bright!

How glo - rious is thy mer - cy - seat, In depths of burn - ing light!

362   *"Herein is Love."*   F. W. FABER.

My God, how wonderful thou art,
  Thy majesty how bright!
How glorious is thy mercy seat,
  In depths of burning light!

2 Yet I may love thee too, O Lord,
  Almighty as thou art;
For thou hast stooped to ask of me
  The love of my poor heart.

3 No earthly father loves like thee,
  No mother half so mild
Bears and forbears, as thou hast done
  With me, thy sinful child.

4 My God, how wonderful thou art,
  Thou everlasting Friend!
On thee I stay my trusting heart,
  Till faith in vision end.

NAOMI. C. M.

LOWELL MASON.

1. Father! whate'er of earthly bliss Thy sovereign will denies, Accepted at thy throne of grace, Let this pe-ti - tion rise:—

363   *Humble Devotion.*   A. STEELE.

FATHER! whate'er of earthly bliss
  Thy sovereign will denies,
Accepted at thy throne of grace,
  Let this petition rise:—

2 "Give me a calm, a thankful heart,
  From every murmur free;
The blessings of thy grace impart,
  And make me live to thee.

3 "Let the sweet hope that thou art mine:
  My life and death attend;
Thy presence through my journey shine,
  And crown my journey's end."

364   *Growth in grace.*   A. NETTLETON.

COME, Holy Ghost, my soul inspire;
  This one great gift impart—
What most I need, and most desire,
  An humble, holy heart.

2 Bear witness I am born again,
  My many sins forgiven:
Nor let a gloomy doubt remain
  To cloud my hope of heaven.

3 More of myself grant I may know,
  From sin's deceit be free;
In all the Christian graces grow,
  And live alone to thee.

GRATITUDE. L. M.   THOS. HASTINGS, arr.

1. My God, how end-less is thy love! Thy gifts are ev - ery eve - ning new;

And morn-ing mer - cies from a - bove, Gen - tly dis - till like ear - ly dew.

365   *Gratitude.*   I. WATTS.

My God, how endless is thy love!
  Thy gifts are every evening new;
And morning mercies from above,
  Gently distill like early dew.

2 Thou spread'st the curtains of the night,
  Great Guardian of my sleeping hours;
Thy sovereign word restores the light,
  And quickens all my drowsy powers.

3 I yield my powers to thy command;
  To thee I consecrate my days;
Perpetual blessings from thine hand
  Demand perpetual songs of praise.

366   *Faith.*   J. NEWTON.

By faith in Christ I walk with God,
  With heaven, my journey's end, in view;
Supported by his staff and rod,
  My road is safe and pleasant too.

2 Though snares and dangers throng my
                              path,
  And earth and hell my course withstand,
I triumph over all by faith,
  Guarded by his almighty hand.

3 The wilderness affords no food,
  But God for my support prepares,
Provides me every needful good,
  And frees my soul from wants and cares.

4 With him sweet converse I maintain;
  Great as he is, I dare be free;
I tell him all my grief and pain,
  And he reveals his love to me.

367   *Contentment.*   W. COWPER, tr.

O LORD, how full of sweet content
  Our years of pilgrimage are spent!
Where'er we dwell, we dwell with thee,
  In heaven, in earth, or on the sea.

2 To us remains nor place nor time:
  Our country is in every clime:
We can be calm and free from care
  On any shore, since God is there.

3 While place we seek, or place we shun,
  The soul finds happiness in none;
But with our God to guide our way,
  'Tis equal joy to go or stay.

4 Could we be cast where thou art not,
  That were indeed a dreadful lot;
But regions none remote we call,
  Secure of finding God in all.

368   *Voiceless Prayer.*   GREEK HYMN.

O BLESSED God, to thee I raise
My voice in thankful hymns of praise;
And when my voice shall silent be,
My silence shall be praise to thee.

2 For voice and silence doth impart
The filial homage of my heart;
And both alike are understood
By thee, thou Parent of all good—

3 Whose grace is all unsearchable,
Whose care for me no tongue can tell,
Who loves my loudest praise to hear,
And loves to bless my voiceless prayer.

DUKE STREET. L. M.　　　　　　　　　　　　　　J. HATTON.

1. 'Tis by the faith of joys to come, We walk through des-erts dark as night;

Till we ar-rive at heaven, our home, Faith is our guide, and faith our light.

369　　*Faith.*　　　i. WATTS.

'Tis by the faith of joys to come,
　We walk through deserts dark as night;
Till we arrive at heaven, our home,
　Faith is our guide, and faith our light.

2 The want of sight she well supplies;
　She makes the pearly gates appear;
Far into distant worlds she pries,
　And brings eternal glories near.

3 Cheerful we tread the desert through,
　While faith inspires a heavenly ray;
Though lions roar, and tempests blow,
　And rocks and dangers fill the way.

370　　*Self-denial.*　　　J. KEBLE.

If on our daily course our mind
Be set, to hallow all we find,
New treasures still, of countless price,
God will provide for sacrifice.

2 Old friends, old scenes, will lovelier be,
As more of heaven in each we see;
Some softening gleam of love and prayer
Shall dawn on every cross and care.

3 The trivial round, the common task,
Will furnish all we ought to ask;—
Room to deny ourselves, a road
To bring us daily nearer God.

4 Only, O Lord, in thy dear love,
Fit us for perfect rest above;
And help us, this and every day,
To live more nearly as we pray.

371　　*Love.*　　　i. WATTS.

Had I the tongues of Greeks and Jews,
And nobler speech than angels use,
If love be absent, I am found
Like tinkling brass, an empty sound.

2 Were I inspired to preach and tell
All that is done in heaven and hell—
Or could my faith the world remove,
Still I am nothing without love.

3 Should I distribute all my store
To feed the hungry, clothe the poor;
Or give my body to the flame,
To gain a martyr's glorious name:—

4 If love to God and love to men
Be absent, all my hopes are vain;
Nor tongues, nor gifts, nor fiery zeal,
The work of love can e'er fulfill.

372　　*Consistency.*　　　l. WATTS.

So let our lips and lives express
The holy gospel we profess;
So let our works and virtues shine,
To prove the doctrine all divine.

2 Thus shall we best proclaim abroad
The honors of our Saviour God;
When his salvation reigns within,
And grace subdues the power of sin.

3 Religion bears our spirits up,
While we expect that blessed hope,—
The bright appearance of the Lord:
And faith stands leaning on his word.

VALENTIA. C. M.   GEO. KINGSLEY, arr.

1. Oh, gift of gifts! oh, grace of faith! My God! how can it be
That thou, who hast dis-cern-ing love, Shouldst give that gift to me?

373   *Faith.*   F. W. FABER.

Oh, gift of gifts! oh, grace of faith!
  My God! how can it be
That thou, who hast discerning love,
  Shouldst give that gift to me?

2 How many hearts thou mightst have had
  More innocent than mine!
How many souls more worthy far
  Of that sweet touch of thine!

3 Ah, grace! into unlikeliest hearts
  It is thy boast to come,
The glory of thy light to find
  In darkest spots a home.

4 The crowd of cares, the weightiest cross,
  Seem trifles less than light—
Earth looks so little and so low
  When faith shines full and bright.

5 Oh, happy, happy that I am!
  If thou canst be, O Faith,
The treasure that thou art in life,
  What wilt thou be in death!

374   *Godly sincerity.*   BARTON.

Walk in the light! so shalt thou know
  That fellowship of love,
His Spirit only can bestow,
  Who reigns in light above,

2 Walk in the light! and thou shalt find
  Thy heart made truly his,
Who dwells in cloudless light enshrined,
  In whom no darkness is.

3 Walk in the light! and ev'n the tomb
  No fearful shade shall wear;
Glory shall chase away its gloom,
  For Christ hath conquered there.

4 Walk in the light! and thou shalt see
  Thy path, though thorny, bright,
For God by grace shall dwell in thee,
  And God himself is light.

375   *Faith.*   D. TURNER.

Faith adds new charms to earthly bliss,
  And saves me from its snares;
Its aid, in every duty, brings,
  And softens all my cares.

2 The wounded conscience knows its power
  The healing balm to give;
That balm the saddest heart can cheer;
  And make the dying live.

3 Wide it unvails celestial worlds,
  Where deathless pleasures reign;
And bids me seek my portion there,
  Nor bids me seek in vain.

4 It shows the precious promise sealed
  With the Redeemer's blood;
And helps my feeble hope to rest
  Upon a faithful God.

5 There—there unshaken would I rest,
  Till this frail body dies;
And then, on faith's triumphant wings,
  To endless glory rise.

BRIDGMAN. C. M.　　　　　　　　　　GEO. KINGSLEY, *arr.*

1. If God is mine, then pres - ent things And things to come are mine; Yea, Christ, his word, and

Spir - it too, And glo - ry all divine.

376　　*"Saints' Inventory."*　　B. BEDDOME.

If God is mine, then present things
　And things to come are mine;
Yea, Christ, his word, and Spirit too,
　And glory all divine.

2 If he is mine, then from his love
　He every trouble sends;
All things are working for my good,
　And bliss his rod attends.

3 If he is mine, let friends forsake,
　Let wealth and honor flee:

Sure he who giveth me himself
　Is more than these to me.

4 Oh, tell me, Lord, that thou art mine;
　What can I wish beside?
My soul shall at the fountain live,
　When all the streams are dried.

377　　　*Perseverance.*　　I. WATTS.

FIRM as the earth thy gospel stands,
　My Lord, my hope, my trust;
If I am found in Jesus' hands,
　My soul can ne'er be lost.

2 His honor is engaged to save
　The meanest of his sheep;
All, whom his heavenly Father gave,
　His hands securely keep.

3 Nor death nor hell shall e'er remove
　His favorites from his breast;
In the dear bosom of his love
　They must for ever rest.

BROWN. C. M.　　　　　　　　　　W. B. BRADBURY.

1. When I can read my ti - tle clear To mansions in the skies, I bid farewell to

ev - ery fear, And wipe my weeping eyes.

378　　　*Assurance.*　　I. WATTS.

WHEN I can read my title clear
　To mansions in the skies,
I bid farewell to every fear,
　And wipe my weeping eyes.

2 Should earth against my soul engage,
　And fiery darts be hurled,
Then I can smile at Satan's rage,
　And face a frowning world.

3 Let cares like a wild deluge come,
　And storms of sorrow fall,
May I but safely reach my home,
　My God, my heaven, my all!—

4 There shall I bathe my weary soul
　In seas of heavenly rest;
And not a wave of trouble roll
　Across my peaceful breast.

LUTHER. S. M.   THOS. HASTINGS.

1. Grace! 'tis a charm-ing sound! Harmonious to mine ear! Heav'n with the ech- -o shall resound, And all the earth shall hear, And all the earth shall hear.

379   *Grace.*   P. DODDRIDGE.

GRACE! 'tis a charming sound!
Harmonious to mine ear!
Heaven with the echo shall resound,
And all the earth shall hear.

2 Grace first contrived a way
To save rebellious man;
And all the steps that grace display,
Which drew the wondrous plan.

3 Grace led my roving feet
To tread the heavenly road;
And new supplies each hour I meet
While pressing on to God.

4 Grace all the work shall crown,
Through everlasting days;
It lays in heaven the topmost stone,
And well deserves the praise.

380   *God our Father.*   C. WINKWORTH, *tr.*

HERE I can firmly rest;
I dare to boast of this,
That God, the highest and the best,
My Friend and Father is.

2 Naught have I of my own,
Naught in the life I lead;
What Christ hath given, that alone
I dare in faith to plead.

3 I rest upon the ground
Of Jesus and his blood;
It is through him that I have found
My soul's eternal good.

4 At cost of all I have,
At cost of life and limb,
I cling to God who yet shall save;
I will not turn from him.

5 His Spirit in me dwells,
O'er all my mind he reigns;
My care and sadness he dispels,
And soothes away my pains.

6 He prospers day by day
His work within my heart,
Till I have strength and faith to say,
"Thou, God, my Father art!"

381   *"It is well."*   J. KENT.

WHAT cheering words are these;
Their sweetness who can tell?
In time, and to eternal days,
"'Tis with the righteous well!"

2 Well when they see his face,
Or sink amidst the flood;
Well in affliction's thorny maze,
Or on the mount with God.

3 'Tis well when joys arise,
'Tis well when sorrows flow,
'Tis well when darkness vails the skies,
And strong temptations grow.

4 'Tis well when Jesus calls,—
"From earth and sin arise,
To join the hosts of ransomed souls,
Made to salvation wise!"

FERGUSON. S. M.

GEO. KINGSLEY.

1. Be-hold what wondrous grace The Fa-ther has be-stowed On sin-ners of a mor-tal race, To call them sons of God!

382   *Adoption.*   I. WATTS.

BEHOLD! what wondrous grace
  The Father has bestowed
On sinners of a mortal race,
  To call them sons of God!

2 Nor doth it yet appear
  How great we must be made;
But when we see our Saviour here,
  We shall be like our Head.

3 A hope so much divine
  May trials well endure,
May purge our souls from sense and sin,
  As Christ the Lord is pure.

4 If in my Father's love
  I share a filial part,
Send down thy Spirit, like a dove,
  To rest upon my heart.

5 We would no longer lie
  Like slaves beneath the throne;
Our faith shall Abba, Father! cry,
  And thou the kindred own.

383   *Peace.*   C. WESLEY.

THOU very present Aid
  In suffering and distress,
The mind which still on thee is stayed,
  Is kept in perfect peace.

2 The soul by faith reclined
  On the Redeemer's breast,
'Mid raging storms, exults to find
  An everlasting rest.

3 Sorrow and fear are gone,
  Whene'er thy face appears;
It stills the sighing orphan's moan,
  And dries the widow's tears.

4 Jesus, to whom I fly,
  Doth all my wishes fill;
What though created streams are dry?
  I have the fountain still.

5 Stripped of each earthly friend,
  I find them all in One,
And peace and joy which never end,
  And heaven, in Christ, alone.

THATCHER. S. M.

FROM G. F. HANDEL.

1. Thou ver - y pres - ent Aid In suf - fering and dis - tress,

The mind which still on thee is stayed, Is kept in per - fect peace.

11

JEWETT. 6s. D.   J. P. HOLBROOK, arr.

1. My Je - sus, as thou wilt! Oh, may thy will be mine! In - to thy hand of love
I would my all re - sign; Through sor - row, or through joy, Con - duct me
as thine own, And help me still to say, My Lord, thy will be done!

384 *"Not my will, but thine."* J. BORTHWICK, tr.

My Jesus, as thou wilt!
  Oh, may thy will be mine;
Into thy hand of love
  I would my all resign;
Through sorrow, or through joy,
  Conduct me as thine own,
And help me still to say,
  My Lord, thy will be done!

2 My Jesus, as thou wilt!
  Though seen through many a tear,
Let not my star of hope
  Grow dim or disappear;
Since thou on earth hast wept,
  And sorrowed oft alone,
If I must weep with thee,
  My Lord, thy will be done!

3 My Jesus, as thou wilt!
  All shall be well for me;
Each changing future scene
  I gladly trust with thee:
Straight to my home above
  I travel calmly on,
And sing, in life or death,
  My Lord, thy will be done!

385 *"He knoweth the way."* H. BONAR.

Thy way, not mine, O Lord,
  However dark it be!
Lead me by thine own hand;
  Choose out my path for me.
I dare not choose my lot:
  I would not, if I might;
Choose thou for me, my God.
  So shall I walk aright.

2 The kingdom that I seek
  Is thine: so let the way
That leads to it be thine,
  Else I must surely stray.
Take thou my cup, and it
  With joy or sorrow fill,
As best to thee may seem;
  Choose thou my good and ill.

3 Choose thou for me my friends,
  My sickness or my health;
Choose thou my cares for me,
  My poverty or wealth.
Not mine, not mine the choice,
  In things or great or small;
Be thou my Guide, my Strength,
  My Wisdom and my All.

MERCY. 7s.   E. P. PARKER, arr.

1. In the dark and cloud-y day, When earth's rich-es flee a - way,

And the last hope will not stay, Sav - iour, com - fort, com - fort me!

386   *Comfort.*   G. RAWSON.

In the dark and cloudy day,
When earth's riches flee away,
And the last hope will not stay,
   Saviour, comfort me!

2 When the secret idol's gone
That my poor heart yearned upon,—
Desolate, bereft, alone,
   Saviour, comfort me!

3 Thou, who wast so sorely tried,
In the darkness crucified,
Bid me in thy love confide;
   Saviour, comfort me!

4 Comfort me; I am cast down:
'Tis my heavenly Father's frown;
I deserve it all, I own:
   Saviour, comfort me!

5 So it shall be good for me
Much afflicted now to be,
If thou wilt but tenderly,
   Saviour, comfort me!

387   *"For he careth."*   R. HILL.

Cast thy burden on the Lord,
Only lean upon his word;
Thou wilt soon have cause to bless
His unchanging faithfulness.

2 He sustains thee by his hand,
He enables thee to stand;
Those, whom Jesus once hath loved,
From his grace are never moved.

3 Heaven and earth may pass away,
God's free grace shall not decay;
He hath promised to fulfil
All the pleasure of his will.

4 Jesus! guardian of thy flock,
Be thyself our constant rock;
Make us by thy powerful hand,
Firm as Zion's mountain stand.

388   *Love seen in trials.*   W. COWPER.

'Tis my happiness below
   Not to live without the cross,
But the Saviour's power to know,
   Sanctifying every loss.

2 Trials must and will befall;
   But with humble faith to see
Love inscribed upon them all,—
   This is happiness to me.

3 God in Israel sows the seeds
   Of affliction, pain and toil;
These spring up and choke the weeds
   Which would else o'erspread the soil.

4 Did I meet no trials here,
   No chastisement by the way,
Might I not with reason fear
   I should prove a castaway?

5 Trials make the promise sweet;
   Trials give new life to prayer;
Trials bring me to his feet,
   Lay me low, and keep me there.

DORRNANCE. 8s, 7s. I. D. WOODBURY.

1. Cease, ye mourners, cease to languish O'er the grave of those you love; Pain and death, and night and anguish Enter not the world above.

389 *Comfort.* W. B. COLLYER.

CEASE, ye mourners, cease to languish
  O'er the grave of those you love;
Pain and death, and night and anguish
  Enter not the world above.

2 While our silent steps are straying
  Lonely through night's deepening shade,
Glory's brightest beams are playing
  Round the happy Christian's head.

3 Light and peace at once deriving
  From the hand of God most high,
In his glorious presence living,
  They shall never, never die.

4 Now, ye mourners, cease to languish
  O'er the grave of those you love;
Far removed from pain and anguish,
  They are chanting hymns above.

TRISTE. 8s, 7s. D. J. P. HOLBROOK.

1. Holy Father, thou hast taught me I should live to thee alone; Year by year thy hand hath brought me
D. S.—Still thine arm has been around me,

On thro' dangers oft unknown. When I wandered, thou hast found me; When I doubted, sent me light;
All my paths were in thy sight.

390 *"Keep me ever."* ANON.

HOLY Father, thou hast taught me
  I should live to thee alone;
Year by year thy hand hath brought me
  On through dangers oft unknown.
When I wandered, thou hast found me;
  When I doubted, sent me light;
Still thine arm has been around me,
  All my paths were in thy sight.

2 In the world will foes assail me,
  Craftier, stronger far than I;
And the strife may never fail me,
  Well I know, before I die.

Therefore, Lord, I come believing
  Thou canst give the power I need;
Through the prayer of faith receiving
  Strength—the Spirit's strength, indeed.

3 I would trust in thy protection,
  Wholly rest upon thine arm;
Follow wholly thy direction,
  Thou, mine only guard from harm!
Keep me from mine own undoing,
  Help me turn to thee when tried,
Still my footsteps, Father, viewing,
  Keep me ever at thy side.

MILWAUKEE. 8s, 7s. J. ZUNDEL.

1. Jesus, while our hearts are bleeding O'er the spoils that death has won, We would at this solemn meeting, Calmly say,—thy will be done.

391 "*Thy will be done.*" T. HASTINGS.

JESUS, while our hearts are bleeding
O'er the spoils that death has won,
We would at this solemn meeting,
Calmly say,—thy will be done.

2 Though cast down, we're not forsaken;
Though afflicted, not alone;
Thou didst give, and thou hast taken;
Blessèd Lord,—thy will be done.

3 Though to-day we're filled with mourning,
Mercy still is on the throne;
With thy smiles of love returning,
We can sing—thy will be done.

4 By thy hands the boon was given,
Thou hast taken but thine own:
Lord of earth, and God of heaven,
Evermore,—thy will be done!

LUX BENIGNA. 10s, 4s. J. B. DYKES.

1. Lead, kindly Light! amid th' encircling gloom, Lead thou me on; The night is dark, and I am far from home,

Lead thou me on; Keep thou my feet; I do not ask to see The distant scene; one step enough for me.

392 "*Lead thou me on!*" J. H. NEWMAN.

LEAD, kindly Light! amid the encircling
Lead thou me on; [gloom,
The night is dark, and I am far from home,
Lead thou me on;
Keep thou my feet; I do not ask to see
The distant scene; one step enough for me.

2 I was not ever thus, nor prayed that thou
Shouldst lead me on;
I loved to choose and see my path; but now
Lead thou me on:

I loved the garish day, and spite of fears,
Pride ruled my will. Remember not past
years.

3 So long thy power has blessed me, sure
Will lead me on [it still
O'er moor and fen, o'er crag and torrent, till
The night is gone;
And with the morn those angel faces smile
Which I have loved long since, and lost
awhile !

DISCIPLINE AND SORROW.

162

FLEMMING. 8s, 6s.   F. FLEMMING.

1. O Ho-ly Sav-iour! Friend un-seen, Since on thine arm thou bid'st me lean, Help me, throughout life's changing scene, By faith to cling to thee.

393 *Clinging to Christ.* C. ELLIOTT.

O Holy Saviour! Friend unseen,
Since on thine arm thou bid'st me lean,
Help me, throughout life's changing scene,
  By faith to cling to thee!

2 What though the world deceitful prove,
And earthly friends and hopes remove;
With patient, uncomplaining love,
  Still would I cling to thee.

3 Though oft I seem to tread alone
Life's dreary waste, with thorns o'ergrown,
Thy voice of love, in gentlest tone,
  Still whispers, "Cling to me!"

4 Though faith and hope are often tried,
I ask not, need not, aught beside;
So safe, so calm, so satisfied,
  The soul that clings to thee!

394 *A will resigned.* J. G. WHITTIER.

I ASK not now for gold to gild,
  With mocking shine, an aching frame;
The yearning of the mind is stilled—
  I ask not now for fame.

2 But, bowed in lowliness of mind,
  I make my humble wishes known;
I only ask a will resigned,
  O Father, to thine own.

3 In vain I task my aching brain,
  In vain the sage's thoughts I scan;
I only feel how weak I am,
  How poor and blind is man.

4 And now my spirit sighs for home,
  And longs for light whereby to see;
And, like a weary child, would come,
  O Father, unto thee.

THY WILL BE DONE. Chant.   LOWELL MASON.

Close. Thy will be done!

395 *Mark* 14 : 36. J. BOWRING.

"Thy will be | done!" ||. In devious way
The hurrying stream of | life may | run; ||
Yet still our grateful hearts shall say, |
  "Thy will be | done."

2 "Thy will be | done!" || If o'er us shine
A gladdening and a | prosperous | sun, ||

This prayer will make it more divine—|
  "Thy will be | done!"

3 "Thy will be | done!" || Tho' shrouded o'er
Our | path with | gloom, | one comfort—one
Is ours:—to breathe, while we adore, |
  "Thy will be | done."

ROMBERG. C. M.

THOS. HASTINGS.

1. O thou, whose boun-ty fills my cup With ev-ery bless-ing meet!

I give thee thanks for ev-ery drop— The bit-ter and the sweet.

396   *Thanks for all.*   J. CREWDSON.

O THOU, whose bounty fills my cup
  With every blessing meet !
I give thee thanks for every drop—
  The bitter and the sweet.

2 I praise thee for the desert road,
  And for the river-side;
For all thy goodness hath bestowed,
  And all thy grace denied.

3 I thank thee for both smile and frown,
  And for the gain and loss;
I praise thee for the future crown,
  And for the present cross.

4 I thank thee for the wing of love,
  Which stirred my worldly nest;
And for the stormy clouds which drove
  The flutterer to thy breast.

5 I bless thee for the glad increase,
  And for the waning joy;
And for this strange, this settled peace,
  Which nothing can destroy.

397   *"I firmly trust."*   J. MONTGOMERY.

ONE prayer I have—all prayers in one—
  When I am wholly thine;
Thy will, my God, thy will be done,
  And let that will be mine.

2 All-wise, almighty, and all-good,
  In thee I firmly trust;
Thy ways, unknown or understood,
  Are merciful and just.

3 May I remember that to thee
  Whate'er I have I owe;
And back, in gratitude, from me
  May all thy bounties flow.

4 And though thy wisdom takes away,
  Shall I arraign thy will?
No, let me bless thy name, and say,
  "The Lord is gracious still."

5 A pilgrim through the earth I roam,
  Of nothing long possessed;
And all must fail when I go home,
  For this is not my rest.

398   *"Sweet to lie passive."*   A. M. TOPLADY.

WHEN languor and disease invade
  This trembling house of clay,
'Tis sweet to look beyond my pain,
  And long to fly away;—

2 Sweet to look inward, and attend
  The whispers of his love;
Sweet to look upward to the place
  Where Jesus pleads above;—

3 Sweet on his faithfulness to rest,
  Whose love can never end;
Sweet on his covenant of grace
  For all things to depend;—

4 Sweet, in the confidence of faith,
  To trust his firm decrees;
Sweet to lie passive in his hands,
  And know no will but his.

STOUGHTON. 8s, 7s. D. · J. P. HOLBROOK.

1. Glo - rious things of thee are spok-en, Zi - on, cit - y of our God!

He, whose word can - not be brok - en, Formed thee for his own a - bode:
D. S.—With sal - va - tion's wall sur - round-ed, Thou may'st smile at all thy foes.

On the Rock of A - ges found - ed, What can shake thy sure re - pose?

399 *" Glorious things."* J. NEWTON.

GLORIOUS things of thee are spoken,
  Zion, city of our God!
He, whose word cannot be broken,
  Formed thee for his own abode:
On the Rock of Ages founded,
  What can shake thy sure repose?
With salvation's walls surrounded,
  Thou may'st smile at all thy foes.

2 See! the streams of living waters,
  Springing from eternal love,
Well supply thy sons and daughters,
  And all fear of want remove:
Who can faint, while such a river
  Ever flows their thirst to assuage?—
Grace, which, like the Lord, the Giver,
  Never fails from age to age.

3 Round each habitation hovering,
  See the cloud and fire appear
For a glory and a covering,
  Showing that the Lord is near!
Thus deriving from their banner,
  Light by night, and shade by day,
Safe they feed upon the manna
  Which he gives them when they pray.

400 *The covenant.* W. COWPER.

HEAR what God, the Lord hath spoken;
  O my people, faint and few,
Comfortless, afflicted, broken,
  Fair abodes I build for you;
Scenes of heartfelt tribulation
  Shall no more perplex your ways;
You shall name your walls "Salvation,"
  And your gates shall all be "Praise."

2 There, like streams that feed the garden,
  Pleasures without end shall flow;
For the Lord, your faith rewarding,
  All his bounty shall bestow.
Still in undisturbed possession
  Peace and righteousness shall reign;
Never shall you feel oppression,
  Hear the voice of war again.

3 Ye, no more your suns descending,
  Waning moons no more shall see,
But, your griefs for ever ending,
  Find eternal noon in me.
God shall rise, and shining o'er you,
  Change to day the gloom of night;
He, the Lord, shall be your Glory,
  God, your everlasting Light.

MIDDLETON, 8s, 7s. D.

ENGLISH AIR.

FINE.

1. { Light of those whose dreary dwell-ing Bor-ders on the shades of death!
Rise on us, thy love re-veal-ing, Dis-si-pate the clouds be-neath: } Thou, of heaven and
D. C.—Scattering all the night of na-ture, Pour-ing day up-on our eyes.

D. C.

earth Cre-a-tor, In our deepest darkness rise,—

401 *"The true Light."* C. WESLEY.

LIGHT of those whose dreary dwelling
Borders on the shades of death !
Rise on us, thy love revealing,
Dissipate the clouds beneath:
Thou, of heaven and earth Creator,
In our deepest darkness rise,—
Scattering all the night of nature,
Pouring day upon our eyes.

2 Still we wait for thine appearing,
Life and joy thy beams impart,
Chasing all our fears, and cheering
Every poor benighted heart:
Come, and manifest thy favor
To the ransomed, helpless race;
Come, thou glorious God and Saviour!
Come, and bring the gospel grace.

3 Save us, in thy great compassion,
O thou mild, pacific Prince!
Give the knowledge of salvation,
Give the pardon of our sins;
By thine all-sufficient merit,
Every burdened soul release;
Every weary, wandering spirit,
Guide into thy perfect peace.

WILSON, 8s, 7s.

FROM MENDELSSOHN.

1. Come, thou long-expect-ed Je-sus, Born to set thy peo-ple free; From our fears and sins re-

lease us, Let us find our rest in thee.

402 *"Come quickly."* C. WESLEY.

COME, thou long-expected Jesus,
Born to set thy people free;
From our fears and sins release us,
Let us find our rest in thee.

2 Israel's Strength and Consolation,
Hope of all the saints thou art:
Dear Desire of every nation,
Joy of every longing heart.

3 Born, thy people to deliver;
Born a child, and yet a King !
Born to reign in us for ever,
Now thy gracious kingdom bring.

4 By thine own eternal Spirit,
Rule in all our hearts alone;
By thine all-sufficient merit,
Raise us to thy glorious throne.

LEIGHTON. S. M.   H. W. GREATOREX.

1. Work while it is to-day! This was our Sav-iour's rule;

With do-cile minds let us o-bey, As learn-ers in his school.

403   *Expedition.*   J. MONTGOMERY.

WORK while it is to-day!
  This was our Saviour's rule;
With docile minds let us obey,
  As learners in his school.

2 Lord Christ, we humbly ask
  Of thee the power and will,
With fear and meekness, every task
  Of duty to fulfill.

3 At home, by word and deed,
  Adorn redeeming grace;
And sow abroad the precious seed
  Of truth in every place:—

4 That thus the wilderness
  May blossom like the rose,
And trees spring up of righteousness,
  Where'er life's river flows.

5 For thee our all to spend,
  Still may we watch and pray,
And, persevering to the end,
  Work while it is to-day.

404   *Contribution.*   W. W. HOW.

WE give thee but thine own,
  Whate'er the gift may be:
All that we have is thine alone,
  A trust, O Lord, from thee.

2 May we thy bounties thus
  As stewards true receive,
And gladly, as thou blessest us,
  To thee our first-fruits give.

3 To comfort and to bless,
  To find a balm for woe,
To tend the lone and fatherless
  Is angel's work below.

4 The captive to release,
  To God the lost to bring,
To teach the way of life and peace—
  It is a Christ-like thing.

5 And we believe thy word,
  Though dim our faith may be;
Whate'er for thine we do, O Lord,
  We do it unto thee.

405   *Reform.*   ANON.

MOURN for the thousands slain,
  The youthful and the strong;
Mourn for the wine-cup's fearful reign,
  And the deluded throng.

2 Mourn for the ruined soul,—
  Eternal life and light
Lost by the fiery, maddening bowl,
  And turned to hopeless night.

3 Mourn for the lost,—but call,
  Call to the strong, the free;
Rouse them to shun the dreadful fall,
  And to the refuge flee.

4 Mourn for the lost,—but pray,
  Pray to our God above,
To break the fell destroyer's sway,
  And show his saving love.

BEDAN. S. M. FROM THE SHAWM.

1. Sow in the morn thy seed, At eve hold not thy hand; To doubt and fear give thou no

heed; To doubt and fear give thou no heed; Broad-cast it o'er the land.

406 *"Harvest home."* J. MONTGOMERY.

Sow in the morn thy seed,
At eve hold not thy hand;
To doubt and fear give thou no heed;
Broad-cast it o'er the land.

2 And duly shall appear
In verdure, beauty, strength,
The tender blade, the stalk, the ear,
And the full corn at length.

3 Thou canst not toil in vain;
Cold, heat, the moist and dry,
Shall foster and mature the grain
For garners in the sky.

4 Then, when the glorious end,
The day of God shall come,
The angel-reapers shall descend,
And heaven sing "Harvest home!"

WORK SONG. P. M. LOWELL MASON.

1. Work, for the night is coming, Work thro' the morning hours; Work, while the dew is sparkling, (*Omit*) .... Work 'mid springing flowers; Work, when the day grows brighter, Work in [the glowing sun;
D.C. Work, for the night is coming, (*Omit*) .... When man's work is done.

407 *"The night cometh."* S. DYER.

Work, for the night is coming;
Work, through the morning hours;
Work, while the dew is sparkling;
Work, 'mid springing flowers;
Work, when the day grows brighter,
Work, in the glowing sun;
Work, for the night is coming,
When man's work is done.

2 Work, for the night is coming,
Work through the sunny noon;
Fill brightest hours with labor,
Rest comes sure and soon.

Give every flying minute
Something to keep in store:
Work, for the night is coming,
When man works no more.

3 Work, for the night is coming,
Under the sunset skies;
While their bright tints are glowing,
Work, for daylight flies.
Work till the last beam fadeth,
Fadeth to shine no more;
Work while the night is darkening,
When man's work is o'er.

1. Hark! the voice of Jesus calling,—Who will go and work to-day? Fields are white, the harvest waiting,
D. S. Who will an-swer, glad-ly saying,

Who will bear the sheaves away? Loud and long the Master calleth, Rich reward he of - fers free;
"Here am I, O Lord, send me."

408   *" The Laborers are few."*   D. MARCH.

HARK! the voice of Jesus calling,—
Who will go and work to-day?
Fields are white, the harvest waiting,—
Who will bear the sheaves away?
Loud and long the Master calleth,
Rich reward he offers free;
Who will answer, gladly saying,
"Here am I, O Lord, send me."

2 If you cannot cross the ocean
And the heathen lands explore,
You can find the heathen nearer,
You can help them at your door;
If you cannot speak like angels,
If you cannot preach like Paul,
You can tell the love of Jesus,
You can say he died for all.

3 While the souls of men are dying,
And the Master calls for you,
Let none hear you idly saying,
"There is nothing I can do!"
Gladly take the task he gives you,
Let his work your pleasure be;
Answer quickly when he calleth,
"Here am I, O Lord, send me."

409   *" What thy hand findeth."*   E. H. GATES.

IF you cannot on the ocean
Sail among the swiftest fleet,

Rocking on the highest billows,
Laughing at the storms you meet,
You can stand among the sailors,
Anchored yet within the bay,
You can lend a hand to help them
As they launch their boat away.

2 If you are too weak to journey
Up the mountain steep and high,
You can stand within the valley,
While the multitude go by;
You can chant in happy measure,
As they slowly pass along;
Though they may forget the singer,
They will not forget the song.

3 If you have not gold and silver
Ever ready to command;
If you cannot toward the needy
Reach an ever open hand,
You can visit the afflicted,
O'er the erring you can weep;
You can be a true disciple
Sitting at the Saviour's feet.

4 If you cannot in the harvest
Garner up the richest sheaf,
Many a grain both ripe and golden
Will the careless reapers leave;
Go and glean among the briers,
Growing rank against the wall,
For it may be that the shadow
Hides the heaviest wheat of all.

SOLNEY. 8s, 7s.   I. A. P. SCHULZ.

1. Cast thy bread up-on the wa-ters, Thinking not 'tis thrown a-way;

God him-self saith, thou shalt gath-er It a-gain some fu-ture day.

410   *Eccl. 11 : 1.*   J. H. HANAFORD.

Cast thy bread upon the waters,
　Thinking not 'tis thrown away;
God himself saith, thou shalt gather
　It again some future day.

2 Cast thy bread upon the waters;
　Wildly though the billows roll,
They but aid thee as thou toilest
　Truth to spread from pole to pole.

3 As the seed by billows floated,
　To some distant island lone,
So to human souls benighted,
　That thou flingest may be borne.

4 Cast thy bread upon the waters;
　Why wilt thou still doubting stand?
Bounteous shall God send the harvest,
　If thou sow'st with liberal hand.

STOCKWELL. 8s, 7s.   D. E. JONES.

1. He that go-eth forth with weep-ing, Bear-ing pre-cious seed in love,

Nev-er tir-ing, nev-er sleep-ing, Find-eth mer-cy from a-bove.

411   *Psalm 126: 6.*   T. HASTINGS.

He that goeth forth with weeping,
　Bearing precious seed in love,
Never tiring, never sleeping,
　Findeth mercy from above.

2 Soft descend the dews of heaven,
　Bright the rays celestial shine;
Precious fruits will thus be given,
　Through an influence all divine

3 Sow thy seed, be never weary,
　Let no fears thy soul annoy;
Be the prospect ne'er so dreary,
　Thou shalt reap the fruits of joy.

4 Lo, the scene of verdure brightening!
　See the rising grain appear;
Look again! the fields are whitening,
　For the harvest time is near.

INVERNESS. S. M.   LOWELL MASON.

1. Great God, now conde - scend To bless our ris-ing race; Soon may their willing spirits bend, The sub-jects of thy grace.

412   *Our children.*   J. FELLOWS.

GREAT God, now condescend
To bless our rising race;
Soon may their willing spirits bend,
The subjects of thy grace.

2 Oh, what a pure delight
Their happiness to see;
Our warmest wishes all unite
To lead their souls to thee.

3 Now bless, thou God of love,
The word of truth divine;
Send thy good Spirit from above,
And make these children thine.

413   *"Suffer them to come."*   H. U. ONDERDONK.

THE Saviour kindly calls
Our children to his breast;
He folds them in his gracious arms,
Himself declares them blest.

2 "Let them approach," he cries,
"Nor scorn their humble claim;
The heirs of heaven are such as these,
For such as these I came."

3 With joy we bring them, Lord,
Devoting them to thee,
Imploring, that, as we are thine,
Thine may our offspring be.

OLIVET. 6s, 4s.   LOWELL MASON.

1. Shepherd of tender youth. Guiding in love and truth Thro' devious ways— { Christ, our triumphant King. } { shout thy praise.
{ We come thy name to sing, } { And here our children bring, To

414   *Ancient Hymn.*   H. M. DEXTER, tr.

SHEPHERD of tender youth,
Guiding in love and truth
  Through devious ways—
Christ, our triumphant King,
We come thy name to sing,
And here our children bring,
  To shout thy praise.

2 Thou art our holy Lord,
The all-subduing Word,
  Healer of strife;
Thou didst thyself abase,
That from sin's deep disgrace
Thou mightest save our race,
  And give us life.

3 Ever be thou our Guide,
Our Shepherd and our pride,
  Our staff and song;
Jesus, thou Christ of God,
By thy perennial word
Lead us where thou hast trod;
  Our faith make strong.

4 So now, and till we die,
Sound we thy praises high,
  And joyful sing:
Let all the holy throng,
Who to thy Church belong,
Unite and swell the song
  To Christ our King!

AZMON. C. M.   LOWELL MASON, arr.

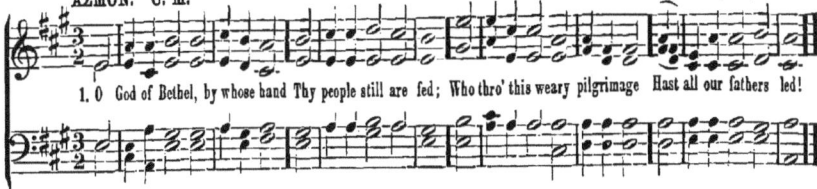

1. O God of Bethel, by whose hand Thy people still are fed; Who thro' this weary pilgrimage Hast all our fathers led!

415   *Genesis* 28: 19–22.   P. DODDRIDGE.

O GOD of Bethel, by whose hand
Thy people still are fed;
Who through this weary pilgrimage
Hast all our fathers led!

2 Our vows, our prayers, we now present
Before thy throne of grace;
God of our fathers! be the God
Of their succeeding race.

3 Through each perplexing path of life
Our wandering footsteps guide;
Give us, each day, our daily bread,
And raiment fit provide.

4 Oh, spread thy covering wings around
Till all our wanderings cease,
And at our Father's loved abode,
Our souls arrive in peace.

5 Such blessings from thy gracious hand
Our humble prayers implore;
And thou shalt be our chosen God,
Our portion evermore.

416   *Christ receiving children.*   P. DODDRIDGE.

SEE Israel's gentle Shepherd stands,
With all engaging charms!
Hark! how he calls the tender lambs,
And folds them in his arms!

2 "Permit them to approach," he cries,
"Nor scorn their humble name;
For 't was to bless such souls as these,
The Lord of angels came."

3 We bring them, Lord, in thankful hands,
And yield them up to thee;
Joyful that we ourselves are thine,—
Thine let our offspring be.

SILOAM. C. M.   I. B. WOODBURY.

1. By cool Si-loam's shady rill How fair the lil-y grows! How sweet the breath, beneath the hill, Of Sharon's dewy rose!

417   *A Christian Child.*   R. HEBER.

By cool Siloam's shady rill
How fair the lily grows!
How sweet the breath beneath the hill
Of Sharon's dewy rose!

2 Lo! such the child whose early feet
The paths of peace have trod;
Whose secret heart, with influence sweet,
Is upward drawn to God.

3 By cool Siloam's shady rill
The lily must decay;
The rose that blooms beneath the hill
Must shortly fade away.

4 And soon, too soon, the wintry hour
Of man's maturer age
May shake the soul with sorrow's power
And stormy passion's rage.

5 O thou, whose infant feet were found
Within thy Father's shrine,
Whose years, with changeless virtue crowned,
Were all alike divine!

6 Dependent on thy bounteous breath,
We seek thy grace alone
In childhood, manhood, age and death,
To keep us still thine own.

1. { Sav-iour, like a shepherd lead us: Much we need thy ten-der care; }
   { In thy pleas-ant pas-tures feed us, For our use thy fold pre-pare: }
D. C.—Keep thy flock, from sin de-fend us, Seek us when we go a-stray.

We are thine: do thou be-friend us, Be the guardian of our way;

418   *Lambs of the Fold.*   D. A. THRUPP.

SAVIOUR, like a shepherd lead us:
  Much we need thy tender care;
In thy pleasant pastures feed us,
  For our use thy fold prepare:
We are thine: do thou befriend us,
  Be the guardian of our way;
Keep thy flock, from sin defend us,
  Seek us when we go astray.

2 Thou hast promised to receive us,
  Poor and sinful though we be;
Thou hast mercy to relieve us,
  Grace to cleanse, and power to free:
Early let us seek thy favor,
  Early help us do thy will;
Holy Lord, our only Saviour!
  With thy grace our bosom fill.

419   *Sabbath School Meeting.*   ANON.

SAVIOUR King, in hallowed union,
  At thy sacred feet we bow;
Heart with heart, in blest communion,
  Join to crave thy favor now!
Though celestial choirs adore thee,
  Let our prayer as incense rise;
And our praise be set before thee,
  Sweet as evening sacrifice.

2 Heavenly Fount, thy streams of blessing,
  Oft have cheered us on our way;
By thy power and grace unceasing,
  We continue to this day:

Raise we then with glad emotion
  Thankful lays: and while we sing,
Vow a pure, a full devotion
  To thy work, O Saviour King!

3 When we tell the wondrous story
  Of thy rich, exhaustless love,
Send thy Spirit, Lord of glory,
  On the youthful heart to move!   •
Oh, that he, the ever-living,
  May descend, as fruitful rain;
Till the wilderness, reviving,
  Blossoms as the rose again!

420   *"These little ones."*   W. A. MUHLENBERG.

SAVIOUR! who thy flock art feeding
  With the shepherd's kindest care,
All the feeble gently leading,
  While the lambs thy bosom share;
Now, these little ones receiving,
  Fold them in thy gracious arm;
There, we know, thy word believing,
  Only there, secure from harm.

2 Never, from thy pasture roving,
  Let them be the lion's prey;
Let thy tenderness, so loving,
  Keep them all life's dangerous way:
Then, within thy fold eternal,
  Let them find a resting-place,
Feed in pastures ever vernal,
  Drink the rivers of thy grace.

NICAEA. P. M.   J. B. DYKES.

1. Holy, holy, ho - ly,   Lord God Almighty!   Early in the morning our song shall rise to thee;

Holy, holy, ho - ly! mer-ci - ful and mighty! God in three persons, blessed Trin-i - ty!

421   *Opening the School.*   R. HEBER.

HOLY, holy, holy, Lord God Almighty!
Early in the morning our song shall rise
    to thee;
Holy, holy, holy, merciful and mighty,
God in three persons, blesséd Trinity!

2 Holy, holy, holy! all the saints adore thee,
Casting down their golden crowns
    around the glassy sea;
Cherubim and seraphim falling down be-
    fore thee,
Which wert and art and evermore
    shalt be.

3 Holy, holy, holy! though the darkness
    hide thee,
Though the eye of sinful man thy glory
    may not see;
Only thou art holy; there is none beside
    thee,
Perfect in power, in love and purity.

4 Holy, holy, holy! Lord God Almighty!
All thy works shall praise thy name, in
    earth and sky and sea;
Holy, holy, holy! merciful and mighty;
God in three persons, blesséd Trinity!

MILWAUKEE. 8s, 7s.   J. ZUNDEL.

1. Saviour! who thy flock art feeding With the shepherd's kindest care, All the feeble gently leading, While the lambs thy bosom share;
2. Now, these little ones re-ceiv-ing, Fold them in thy gracious arm; There, we know, thy word believing, Only there, secure from harm.

12

PAULINA. 11s.   L. W. BACON, arr.

1. O thou who in Jordan didst bow thy meek head, And whelmed in our sorrow didst sink to the dead,

Then rose from the darkness to glo-ry a-bove, And claimed for thy chosen the kingdom of love;—

422   *Following Jesus.*   G. W. BETHUNE.

O thou who in Jordan didst bow thy meek head,
And whelmed in our sorrow didst sink to the dead,
Then rose from the darkness to glory above,
And claimed for thy chosen the kingdom of love;—

2 Thy footsteps we follow, to bow in the tide,
And are buried with thee in the death thou hast died,
Then wake with thy likeness to walk in the way
That brightens and brightens to shadowless day.

3 O Jesus, our Saviour, O Jesus, our Lord,
By the life of thy passion, the grace of thy word,
Accept us, redeem us, dwell ever within,
To keep, by thy Spirit, our spirits from sin;—

4 Till, crowned with thy glory, and waving the palm,
Our garments all white from the blood of the Lamb,
We join the bright millions of saints gone before,
And bless thee, and wonder, and praise evermore.

BELIEF. C. M.   ANON.   D. C.

1. Meek-ly in Jordan's holy stream The great Redeemer bowed; Bright was the glory's sacred beam That hushed the wond'ring crowd.
CHO.—I do believe, I now believe That Je-sus died for me; And through his blood, his precious blood, I shall from sin be free.

423   *Jesus' Baptism.*   S. F. SMITH.

MEEKLY in Jordan's holy stream
The great Redeemer bowed;
Bright was the glory's sacred beam
That hushed the wondering crowd.

CHO.—I do believe, I now believe
That Jesus died for me;
And through his blood, his precious blood,
I shall from sin be free.

2 Thus God descended to approve
The deed that Christ had done;
Thus came the emblematic Dove,
And hovered o'er the Son.—CHO.

3 So, blessèd Spirit, come to-day
To our baptismal scene;
Let thoughts of earth be far away,
And every mind serene.—CHO.

COMMUNION. [No. 2.] C. M.   CHARLES ZEUNER.

1. In all my Lord's appointed ways My journey I'll pur - sue; Hinder me not, ye much-loved saints, For I must go with you.

424   *Gen. 24: 56.*   J. RYLAND.

In all my Lord's appointed ways
  My journey I'll pursue;
Hinder me not, ye much-loved saints,
  For I must go with you.

2 Through floods and flames, if Jesus lead,
  I'll follow where he goes;
Hinder me not! shall be my cry,
  Though earth and hell oppose.

3 Through duties, and through trials too,
  I'll go at his command;
Hinder me not, for I am bound
  To my Immanuel's land.

4 And when my Saviour calls me home,
  Still this my cry shall be,
Hinder me not! come, welcome death;
  I'll gladly go with thee!

425   *"This is my Son."*   ENG. BAP. COLL.

'Tis God the Father we adore
  In this baptismal sign;
'Tis he whose voice on Jordan's shore
  Proclaimed the Son divine.

2 The Father owned him; let our breath
  In answering praise ascend,
As in the image of his death
  We own our heavenly Friend.

3 We seek the consecrated grave
  Along the path he trod;
Receive us in the hallowed wave,
  Thou holy Son of God.

4 Let earth and heaven our zeal record,
  And future witness bear;
That we to Zion's mighty Lord
  Our full allegiance swear.

426   *"All righteousness."*   B. BEDDOME.

Buried beneath the yielding wave,
  The great Redeemer lies;
Faith views him in the watery grave,
  And thence beholds him rise.

2 Thus do his willing saints, to-day,
  Their ardent zeal express,
And, in the Lord's appointed way,
  Fulfill all righteousness.

3 With joy we in his footsteps tread,
  And would his cause maintain;
Like him be numbered with the dead,
  And with him rise and reign.

4 Now we, blest Saviour, would to thee
  Our grateful voices raise;
Washed in the fountain of thy blood,
  Our lives shall be thy praise.

427   *Consecration.*   B. BEDDOME.

Witness, ye men and angels, now
  Before the Lord we speak;
To him we make our solemn vow,
  A vow we dare not break:—

2 That, long as life itself shall last,
  Ourselves to Christ we yield;
Nor from his cause will we depart,
  Or ever quit the field.

3 We trust not in our native strength,
  But on his grace rely,
That with returning wants the Lord
  Will all our need supply.

4 Oh, guide our doubtful feet aright,
  And keep us in thy ways;
And, while we turn our vows to prayers,
  Turn thou our prayers to praise.

1. Come, happy souls, a-dore the Lamb, Who loved our race ere time began, Who vailed his Godhead

in our clay, And in an humble manger lay, And in an hum-ble man-ger lay.

428   *Imitation of Christ.*   T. BALDWIN.

COME, happy souls, adore the Lamb,
Who loved our race ere time began,
Who vailed his Godhead in our clay,
And in an humble manger lay.

2 To Jordan's stream the Spirit led,
To mark the path his saints should tread;
With joy they trace the sacred way,
To see the place where Jesus lay.

3 Baptized by John in Jordan's wave,
The Saviour left his watery grave;
Heaven owned the deed, approved the way,
And blessed the place where Jesus lay.

4 Come, all who love his precious name,
Come, tread his steps, and learn of him;
Happy beyond expression they
Who find the place where Jesus lay.

429   *'Buried with him."*   MORAVIAN.

BURIED in baptism with our Lord,
We rise with him, to life restored;
Not the bare life in Adam lost,
But richer far, for more it cost.

2 Water can cleanse the flesh, we own,
But Christ well knows, and Christ alone,
How dear to him our cleansing stood,
Baptized in fire, and bathed in blood.

3 He by his blood atoned for sin;
This precious blood can wash us clean;
And he arrays us in the dress
Of his unspotted righteousness.

430   *The pleasant path.*   A. JUDSON.

OUR Saviour bowed beneath the wave,
And meekly sought a watery grave;
Come, see the sacred path he trod,
A path well pleasing to our God.

2 His voice we hear, his footsteps trace,
And hither come to seek his face,
To do his will, to feel his love,
And join our songs with songs above.

3 Hosanna to the Lamb divine!
Let endless glories round him shine!
High o'er the heavens for ever reign,
O Lamb of God, for sinners slain!

431   *Invocation.*   A. JUDSON.

COME, Holy Spirit, Dove divine,
On these baptismal waters shine,
And teach our hearts, in highest strain,
To praise the Lamb for sinners slain.

2 We love thy name, we love thy laws,
And joyfully embrace thy cause;
We love thy cross, the shame, the pain,
O Lamb of God, for sinners slain!

3 We sink beneath thy mystic flood,
Oh, bathe us in thy cleansing blood;
We die to sin, and seek a grave
With thee, beneath the yielding wave.

4 And as we rise, with thee to live
Oh, let the Holy Spirit give
The sealing unction from above,
The breath of life, the fire of love!

WELTON. L. M.

C. H. A. MALAN.

1. O thou, my soul, for - get no more The Friend who all thy sor - rows bore,

Let eve - ry i - dol be for - got, But, O my soul, for - get him not.

432 *"Forget him not."* J. MARSHMAN, *tr.*

O THOU, my soul, forget no more,
The Friend who all thy sorrows bore,
Let every idol be forgot,
But, O my soul, forget him not.

2 Renounce thy works and ways, with grief,
And fly to this divine relief;
Nor him forget, who left his throne,
And for thy life gave up his own.

3 Eternal truth and mercy shine
In him, and he himself is thine:
And canst thou, then, with sin beset,
Such charms, such matchless charms forget?

4 Oh, no: till life itself depart,
His name shall cheer and warm my heart;
And, lisping this, from earth I'll rise,
And join the chorus of the skies.

LUTON. L. M.

G. BURDER.

1. Come in, thou bless - ed of the Lord, Oh, come in Je - sus' pre - cious name;

We wel - come thee with one ac - cord, And trust the Sav - iour does the same.

433 *"Come in!"* T. KELLY.

COME in, thou blessèd of the Lord,
Oh, come in Jesus' precious name;
We welcome thee with one accord,
And trust the Saviour does the same.

2 Those joys which earth cannot afford,
We'll seek in fellowship to prove;
Joined in one spirit to our Lord,
Together bound by mutual love.

434 *"At thy command."* I. WATTS.

AT thy command, our dearest Lord,
Here we attend thy dying feast;
Thy blood, like wine, adorns thy board,
And thine own flesh feeds every guest.

2 Our faith adores thy bleeding love,
And trusts for life in One that died;
We hope for heavenly crowns above,
From a Redeemer crucified.

HAMBURG. L. M. LOWELL MASON, arr.

1. Oh, the sweet wonders of that cross Where my Redeemer loved and died! Her noblest life my spirit draws From his dear wounds, and bleeding side.

435 *Parting Song.* I. WATTS.

Oh, the sweet wonders of that cross
  Where my Redeemer loved and died!
Her noblest life my spirit draws
  From his dear wounds, and bleeding side.

2 I would for ever speak his name
  In sounds to mortal ears unknown;
With angels join to praise the Lamb,
  And worship at his Father's throne.

436 *"Bought with a price."* S. DAVIES.

Lord, I am thine, entirely thine,
Purchased and saved by blood divine,
With full consent thine I would be,
And own thy sovereign right in me.

2 Grant one poor sinner more a place
Among the children of thy grace;
A wretched sinner, lost to God,
But ransomed by Immanuel's blood.

3 Thine would I live, thine would I die.
Be thine through all eternity;
The vow is past beyond repeal;
And now I set the solemn seal.

4 Here at that cross where flows the blood
That bought my guilty soul for God,
Thee, my new Master now I call,
And consecrate to thee my all.

HAPPY DAY. L. M. FROM E. F. RIMBAULT.

1. Oh, happy day, that fixed my choice On thee, my Saviour, and my God! Well may this glowing heart re-joice, And tell its rap-tures all a-broad. Hap-py day, hap-py day, When Jesus wash'd my sins a-way! He taught me how to watch and pray, And live re-joic-ing ev-ery day;

437 *"Happy Day."* P. DODDRIDGE.

Oh, happy day, that fixed my choice
  On thee, my Saviour, and my God!
Well may this glowing heart rejoice,
  And tell its raptures all abroad.

Cho.—Happy day, happy day,
  When Jesus washed my sins away!
He taught me how to watch and pray,
  And live rejoicing every day:

Happy day, happy day,
  When Jesus washed my sins away!

2 Oh, happy bond, that seals my vows
  To him who merits all my love!
Let cheerful anthems fill his house,
  While to that sacred shrine I move.—Cho

3 'Tis done, the great transaction's done:
  I am my Lord's, and he is mine:
He drew me, and I followed on,
  Charmed to confess the voice divine—Cho.

NETTLETON. 8s, 7s. D.

ANON.

1. { Come, thou Fount of ev-ery blessing, Tune my heart to sing thy grace; }
{ Streams of mercy, nev-er ceasing. Call for songs of loudest praise; } Teach me some melodious

D. C.—Praise the mount—I'm fixed upon it!—Mount of thy redeeming love.

son-net, Sung by flaming tongues above:

438   *"Eben-ezer."*   R. ROBINSON.

Come, thou Fount of every blessing,
  Tune my heart to sing thy grace;
Streams of mercy, never ceasing,
  Call for songs of loudest praise;
Teach me some melodious sonnet,
  Sung by flaming tongues above;
Praise the mount—I'm fixed upon it!—
  Mount of thy redeeming love.

2 Here I'll raise mine Eben-ezer;
  Hither by thy help I'm come;
And I hope, by thy good pleasure,
  Safely to arrive at home.
Jesus sought me when a stranger,
  Wandering from the fold of God;
He, to rescue me from danger,
  Interposed his precious blood.

3 Oh, to grace how great a debtor
  Daily I'm constrained to be!
Let thy goodness, like a fetter,
  Bind my wandering heart to thee;
Prone to wander, Lord, I feel it;
  Prone to leave the God I love;
Here's my heart; oh, take and seal it:
  Seal it for thy courts above.

NAUFORD. P. M.

A. S. SULLIVAN.

1. By Christ redeemed, in Christ restored, We keep the mem-o-ry a-dored, And show the death of our dear Lord, Un-til he come.

439   *"Till he come."*   G. RAWSON.

By Christ redeemed, in Christ restored,
We keep the memory adored,
And show the death of our dear Lord,
  Until he come.

2 His body broken in our stead
Is here, in this memorial bread;
And so our feeble love is fed,
  Until he come.

3 His fearful drops of agony,
His life-blood shed for us we see:
The wine shall tell the mystery,
  Until he come.

4 And thus that dark betrayal night,
With the last advent we unite—
The shame, the glory, by this rite,
  Until he come.

5 Until the trump of God be heard,
Until the ancient graves be stirred,
And with the great commanding word,
  The Lord shall come.

6 Oh, blessèd hope! with this elate,
Let not our hearts be desolate,
But, strong in faith, in patience wait,
  Until he come!

C. C. CONVERSE.

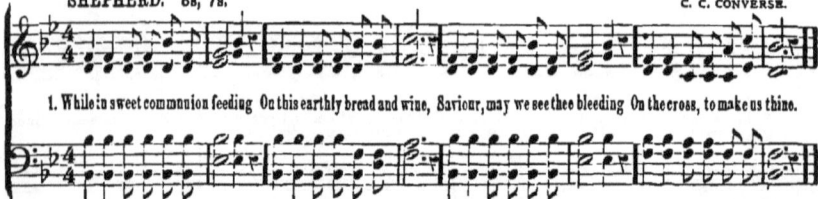

1. While in sweet communion feeding On this earthly bread and wine, Saviour, may we see thee bleeding On the cross, to make us thine.

440   *"In remembrance."*   E. DENNY.

WHILE in sweet communion feeding
  On this earthly bread and wine,
Saviour, may we see thee bleeding
  On the cross, to make us thine.

2 Though unseen, now be thou near us,
  With the still small voice of love;
Whispering words of peace to cheer us—
  Every doubt and fear remove.

3 Bring before us all the story,
  Of thy life, and death of woe;
And, with hopes of endless glory,
  Wean our hearts from all below.

441   *"His banner."*   R. PARK.

JESUS spreads his banner o'er us,
  Cheers our famished souls with food;
He the banquet spreads before us,
  Of his mystic flesh and blood.

2 Precious banquet; bread of heaven;
  Wine of gladness, flowing free;
May we taste it, kindly given
  In remembrance, Lord, of thee!

3 In thy trial and rejection;
  In thy sufferings on the tree;
In thy glorious resurrection;
  May we, Lord, remember thee!

DORRNANCE. 8s, 7s.   I. B. WOODBURY.

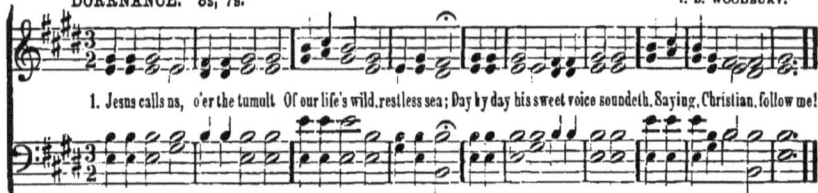

1. Jesus calls us, o'er the tumult Of our life's wild, restless sea; Day by day his sweet voice soundeth, Saying, Christian, follow me!

442   *"Follow me."*   ANON.

JESUS calls us, o'er the tumult
  Of our life's wild, restless sea;
Day by day his sweet voice soundeth,
  Saying, Christian, follow me!

2 Jesus calls us—from the worship
  Of the vain world's golden store;
From each idol that would keep us,—
  Saying, Christian, love me more!

3 In our joys and in our sorrows,
  Days of toil and hours of ease,
Still he calls, in cares and pleasures,—
  Christian, love me more than these!

4 Jesus calls us! by thy mercies,
  Saviour, may we hear thy call;
Give our hearts to thy obedience,
  Serve and love thee best of all!

443   *"Take my heart."*   ANON.

TAKE my heart, O Father! take it;
  Make and keep it all thine own;
Let thy Spirit melt and break it—
  This proud heart of sin and stone.

2 Father, make me pure and lowly,
  Fond of peace and far from strife;
Turning from the paths unholy
  Of this vain and sinful life.

3 Ever let thy grace surround me,
  Strengthen me with power divine,
Till thy cords of love have bound me:
  Make me to be wholly thine.

4 May the blood of Jesus heal me,
  And my sins be all forgiven;
Holy Spirit, take and seal me,
  Guide me in the path to heaven.

PEARL STREET 8s, 7s.

1. Sweet the mo-ments, rich in blessing, Which be-fore the cross we spend; Life, and health, and

peace possessing, From the sinner's dying Friend.

444 *Before the cross.* J. ALLEN.

SWEET the moments, rich in blessing,
  Which before the cross we spend;
Life, and health, and peace possessing,
  From the sinner's dying Friend.

2 Truly bléssed is this station,
  Low before his cross to lie,
While we see divine compassion,
  Beaming in his gracious eye.

3 Love and grief our hearts dividing,
  With our tears his feet we bathe;
Constant still, in faith abiding,
  Life deriving from his death.

4 For thy sorrows we adore thee,
  For the pains that wrought our peace,
Gracious Saviour! we implore thee
  In our souls thy love increase.

5 Here we feel our sins forgiven,
  While upon the Lamb we gaze;
And our thoughts are all of heaven,
  And our lips o'erflow with praise.

6 Still in ceaseless contemplation,
  Fix our hearts and eyes on thee,
Till we taste thy full salvation,
  And, unvailed, thy glories see.

SICILY. 8s, 7s. SICILIAN MELODY.

1. From the ta - ble now re - tir - ing, Which for us the Lord hath spread, May our souls, refreshment

finding, Grow in all things like our Head!

445 *Parting Hymn.* J. ROWE.

FROM the table now retiring,
  Which for us the Lord hath spread,
May our souls refreshment finding,
  Grow in all things like our Head!

2 His example while beholding,
  May our lives his image bear;
Him our Lord and Master calling,
  His commands may we revere.

3 Love to God and man displaying,
  Walking steadfast in his way,
Joy attend us in believing,
  Peace from God, through endless day.

4 Praise and honor to the Father,
  Praise and honor to the Son,
Praise and honor to the Spirit,
  Ever Three and ever One.

1. Rock of A - ges, cleft for me! Let me hide my - self in thee;
D. C.—Be of sin the per - fect cure; Save me, Lord! and make me pure.

Let the wa - ter and the blood, From thy wound - ed side that flowed,

446   *The Rock of Ages.*   A. M. TOPLADY.

Rock of Ages, cleft for me!
Let me hide myself in thee;
Let the water and the blood,
From thy wounded side that flowed,
Be of sin the perfect cure;
Save me, Lord! and make me pure.

2 Should my tears for ever flow,
Should my zeal no languor know,
This for sin could not atone,
Thou must save and thou alone:
In my hand no price I bring;
Simply to thy cross I cling.

3 While I draw this fleeting breath,
When mine eye-lids close in death,
When I rise to worlds unknown,
And behold thee on thy throne,
Rock of ages, cleft for me!
Let me hide myself in thee.

447   *" Manifest thyself."*   R. MANT.

Son of God! to thee I cry:
By the holy mystery
Of thy dwelling here on earth,
By thy pure and holy birth,
Lord, thy presence let me see,
Manifest thyself to me.

2 Lamb of God! to thee I cry:
By thy bitter agony,
By thy pangs to us unknown,
By thy spirit's parting groan,
Lord, thy presence let me see,
Manifest thyself to me.

3 Prince of Life! to thee I cry:
By thy glorious majesty,
By thy triumph o'er the grave,
Meek to suffer, strong to save,
Lord, thy presence let me see,
Manifest thyself to me.

4 Lord of glory, God most high,
Man exalted to the sky!
With thy love my bosom fill,
Prompt me to perform thy will;
Then thy glory I shall see,
Thou wilt bring me home to thee.

448   *"Till he come."*   E. H. BICKERSTETH.

"Till He come:" oh, let the words
Linger on the trembling chords;
Let the little while between
In their golden light be seen;
Let us think how heaven and home
Lie beyond that—"Till he come."

2 When the weary ones we love
Enter on their rest above,
Seems the earth so poor and vast,
All our life joy overcast?
Hush, be every murmur dumb;
It is only—"Till he come."

3 See, the feast of love is spread,
Drink the wine, and break the bread;
Sweet memorials,—till the Lord
Call us round his heavenly board;
Some from earth, from glory some,
Severed only—"Till he come."

MISSIONARY HYMN. 7s, 6. D.   LOWELL MASON.

1. From Greenland's icy mountains, From India's coral strand,
Where Afric's sunny fountains (Omit).................... Roll down their golden sand; From [many an
ancient riv-er, From many a palmy plain, They call us to de-liv-er Their land from error's chain.

449   *"Come over, and help us."*   R. HEBER.

FROM Greenland's icy mountains,
  From India's coral strand,
Where Afric's sunny fountains
  Roll down their golden sand,—
From many an ancient river,
  From many a palmy plain,
They call us to deliver
  Their land from error's chain.

2 What though the spicy breezes
  Blow soft o'er Ceylon's isle;
Though every prospect pleases,
  And only man is vile;
In vain with lavish kindness
  The gifts of God are strown;
The heathen, in his blindness,
  Bows down to wood and stone!

3 Shall we, whose souls are lighted
  With wisdom from on high,—
Shall we, to men benighted,
  The lamp of life deny?
Salvation, oh, salvation!
  The joyful sound proclaim,
Till earth's remotest nation
  Has learned Messiah's name.

4 Waft, waft, ye winds, his story,
  And you, ye waters, roll,
Till, like a sea of glory,
  It spreads from pole to pole;

Till o'er our ransomed nature
  The Lamb for sinners slain,
Redeemer, King, Creator,
  In bliss returns to reign!

450   *The day of Jubilee.*   B. GOUGH.

HOW BEAUTEOUS on the mountains,
  The feet of him that brings,
Like streams from living fountains,
  Good tidings of good things;
That publisheth salvation,
  And jubilee release,
To every tribe and nation,
  God's reign of joy and peace!

2 Lift up thy voice, O watchman!
  And shout, from Zion's towers,
Thy hallelujah chorus,—
  "The victory is ours!"
The Lord shall build up Zion
  In glory and renown,
And Jesus, Judah's lion,
  Shall wear his rightful crown.

3 Break forth in hymns of gladness;
  O waste Jerusalem!
Let songs, instead of sadness,
  Thy jubilee proclaim;
The Lord, in strength victorious,
  Upon thy foes hath trod;
Behold, O earth! the glorious
  Salvation of our God!

WEBB.   7s, 6s. D.   G. J. WEBB.

1. Hail to the Lord's anointed,   Great David's greater Son ! Hail, in   the time ap - pointed,
D. S.—To take a - way transgression,

FINE.   D. S.

His reign on earth begun !   He comes to break oppres - sion, To set the captive free,
And rule in eq - ui - ty.

---

451   *Psalm 72.*   J. MONTGOMERY.

HAIL to the Lord's anointed,
  Great David's greater Son !
Hail, in the time appointed,
  His reign on earth begun !
He comes to break oppression,
  To set the captive free,
To take away transgression,
  And rule in equity.

2 He comes, with succor speedy,
  To those who suffer wrong;
To help the poor and needy,
  And bid the weak be strong;
To give them songs for sighing,
  Their darkness turn to light,
Whose souls, condemned and dying,
  Were precious in his sight.

3 He shall come down like showers
  Upon the fruitful earth,
And love, and joy, like flowers,
  Spring in his path to birth:
Before him, on the mountains,
  Shall peace the herald go,
And righteousness in fountains
  From hill to valley flow.

4 Arabia's desert-ranger
  To him shall bow the knee;
The Ethiopian stranger
  His glory come to see:

With offerings of devotion,
  Ships from the isles shall meet,
To pour the wealth of ocean
  In tribute at his feet.

5 Kings shall fall down before him,
  And gold and incense bring:
All nations shall adore him;
  His praise all people sing;
For he shall have dominion
  O'er river, sea, and shore,
Far as the eagle's pinion
  Or dove's light wing can soar.

6 For him shall prayer unceasing
  And daily vows ascend;
His kingdom still increasing,
  A kingdom without end.
The heavenly dew shall nourish
  A seed in weakness sown,
Whose fruit shall spread and flourish,
  And shake like Lebanon.

7 O'er every foe victorious,
  He on his throne shall rest;
From age to age more glorious,
  All-blessing and all-blessed.
The tide of time shall never
  His covenant remove;
His name shall stand for ever;
  His great, best name of Love!

452 7s, 6s. *The morning light.*   S. F. SMITH.

THE morning light is breaking;
  The darkness disappears!
The sons of earth are waking
  To penitential tears;
Each breeze that sweeps the ocean
  Brings tidings from afar,
Of nations in commotion,
  Prepared for Zion's war.

2 See heathen nations bending
    Before the God we love,
  And thousand hearts ascending
    In gratitude above;

While sinners, now confessing,
  The gospel call obey,
And seek the Saviour's blessing—
  A nation in a day.

3 Blest river of salvation!
  Pursue thine onward way;
Flow thou to every nation,
  Nor in thy richness stay:
Stay not till all the lowly
  Triumphant reach their home:
Stay not till all the holy
  Proclaim—"The Lord is come!"

WESLEY. 11s, 10s.   LOWELL MASON.

1. Hail to the brightness of Zion's glad morning! Joy to the lands that in darkness have lain!

Hushed be the accents of sorrow and mourning; Zi-on in tri-umph begins her mild reign.

453   *The Promise.*   T. HASTINGS.

HAIL to the brightness of Zion's glad
    morning!
Joy to the lands that in darkness have lain!
Hushed be the accents of sorrow and
    mourning;
  Zion in triumph begins her mild reign.

2 Hail to the brightness of Zion's glad
    morning,
  Long by the prophets of Israel foretold;
Hail to the millions from bondage returning;
  Gentile and Jew the blest vision behold.

3 Lo! in the desert rich flowers are springing,
    Streams ever copious are gliding along;
Loud from the mountain-tops echoes are
    ringing,
  Wastes rise in verdure, and mingle in
    song.

4 See, from all lands—from the isles of the
    ocean,
  Praise to Jehovah ascending on high;
Fallen are the engines of war and commo-
    tion,
  Shouts of salvation are rending the sky.

RATHBUN. 8s, 7s.   I. CONKEY.

1. Sav-iour, vis-it thy plant-a-tion! Grant us, Lord, a gra-cious rain:

All will come to des-o-la-tion, Un-less thou re-turn a-gain.

454   *Revival Implored.*   J. NEWTON.

SAVIOUR, visit thy plantation!
  Grant us, Lord, a gracious rain:
All will come to desolation,
  Unless thou return again.

2 Keep no longer at a distance,
  Shine upon us from on high,
Lest, for want of thine assistance,
  Every plant should droop and die.

3 Once, O Lord, thy garden flourished;
  Every part looked gay and green;
Then thy word our spirits nourished:
  Happy seasons we have seen.

4 But a drought has since succeeded,
  And a sad decline we see:
Lord, thy help is greatly needed:
  Help can only come from thee.

5 Let our mutual love be fervent:
  Make us prevalent in prayer;
Let each one esteemed thy servant
  Shun the world's bewitching snare.

6 Break the tempter's fatal power,
  Turn the stony heart to flesh,
And begin from this good hour
  To revive thy work afresh.

455   '*Westward.*'   ANON.

HARK! the sound of angel-voices,
  Over Bethlehem's star-lit plain;
Hark! the heavenly host rejoices,
  Jesus comes on earth to reign.

2 See celestial radiance beaming,
  Lighting up the midnight sky;
'Tis the promised day-star gleaming,
  'Tis the day-spring from on high.

3 Westward, all along the ages,
  Trace its pathway clear and bright;
Star of hope to Eastern sages,
  Radiant now with gospel light.

4 Angels from the realms of glory,
  Peace on earth delight to sing;
Christian, tell the wondrous story,
  Go proclaim the Saviour King!

456   *Home Missions.*   ANON.

WHERE the woodman's axe is ringing,
  Where the hunter roams alone,
Where the prairie-flowers are springing,
  Make the great Redeemer known.

2 While, from California's mountains,
  Pure and sweet the anthem swells;
Oregon's dark wilds and fountains
  Hail the sound of Sabbath-bells.

3 Like an arméd host with banners,
  Terrible in war array,
Zion comes with glad hosannas,
  To prepare her Monarch's way.

4 Unto him all power is given,
  All the world his sway shall own,
And on earth, as now in heaven,
  Shall his will be done alone.

ZION. 8s, 7s, 4s.   THOS. HASTINGS.

1. {On the mountain's top ap-pear-ing, Lo! the sa-cred her-ald stands,}
{Welcome news to Zi-on bear-ing— Zi-on long in hos-tile lands:} Mourning

cap-tive! God himself shall loose thy bands, Mourning captive! God himself shall loose thy bands.

457 *The gospel herald.* T. KELLY.

On the mountain's top appearing,
  Lo ! the sacred herald stands,
Welcome news to Zion bearing—
  Zion long in hostile lands:
    Mourning captive !
  God himself shall loose thy bands.

2 Has thy night been long and mournful?
  Have thy friends unfaithful proved?
Have thy foes been proud and scornful?
  By thy sighs and tears unmoved?
    Cease thy mourning,
  Zion still is well beloved.

3 God, thy God, will now restore thee;
  He himself appears thy Friend;
All thy foes shall flee before thee;
  Here their boasts and triumphs end:
    Great deliverance
  Zion's King will surely send.

458 *Sun of Righteousness.* W. WILLIAMS.

O'er the gloomy hills of darkness,
  Cheered by no celestial ray,
Sun of righteousness ! arising,
  Bring the bright, the glorious day;
    Send the gospel
  To the earth's remotest bound.

2 Kingdoms wide that sit in darkness,—
  Grant them, Lord ! the glorious light:
And, from eastern coast to western,
  May the morning chase the night;
    And redemption,
  Freely purchased, win the day.

3 Fly abroad, thou mighty gospel !
  Win and conquer, never cease;
May thy lasting, wide dominions
  Multiply and still increase;
    Sway thy sceptre,
  Saviour ! all the world around.

HAMDEN. 8s, 7s, 4s.   LOWELL MASON.

1. { O'er the gloomy hills of darkness, Cheered by no celestial ray, }
{ Sun of righteousness ! a-ris-ing, Bring the bright, the glorious day; } Send the gospel To the earth's re-mot-est bound.

APPLETON. L. M.   WILLIAM BOYCE.

1. God is the ref-uge of his saints, When storms of sharp dis-tress in-vade;

Ere we can of-fer our complaints, Be-hold him pres-ent with his aid.

459   *Psalm 46.*   I. WATTS.

God is the refuge of his saints,
  When storms of sharp distress invade;
Ere we can offer our complaints,
  Behold him present with his aid.

2 Let mountains from their seats be hurled
  Down to the deep, and buried there,
Convulsions shake the solid world—
  Our faith shall never yield to fear.

3 Loud may the troubled ocean roar—
  In sacred peace our souls abide;
While every nation, every shore,
  Trembles, and dreads the swelling tide.

4 There is a stream, whose gentle flow
  Supplies the city of our God;
Life, love, and joy, still gliding through,
  And watering our divine abode.

5 That sacred stream, thy holy word,
  Our grief allays, our fear controls;
Sweet peace thy promises afford,
  And give new strength to fainting souls.

6 Zion enjoys her Monarch's love,
  Secure against a threatening hour;
Nor can her firm foundation move,
  Built on his truth, and armed with power.

460   *Psalm 72.*   I. WATTS.

Great God! whose universal sway
The known and unknown worlds obey;
Now give the kingdom to thy Son;
Extend his power, exalt his throne.

2 As rain on meadows newly mown,
So shall he send his influence down;
His grace, on fainting souls, distills
Like heavenly dew on thirsty hills.

3 The heathen lands, that lie beneath
The shades of overspreading death,
Revive at his first dawning light,
And deserts blossom at the sight.

4 The saints shall flourish in his days,
Dressed in the robes of joy and praise;
Peace, like a river, from his throne,
Shall flow to nations yet unknown.

WARD. L. M.   LOWELL MASON, arr.

1. God is the refuge of his saints, When storms of sharp distress invade; Ere we can offer our complaints, Behold him present with his aid.

ANVERN. L. M.　　　　　　　　　　　　LOWELL MASON, arr.

1. Triumphant Zi - on, lift thy head From dust, and darkness, and the dead; Tho' humbled

long, awake at length, And gird thee with thy Saviour's strength, And gird thee with thy Saviour's strength.

461　　*"Triumphant Zion."*　P. DODDRIDGE.

TRIUMPHANT Zion, lift thy head
From dust, and darkness, and the dead;
Though humbled long, awake at length,
And gird thee with thy Saviour's strength.

2 Put all thy beauteous garments on,
And let thy various charms be known:
The world thy glories shall confess,
Decked in the robes of righteousness.

3 No more shall foes unclean invade,
And fill thy hallowed walls with dread;
No more shall hell's insulting host
Their victory and thy sorrows boast.

4 God, from on high, thy groans will hear;
His hand thy ruins shall repair;
Nor will thy watchful Monarch cease
To guard thee in eternal peace.

462　　*Ancient Israel.*　J. JOYCE.

WHY on the bending willows hung,
Israel! still sleeps thy tuneful string?—
Still mute remains thy sullen tongue,
And Zion's song denies to sing?

2 Awake! thy sweetest raptures raise;
Let harp and voice unite their strains:
Thy promised King his sceptre sways:
Jesus, thine own Messiah, reigns!

3 No taunting foes the song require;
No strangers mock thy captive chain;
But friends provoke the silent lyre,
And brethren ask the holy strain.

13

4 Nor fear thy Salem's hills to wrong,
If other lands thy triumphs share:
A heavenly city claims thy song;
A brighter Salem rises there.

5 By foreign streams no longer roam;
Nor, weeping, think of Jordan's flood:
In every clime behold a home,
In every temple see thy God.

463　　*Home Missions.*　W. C. BRYANT.

LOOK from thy sphere of endless day,
O God of mercy and of might!
In pity look on those who stray,
Benighted in this land of light.

2 In peopled vale, in lonely glen,
In crowded mart, by stream or sea,
How many of the sons of men
Hear not the message sent from thee!

3 Send forth thy heralds, Lord, to call
The thoughtless young, the hardened old,
A scattered, homeless flock, till all
Be gathered to thy peaceful fold.

4 Send them thy mighty word to speak,
Till faith shall dawn, and doubt depart,
To awe the bold, to stay the weak,
And bind and heal the broken heart.

5 Then all these wastes, a dreary scene,
That makes us sadden as we gaze,
Shall grow with living waters green,
And lift to heaven the voice of praise.

LUTHER. S. M.   THOS. HASTINGS.

1. O thou whom we.... a-dore! To bless our earth again, As-sume thine own al-

might-y power, And o'er the na-tions reign, And o'er the na-tions reign.

464   *Phillipians 2: 10, 11.*   C. WESLEY.

O THOU whom we adore!
   To bless our earth again,
Assume thine own almighty power,
   And o'er the nations reign.

2 The world's Desire and Hope,
   All power to thee is given;
Now set the last great empire up,
   Eternal Lord of heaven!

3 A gracious Saviour, thou
   Wilt all thy creatures bless;
And every knee to thee shall bow,
   And every tongue confess.

4 According to thy word,
   Now be thy grace revealed;
And with the knowledge of the Lord,
   Let all the earth be filled.

465   *"Thy kingdom come!"*   H. B. JOHNS.

COME, kingdom of our God,
   Sweet reign of light and love!
Shed peace and hope and joy abroad,
   And wisdom from above.

2 Over our spirits first
   Extend thy healing reign;
There raise and quench the sacred thirst,
   That never pains again.

3 Come, kingdom of our God!
   And make the broad earth thine;
Stretch o'er her lands and isles the rod
   That flowers with grace divine.

4 Soon may all tribes be blest
   With fruit from life's glad tree;
And in its shade like brothers rest,
   Sons of one family.

DOVER. S. M.   FROM AARON WILLIAMS.

1. Come, kingdom of our God, Sweet reign of light and love! Shed peace, and hope, and joy abroad, And wisdom from a-bove.

ST. BRIDE. S. M.   S. HOWARD.

1. Come, Lord, and tar - ry not! Bring the long - looked - for day!

Oh, why these years of wait - ing here, These a - ges of de - lay?

466   *"Come, Lord Jesus."*   H. BONAR.

Come, Lord, and tarry not!
    Bring the long-looked-for day;
Oh, why these years of waiting here,
    These ages of delay?

2 Come, for thy saints still wait;
    Daily ascends their sigh;
The Spirit and the Bride say, Come!
    Dost thou not hear the cry?

3 Come, for creation groans,
    Impatient of thy stay,
Worn out with these long years of ill,
    These ages of delay.

4 Come, and make all things new,
    Build up this ruined earth,
Restore our faded paradise,—
    Creation's second birth.

5 Come, and begin thy reign
    Of everlasting peace;
Come, take the kingdom to thyself,
    Great King of Righteousness!

467   *Declension.—*   G. W. BETHUNE.

Oh, for the happy hour
    When God will hear our cry,
And send, with a reviving power,
    His Spirit from on high.

2 We meet, we sing, we pray,
    We listen to the word,
In vain;—we see no cheering ray,
    No cheering voice is heard.

3 While many crowd thy house,
    How few, around thy board,
Meet to recount their solemn vows,
    And bless thee as their Lord!

4 Thou, thou alone canst give
    Thy gospel sure success;
Canst bid the dying sinner live
    Anew in holiness.

5 Come, then, with power divine,
    Spirit of life and love!
Then shall this people all be thine,
    This church like that above.

468   *"Revive thy work."*   P. H. BROWN, *alt.*

O Lord, thy work revive,
    In Zion's gloomy hour,
And make her dying graces live
    By thy restoring power.

2 Awake thy chosen few
    To fervent earnest prayer;
Again may they their vows renew,
    Thy blessèd presence share.

3 Thy Spirit then will speak
    Through lips of feeble clay,
And hearts of adamant will break,
    And rebels will obey.

4 Lord, lend thy gracious ear;
    Oh, listen to our cry;
Oh, come and bring salvation here:
    Our hopes on thee rely

GROSTETTE. L. M.   H. W. GREATOREX.

1. Soon may the last glad song a - rise Through all the mill - ions of the skies—

That song of tri - umph which re - cords That all the earth is now the Lord's!

469   *The last song.*   MRS. VOKE.

Soon may the last glad song arise
Through all the millions of the skies—
That song of triumph which records
That all the earth is now the Lord's!

2 Let thrones and powers and kingdoms be
Obedient, mighty God, to thee!
And, over land and stream and main,
Wave thou the sceptre of thy reign!

3 Oh, let that glorious anthem swell,
Let host to host the triumph tell,
That not one rebel heart remains,
But over all the Saviour reigns!

470   *Missionary Convocation.*   W. B. COLLYER.

Assembled at thy great command,
Before thy face, dread King, we stand;
The voice that marshaled every star,
Has called thy people from afar.

2 We meet, through distant lands to spread
The truth for which the martyrs bled;
Along the line, to either pole,
The thunder of thy praise to roll.

3 Our prayers assist, accept our praise,
Our hopes revive, our courage raise;
Our counsels aid, to each impart
The single eye, the faithful heart.

4 Forth with thy chosen heralds come,
Recall the wandering spirits home;
From Zion's mount send forth the sound,
To spread the spacious earth around.

471   *Christ's coming.*   W. H. BATHURST.

Jesus! thy church, with longing eyes,
For thine expected coming waits;
When will the promised light arise,
And glory beam from Zion's gates?

2 Ev'n now, when tempests round us fall,
And wintry clouds o'ercast the sky,
Thy words with pleasure we recall,
And deem that our redemption's nigh

3 Oh, come and reign o'er every land;
Let Satan from his throne be hurled;
All nations bow to thy command,
And grace revive a dying world.

4 Teach us, in watchfulness and prayer,
To wait for the appointed hour;
And fit us, by thy grace, to share
The triumphs of thy conquering power.

472   *"Ascend thy throne."*   B. BEDDOME.

Ascend thy throne, almighty King,
And spread thy glories all abroad;
Let thine own arm salvation bring,
And be thou known the gracious God

2 Let millions bow before thy seat,
Let humble mourners seek thy face,
Bring daring rebels to thy feet,
Subdued by thy victorious grace.

3 Oh, let the kingdoms of the world
Become the kingdoms of the Lord!
Let saints and angels praise thy name,
Be thou through heaven and earth adored.

MISSIONARY CHANT. L. M.   C. ZEUNER.

1. Jesus shall reign where'er the sun
Does his successive journeys run;
His kingdom stretch from shore to shore,
Till moons shall wax and wane no more.

473 *Psalm 72.* I. WATTS.

JESUS shall reign where'er the sun
Does his successive journeys run;
His kingdom stretch from shore to shore,
Till moons shall wax and wane no more.

2 For him shall endless prayer be made,
And endless praises crown his head;
His name, like sweet perfume, shall rise
With every morning-sacrifice.

3 People and realms of every tongue
Dwell on his love, with sweetest song;
And infant voices shall proclaim
Their early blessings on his name.

4 Blessings abound where'er he reigns;
The prisoner leaps to lose his chains;
The weary find eternal rest,
And all the sons of want are blest.

5 Let every creature rise and bring
Peculiar honors to our King;
Angels descend with songs again,
And earth repeat the loud Amen!

474 *Conversion of the World.* MRS. VOKE.

SOVEREIGN of worlds! display thy power;
Be this thy Zion's favored hour;
Bid the bright morning Star arise,
And point the nations to the skies.

2 Set up thy throne where Satan reigns,—
On Afric's shore, on India's plains,
On wilds and continents unknown,—
And make the nations all thine own.

3 Speak! and the world shall hear thy voice;
Speak! and the desert shall rejoice;
Scatter the gloom of heathen night,
And bid all nations hail the light.

475 *"Sun of Righteousness."* P. DODDRIDGE, alt.

O SUN of righteousness, arise,
With gentle beams on Zion shine;
Dispel the darkness from our eyes,
And souls awake to life divine.

2 On all around, let grace descend,
Like heavenly dew, or copious showers:
That we may call our God our friend;
That we may hail salvation ours.

EISENACH. L. M.   JOHANN HERMANN SCHEIN.

1. O Sun of right-eous-ness, a-rise, With gen-tle beams on Zi-on shine;
Dis-pel the darkness from our eyes, And souls a-wake to life di-vine.

THE CHRISTIAN'S DEATH.

FREDERICK. 11s.

GEO. KINGSLEY.

1. { I would not live alway; I ask not to stay }
{ Where storm af-ter storm rises (*Omit*).......... } dark o'er the way: The few lu-rid

mornings that dawn on us here Are e-nough for life's woes, full e-nough for its cheer.

476 *" I would not live alway."* W. A. MUHLENBERG.

I WOULD not live alway: I ask not to stay
Where storm after storm rises dark o'er
the way;
The few lurid mornings that dawn on us here
Are enough for life's woes, full enough for
its cheer.

2 I would not live alway, thus fettered by sin—
Temptation without and corruption within:
Ev'n the rapture of pardon is mingled with
fears,
And the cup of thanksgiving with penitent
tears.

3 I would not live alway; no, welcome the
tomb;
Since Jesus hath lain there, I dread not its
gloom;
There sweet be my rest till he bid me arise
To hail him in triumph descending the skies.

4 Who, who would live alway, away from his
God,
Away from yon heaven, that blissful abode,
Where the rivers of pleasure flow o'er the
bright plains,
And the nooitide of glory eternally reigns?

5 Where the saints of all ages in harmony
meet,
Their Saviour and brethren transported to
greet;
While the anthems of rapture unceasingly
roll,
And the smile of the Lord is the feast of
the soul.

477 (*See also* SCOTLAND, *p.* 88) R. HEBER.

THOU art gone to the grave! but we will
not deplore thee,
Though sorrows and darkness encompass
the tomb;
The Saviour hath passed through its portals
before thee,
And the lamp of his love is thy guide
through the gloom.

2 Thou art gone to the grave! we no
longer behold thee,
Nor tread the rough paths of the world by
thy side;
But the wide arms of mercy are spread to
enfold thee,
And sinners may hope, for the Sinless hath
died.

3 Thou art gone to the grave! and, its
mansion forsaking,
Perchance thy weak spirit in doubt lingered
long;
But the sunshine of glory beamed bright
on thy waking,
And the sound thou didst hear was the
seraphim's song.

4 Thou art gone to the grave! but we
will not deplore thee,
Since God was thy ransom, thy guardian,
and guide:
He gave thee, he took thee, and he will restore thee,
And death has no sting, since the Saviour
hath died.

AMSTERDAM. 7s, 6s. D.   JAMES NARES.

1. Rise, my soul, and stretch thy wings, Thy better por - tion trace;
Rise from transi-tory things Tow'rd heaven, thy na - tive place: } Sun and moon and stars decay;

Time shall soon this earth remove; Rise, my soul, and haste away   To seats prepared   a - bove.

478   *The better portion.*   R. SEAGRAVE.

Rise, my soul, and stretch thy wings,
   Thy better portion trace;
Rise from transitory things
   Toward heaven, thy native place:
Sun and moon and stars decay;
   Time shall soon this earth remove;
Rise, my soul, and haste away
   To seats prepared above.

2 Rivers to the ocean run,
   Nor stay in all their course;
Fire ascending seeks the sun;
   Both speed them to their source:
So a soul that's born of God,
   Pants to view his glorious face;
Upward tends to his abode,
   To rest in his embrace.

3 Cease, ye pilgrims, cease to mourn,
   Press onward to the prize;
Soon our Saviour will return
   Triumphant in the skies:

Yet a season,—and you know
   Happy entrance will be given,
All our sorrows left below,
   And earth exchanged for heaven.

479   *"Our earthly house."*   J. BURTON

Time is winging us away
   To our eternal home;
Life is but a winter's day—
   A journey to the tomb;
Youth and vigor soon will flee,
   Blooming beauty lose its charms;
All that's mortal soon shall be
   Enclosed in death's cold arms.

2 Time is winging us away
   To our eternal home;
Life is but a winter's day—
   A journey to the tomb;
But the Christian shall enjoy
   Health and beauty, soon, above,
Far beyond the world's annoy,
   Secure in Jesus' love.

GENEVA. 7s, 6s. D.   LOWELL MASON.

1. Time is winging us a - way   To our e - ter-nal home;
Life is but a winter's day—   A journey to the tomb; } Youth and vig-or soon will flee,

Blooming beauty lose its charms; All that's mortal soon shall be   Enclosed in death's cold arms.

ZEPHYR. L. M.   W. B. BRADBURY.

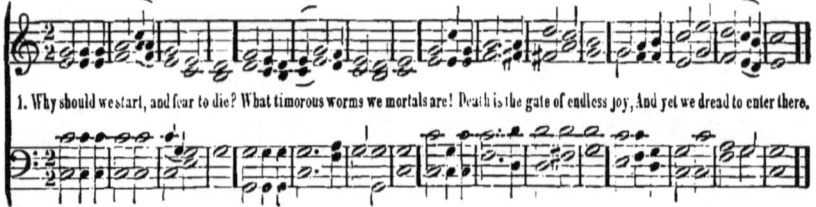

1. Why should we start, and fear to die? What timorous worms we mortals are! Death is the gate of endless joy, And yet we dread to enter there.

480   *"His beloved sleep."*   I. WATTS.

Why should we start, and fear to die?
    What timorous worms we mortals are !
Death is the gate of endless joy,
    And yet we dread to enter there.

2 The pains, the groans, the dying strife
    Fright our approaching souls away ;
We still shrink back again to life,
    Fond of our prison and our clay.

3 Oh, if my Lord would come and meet,
    My soul should stretch her wings in haste,
Fly fearless through death's iron gate,
    Nor feel the terrors as she passed.

4 Jesus can make a dying bed
    Feel soft as downy pillows are,
While on his breast I lean my head,
    And breathe my life out sweetly there !

ST. EDMUND'S. L. M.   F. J. HAYDN.

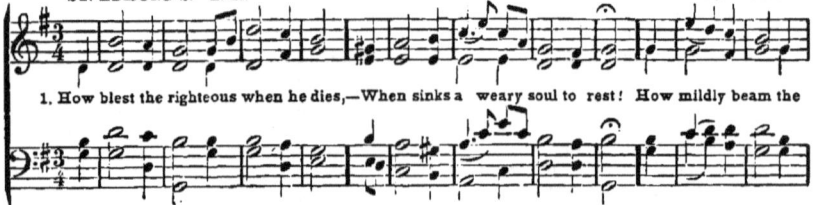

1. How blest the righteous when he dies,—When sinks a weary soul to rest! How mildly beam the

closing eyes! How gently heaves th'expiring breast !

4 Life's labor done, as sinks the clay,
    Light from its load the spirit flies;
While heaven and earth combine to say,—
    "How blest the righteous when he dies !"

482   *Psalm 90.*   I. WATTS.

Through every age, eternal God !
Thou art our Rest, our safe Abode;
High was thy throne, ere heaven was made,
Or earth thy humble footstool laid.

2 Long hadst thou reigned, ere time began,
Or dust was fashioned into man;
And long thy kingdom shall endure,
When earth and time shall be no more.

3 Death, like an overflowing stream,
Sweeps us away; our life's a dream;
An empty tale; a morning flower,
Cut down, and withered in an hour.

4 Teach us, O Lord, how frail is man;
And kindly lengthen out our span,
Till thine own grace, so rich, so free,
Fit us to die and dwell with thee.

481   *Death of the Righteous.* A. L. BARBAULD.

How blest the righteous when he dies,—
    When sinks a weary soul to rest !
How mildly beam the closing eyes !
    How gently heaves the expiring breast !

2 So fades a summer-cloud away;
    So sinks the gale when storms are o'er;
So gently shuts the eye of day;
    So dies a wave along the shore.

3 A holy quiet reigns around,—
    A calm which life nor death destroys;
And naught disturbs that peace profound,
    Which his unfettered soul enjoys.

REST. L. M. W. B. BRADBURY.

1. A - sleep in Je - sus! blessed sleep! From which none ev - er wake to weep;

A calm and un - dis - turbed re - pose, Un - brok - en by the last of foes.

483 *"Asleep in Jesus."* M. MACKAY.

ASLEEP in Jesus! blessèd sleep!
From which none ever wake to weep;
A calm and undisturbed repose,
Unbroken by the last of foes.

2 Asleep in Jesus! oh, how sweet
To be for such a slumber meet!
With holy confidence to sing
That death hath lost its venomed sting!

3 Asleep in Jesus! peaceful rest!
Whose waking is supremely blest;
No fear—no woe, shall dim the hour
That manifests the Saviour's power.

4 Asleep in Jesus! oh, for me
May such a blissful refuge be:
Securely shall my ashes lie,
And wait the summons from on high.

FEDERAL STREET. L. M. H. K. OLIVER.

1. So fades the love - ly, bloom - ing flower,—Frail, smiling sol - ace of an hour!

So soon our tran - sient com - forts fly, And pleasure on - ly blooms to die.

484 *Death of an Infant.* A. STEELE.

So FADES the lovely, blooming flower,—
Frail smiling solace of an hour!
So soon our transient comforts fly,
And pleasure only blooms to die.

2 Is there no kind, no lenient art,
To heal the anguish of the heart?
Spirit of grace! be ever nigh,
Thy comforts are not made to die.

3 Thy powerful aid supports the soul,
And nature owns thy kind control;
While we peruse the sacred page,
Our fiercest griefs resign their rage.

4 Then gentle patience smiles on pain,
And dying hope revives again;
Hope wipes the tear from sorrow's eye,
And faith points upward to the sky.

OLMUTZ. S. M.   LOWELL MASON, arr.

1. "For - ev - er with the Lord!" So, Je - sus! let it be;
Life from the dead is in that word; 'Tis im - mor - tal - i - ty.

485   *"For ever."*   J. MONTGOMERY.

"FOR ever with the Lord!"
   So, Jesus! let it be;
Life from the dead is in that word;
   'Tis immortality.

2 Here, in the body pent,
   Absent from thee I roam: ·
Yet nightly pitch my moving tent
   A day's march nearer home.

3 My Father's house on high,
   Home of my soul! how near,
At times, to faith's aspiring eye,
   Thy golden gates appear!

4 "For ever with the Lord!"
   Father, if 'tis thy will,
The promise of thy gracious word
   Ev'n here to me fulfill.

5 So, when my latest breath
   Shall rend the vail in twain,
By death I shall escape from death,
   And life eternal gain.

6 Knowing as I am known,
   How shall I love that word,
And oft repeat before the throne,
   "For ever with the Lord!"

486   *Resurrection.*   S. F. SMITH.

OH, for the death of those
   Who slumber in the Lord!
Oh, be like theirs my last repose,
   Like theirs my last reward!

2 Their bodies in the ground,
   In silent hope may lie,
Till the last trumpet's joyful sound
   Shall call them to the sky.

3 Their ransomed spirits soar
   On wings of faith and love,
To meet the Saviour they adore,
   And reign with him above.

4 With us their names shall live
   Through long succeeding years,
Embalmed with all our hearts can give,
   Our praises and our tears.

487   *"I will wait."*   H. BONAR.

A FEW more years shall roll,
   A few more seasons come;
And we shall be with those that rest,
   Asleep within the tomb;—

2 A few more storms shall beat
   On this wild rocky shore;
And we shall be where tempests cease,
   And surges swell no more:—

3 A few more struggles here,
   A few more partings o'er,
A few more toils, a few more tears,
   And we shall weep no more.

4 Then, O my Lord, prepare
   My soul for that glad day;
Oh, wash me in thy precious blood,
   And take my sins away!

DAWN. S. M.

E. P. PARKER.

1. One sweet-ly sol-emn thought Comes to me o'er and o'er,—

Near-er my home, to-day am I Than e'er I've been be-fore.

488 *"Nearer."* P. CARY.

ONE sweetly solemn thought
Comes to me o'er and o'er,—
Nearer my home, to-day, am I
Than e'er I've been before.

2 Nearer my Father's house,
Where many mansions be;
Nearer to-day the great white throne,
Nearer the crystal sea.

3 Nearer the bound of life,
Where burdens are laid down;
Nearer to leave the heavy cross;
Nearer to gain the crown.

4 But, lying dark between,
Winding down through the night,
There rolls the deep and unknown stream
That leads at last to light.

5 Ev'n now, perchance, my feet
Are slipping on the brink,
And I, to-day, am nearer home,—
Nearer than now I think.

6 Father, perfect my trust!
Strengthen my power of faith!
Nor let me stand, at last, alone
Upon the shore of death.

DUNBAR S. M.

E. W. DUNBAR.

1. One sweet-ly sol-emn thought Comes to me o'er and o'er,—
CHO.—There'll be no sor-row there, There'll be no sor-row there;

D. C.

Near-er my home, to-day, am I Than e'er I've been be-fore.
In heaven a-bove, where all is love, There'll be no sor-row there.

BARBY. C. M.   W. TANSUR.

1. Oh, for an o - ver - com - ing faith, To cheer my dy - ing hours;

To tri - umph o'er ap - proach - ing death, And all his fright - ful powers!

489   *"Where is thy sting?"*   I. WATTS.

OH, for an overcoming faith,
   To cheer my dying hours;
To triumph o'er approaching death,
   And all his frightful powers!

2 Joyful, with all the strength I have,
   My quivering lip should sing,—
"Where is thy boasted victory, grave;
   And where, O death, thy sting?"

3 Now to the God of victory
   Immortal thanks be paid;—
Who makes us conquerors, while we die,
   Through Christ, our living Head!

490   *"I shall go to him."*   H. K. WHITE.

THROUGH sorrow's night, and danger's path,
   Amid the deepening gloom,
We, followers of our suffering Lord,
   Are marching to the tomb.

2 There, when the turmoil is no more,
   And all our powers decay,
Our cold remains, in solitude,
   Shall sleep the years away.

3 Our labors done, securely laid
   In this our last retreat,
Unheeded o'er our silent dust
   The storms of earth shall beat.

4 Yet not thus buried or extinct,
   The vital spark shall lie:
For o'er life's wreck that spark shall rise
   To seek its kindred sky.

5 These ashes, too, this little dust,
   Our Father's care shall keep,
Till the last angel rise and break
   The long and dreary sleep.

6 Then love's soft dew o'er every eye
   Shall shed its mildest rays,
And the long silent voice awake
   With shouts of endless praise.

491   *Resurrection sure.*   RAY PALMER.

WHEN downward to the darksome tomb
   I thoughtful turn my eyes,
Frail nature trembles at the gloom,
   And anxious fears arise.

2 Why shrinks my soul?—in death's embrace
   Once Jesus captive slept:
And angels, hovering o'er the place,
   His lowly pillow kept.

3 Thus shall they guard my sleeping dust,
   And, as the Saviour rose,
The grave again shall yield her trust,
   And end my deep repose.

4 My Lord, before to glory gone,
   Shall bid me come away;
And calm and bright shall break the dawn
   Of heaven's eternal day,

5 Then let my faith each fear dispel,
   And gild with light the grave;
To him my loftiest praises swell,
   Who died, from death to save.

CHINA. C. M.   T. SWAN.

1. Why do we mourn de - part - ing friends, Or shake at death's a - larms?

'Tis but the voice that Je - sus sends, To call them to his arms.

492 *"We are confident."* I. WATTS.

WHY do we mourn departing friends,
  Or shake at death's alarms?
'Tis but the voice that Jesus sends,
  To call them to his arms.

2 Are we not tending upward, too,
  As fast as time can move?
Nor would we wish the hours more slow,
  To keep us from our love.

3 Why should we tremble to convey
  Their bodies to the tomb?
There the dear flesh of Jesus lay,
  And scattered all the gloom.

4 The graves of all the saints he blessed,
  And softened every bed;
Where should the dying members rest,
  But with the dying Head?

5 Thence he arose, ascending high,
  And showed our feet the way;
Up to the Lord we, too, shall fly
  At the great rising-day.

6 Then let the last loud trumpet sound,
  And bid our kindred rise;
Awake! ye nations under ground;
  Ye saints! ascend the skies.

ST. AGNES. C. M.   J. B. DYKES.

1. When downward to the dark - some tomb I thoughtful turn my eyes,

Frail na - ture trem - bles at the gloom, And anxious fears a - rise.

NUNDA. L. M. D.   LOWELL MASON.

1. How vain is all beneath the skies! How transient every earthly bliss! / How slender all the fondest ties That bind us to a world like this! 2. The evening / The withering

cloud, the morning dew, / grass, the fading flower, Of earthly hopes are emblems true,—The glory of a passing hour.

493 *Heaven alone unfading.* D. E. FORD.

How vain is all beneath the skies!
How transient every earthly bliss!
How slender all the fondest ties
That bind us to a world like this!

2 The evening-cloud, the morning dew,
The withering grass, the fading flower,
Of earthly hopes are emblems true,—
The glory of a passing hour.

3 But, though earth's fairest blossoms die,
And all beneath the skies is vain,
There is a land whose confines lie
Beyond the reach of care and pain.

4 Then let the hope of joys to come
Dispel our cares and chase our fears;
If God be ours, we're traveling home,
Though passing through a vale of tears.

494 *Psalm 17.* I. WATTS.

What sinners value I resign;
Lord! 'tis enough that thou art mine;
I shall behold thy blissful face,
And stand complete in righteousness.

2 This life's a dream—an empty show;
But the bright world, to which I go,
Hath joys substantial and sincere;
When shall I wake, and find me there?

3 Oh, glorious hour! oh, blest abode!
I shall be near, and like my God;
And flesh and sin no more control
The sacred pleasures of the soul.

4 My flesh shall slumber in the ground,
Till the last trumpet's joyful sound;
Then burst the chains, with sweet surprise,
And in my Saviour's image rise!

MERIBAH. C. P. M.   LOWELL MASON.

1. When thou, my righteous Judge, shalt come   To bring thy ransomed people home, Shall

I among them stand? / Shall such a worthless worm as I, / Who sometimes am afraid to die, Be found at thy right hand?

THE ROCK THAT IS HIGHER. P. M.   W. G. FISCHER.

1. Oh, sometimes the shadows are deep, And rough seems the path to the goal; And sorrows sometimes how they sweep

REFRAIN.

Like tempests down o-ver the soul. Oh, then, to the Rock let me fly, (let me fly,) To the Rock that is high-er than

I: Oh, then to the Rock let me fly, (let me fly,) To the Rock that is high-er than I.

higher than I:)

495   *"To the Rock."*   E. JOHNSON.

Oh, sometimes the shadows are deep,
  And rough seems the path to the goal;
And sorrows sometimes how they sweep
  Like tempests down over the soul.
REF. —||: Oh, then, to the Rock let me fly,
  To the Rock that is higher than I. :||

2 Oh, sometimes how long seems the day,
And sometimes how weary my feet;

But toiling in life's dusty way,
  The Rock's blessèd shadow how sweet.
REF.—||: Oh, then, to the Rock let me fly,
  To the Rock that is higher than I. :||

3 Oh, near to the Rock let me keep,
  If blessings, or sorrows prevail;
Or climbing the mountain way steep,
  Or walking the shadowy vale.
REF.—||: Then, quick to the Rock I can fly,
  To the Rock that is higher than I. :||

496 c. p. m. *The Tribunal.* LADY HUNTINGTON.

When thou, my righteous Judge, shalt come
To take thy ransomed people home,
  Shall I among them stand?
Shall such a worthless worm as I,
Who sometimes am afraid to die,
  Be found at thy right hand?

2 I love to meet thy people now,
Before thy feet with them to bow,
  Though vilest of them all;
But, can I bear the piercing thought,
What if my name should be left out,
  When thou for them shalt call?

3 O Lord, prevent it by thy grace;
Be thou my only hiding-place,
  In this the accepted day;
Thy pardoning voice, oh, let me hear,
To still my unbelieving fear,
  Nor let me fall, I pray.

4 Among thy saints let me be found,
Whene'er the archangel's trump shall sound,
  To see thy smiling face;
Then loudest of the throng I'll sing,
While heaven's resounding mansions ring
  With shouts of sovereign grace

AUGUSTUS. C. M. WM. F. SHERWIN.

1. That aw - ful day will sure - ly come, Th'ap - point - ed hour makes haste,

When I must stand be - fore my Judge, And pass the sol - emn test.

497 *"That awful day."* I. WATTS.

THAT awful day will surely come,
 The appointed hour makes haste,
When I must stand before my Judge,
 And pass the solemn test.

2 Thou lovely Chief of all my joys,
 Thou Sovereign of my heart!
How could I bear to hear thy voice
 Pronounce the sound, "Depart!"

3 Jesus, I throw my arms around,
 And hang upon thy breast:

Without one gracious smile from thee,
 My spirit cannot rest.

4 Oh, tell me that my worthless name
 Is graven on thy hands!
Show me some promise in thy book,
 Where my salvation stands.

5 Give me one kind, assuring word,
 To sink my fears again;
And cheerfully my soul shall wait
 Her threescore years and ten.

HOWARD. C. M. S. HOWARD.

1. When, ris - ing from the bed of death, O'erwhelmed with guilt and fear,

I see my Mak - er face to face, Oh, how shall I........ ap - pear?

498 *The Test.* J. ADDISON.

WHEN, rising from the bed of death,
 O'erwhelmed with guilt and fear,
I see my Maker face to face,
 Oh, how shall I appear?

2 If yet while pardon may be found
 And mercy may be sought,

My heart with inward horror shrinks,
 And trembles at the thought;—

2 When thou, O Lord! shalt stand disclosed
 In majesty severe,
And sit in judgment on my soul,
 Oh, how shall I appear?

JUDGMENT HYMN. P. M.   JOSEPH KLUG'S GESANGBUCH.

1. Great God, what do I see and hear! The end of things cre-a-ted! The Judge of man I see appear, On clouds of glo-ry seat-ed: The trumpet sounds; the

graves restore The dead which they contained before; Prepare, my soul, to meet him.

499 *Prepare to meet God.* W. B. COLLYER, tr.

GREAT God, what do I see and hear!
  The end of things created!
The Judge of man I see appear,
  On clouds of glory seated:
The trumpet sounds; the graves restore
The dead which they contained before;
  Prepare, my soul, to meet him.

2 The dead in Christ shall first arise,
  At the last trumpet's sounding—
Caught up to meet him in the skies,
  With joy their Lord surrounding;
No gloomy fears their souls dismay,
His presence sheds eternal day
  On those prepared to meet him.

3 But sinners, filled with guilty fears,
  Behold his wrath prevailing;
For they shall rise, and find their tears
  And sighs are unavailing:
The day of grace is past and gone;
Trembling they stand before the throne,
  All unprepared to meet him.

4 Great God! what do I see and hear!
  The end of things created!
The Judge of man I see appear,
  On clouds of glory seated:
Beneath his cross I view the day
When heaven and earth shall pass away,
  And thus prepare to meet him.
14

500 *"Into thine hand."* GERMAN.

WHEN my last hour is close at hand,
  My last sad journey taken,
Do thou, Lord Jesus! by me stand;
  Let me not be forsaken:
O Lord! my spirit I resign
Into thy loving hands divine;
  'Tis safe within thy keeping.

2 Countless as sands upon the shore,
  My sins may then appall me;
Yet, though my conscience vex me sore,
  Despair shall not enthrall me;
For as I draw my latest breath,
I'll think, Lord Christ! upon thy death,
  And there find consolation.

3 I shall not in the grave remain,
  Since thou death's bonds hast severed:
By hope with thee to rise again,
  From fear of death delivered,
I'll come to thee, where'er thou art,—
Live with thee, from thee never part;
  Therefore I die in rapture.

4 And so to Jesus Christ I'll go,
  My longing arms extending;
So fall asleep, in slumber deep,
  Slumber that knows no ending;
Till Jesus Christ, God's only Son,
Opens the gates of bliss, leads on
  To heaven, to life eternal.

VIGIL. S. M.   ST. ALBAN'S TUNE BOOK.

1. I have a home a - bove, From sin and sorrow free; A mansion which e-ter-nal love Designed and formed for me.

501   *"A place for you."*   H. BENNETT.

I HAVE a home above,
  From sin and sorrow free;
A mansion which eternal love
  Designed and formed for me.

2 My Father's gracious hand
  Has built this sweet abode;
From everlasting it was planned—
  My dwelling-place with God.

3 My Saviour's precious blood
  Has made my title sure;
He passed thro' death's dark raging flood
  To make my rest secure.

4 The Comforter has come,
  The earnest has been given;
He leads me onward to the home
  Reserved for me in heaven.

HAVERHILL. S. M.   LOWELL MASON.

1. And is there, Lord, a rest For weary souls designed, Where not a care shall stir the breast, Or sorrow entrance find?

502   *"A rest."*   RAY PALMER.

AND is there, Lord, a rest
  For weary souls designed,
Where not a care shall stir the breast,
  Or sorrow entrance find?

2 Is there a blissful home,
  Where kindred minds shall meet,
And live, and love, nor ever roam
  From that serene retreat?

3 For ever blessèd they,
  Whose joyful feet shall stand,
While endless ages waste away,
  Amid that glorious land!

4 My soul would thither tend,
  While toilsome years are given;
Then let me, gracious God, ascend
  To sweet repose in heaven!

VARINA. C. M. D.   G. F. ROOT, arr.

1. { There is a land of pure delight, Where saints immortal reign; }
   { In - finite day excludes the night, And pleasures banish pain, } There ever-lasting spring abides,

And never-withering flowers: Death, like a narrow sea, divides This heavenly land from ours.

JORDAN. C. M. D.   W. BILLINGS.

503   *"Go over this Jordan."*   L. WATTS.

THERE is a land of pure delight,
  Where saints immortal reign;
Infinite day excludes the night,
  And pleasures banish pain.
There everlasting spring abides,
  And never-withering flowers;
Death, like a narrow sea, divides
  This heavenly land from ours.

2 Sweet fields beyond the swelling flood
  Stand dressed in living green;
So to the Jews old Canaan stood,
  While Jordan rolled between.
But timorous mortals start and shrink
  To cross this narrow sea;
And linger, shivering on the brink,
  And fear to launch away.

3 Oh, could we make our doubts remove,
  These gloomy doubts that rise,
And see the Canaan that we love
  With unbeclouded eyes:—
Could we but climb where Moses stood,
  And view the landscape o'er,
Not Jordan's stream, nor death's cold flood,
  Should fright us from the shore.

504   *"Hold fast."*   C. F. ALEXANDER.

THE roseate hues of early dawn,
  The brightness of the day,
The crimson of the sunset sky,
  How fast they fade away!
Oh, for the pearly gates of heaven!
  Oh, for the golden floor!
Oh, for the Sun of Righteousness,
  That setteth nevermore!

2 The highest hopes we cherish here,
  How soon they tire and faint!
How many a spot defiles the robe
  That wraps an earthly saint!
Oh, for a heart that never sins!
  Oh, for a soul washed white!
Oh, for a voice to praise our King,
  Nor weary day or night!

3 Here faith is ours, and heavenly hope,
  And grace to lead us higher;
But there are perfectness and peace,
  Beyond our best desire.
Oh, by thy love and anguish, Lord,
  And by thy life laid down,
Grant that we fall not from thy grace,
  Nor fail to reach our crown!

RHINE. C. M.

GERMAN MELODY.

1. O moth-er dear, Je-ru-sa-lem, When shall I come to thee? When shall my sor-rows

have an end? Thy joys when shall I see? Thy joys when shall I see?

505 *The New Jerusalem.* D. DICKSON.

O MOTHER dear, Jerusalem,
  When shall I come to thee?
When shall my sorrows have an end?
  Thy joys when shall I see?

2 O happy harbor of God's saints!
  O sweet and pleasant soil!
In thee no sorrow can be found,
  Nor grief, nor care, nor toil.

3 No dimly cloud o'ershadows thee,
  Nor gloom, nor darksome night;
But every soul shines as the sun,
  For God himself gives light.

4 Thy walls are made of precious stone,
  Thy bulwarks diamond-square,
Thy gates are all of orient pearl—
  O God! if I were there!

506 *Faith and the Future.* W. H. BATHURST.

Oh, for a faith that will not shrink
  Though pressed by every foe,
That will not tremble on the brink
  Of any earthly woe!—

2 That will not murmur nor complain
  Beneath the chastening rod,
But, in the hour of grief or pain,
  Will lean upon its God;—

3 A faith that shines more bright and clear
  When tempests rage without;
That, when in danger, knows no fear,
  In darkness, feels no doubt;—

4 Lord, give us such a faith as this,
  And then, whate'er may come,
We'll taste, ev'n here, the hallowed bliss
  Of an eternal home.

SHINING SHORE. P. M.

GEO. F. ROOT.

1. My days are swiftly gliding by, And I, a pilgrim stranger, Would not detain them as they fly,
D. S.—just before, the Shining Shore

FINE.

D. S.

Those hours of toil and danger. For, oh, we stand on Jordan's strand, Our friends are passing over; And
We may al-most dis-cov-er.

JOYFUL SOUND. C. M. D.   E. L. WHITE.

1. { Je - ru - sa - lem! my hap - py home! Name ev - er dear to me!
   { When shall my la - bors have an end, (Omit).... .... } In
D.C.—Where con - gre - ga - tions ne'er break up, (Omit)................................ And

joy, and peace, in thee? Oh, when, thou cit-y of my God, Shall I thy courts as-cend,
Sab-baths have no end.

507   *The New Jerusalem.*   ANON.

JERUSALEM! my happy home!
Name ever dear to me!
When shall my labors have an end,
In joy, and peace, in thee!
Oh, when, thou city of my God,
Shall I thy courts ascend,
Where congregations ne'er break up,
And Sabbaths have no end?

2 There happier bowers than Eden's bloom,
Nor sin nor sorrow know:
Blest seats! thro' rude and stormy scenes,
I onward press to you.

Why should I shrink at pain and woe!
Or feel, at death, dismay?
I've Canaan's goodly land in view,
And realms of endless day.

3 Apostles, martyrs, prophets there,
Around my Saviour stand;
And soon my friends in Christ below,
Will join the glorious band.
Jerusalem! my happy home!
My soul still pants for thee;
Then shall my labors have an end,
When I thy joys shall see.

508   P. M.   *"Jordan's Strand."*   D. NELSON.

My days are gliding swiftly by,
And I, a pilgrim stranger,
Would not detain them as they fly,
Those hours of toil and danger.
For, oh, we stand on Jordan's strand,
Our friends are passing over;
And just before, the Shining Shore
We may almost discover!

2 We'll gird our loins, my brethren dear,
Our heavenly home discerning;
Our absent Lord has left us word,
Let every lamp be burning.—REF.

3 Should coming days be cold and dark,
We need not cease our singing;
That perfect rest naught can molest,
Where golden harps are ringing.—REF.

4 Let sorrow's rudest tempest blow,
Each cord on earth to sever;
Our King says, Come, and there's our home
For ever, oh, for ever!
For, oh, we stand on Jordan's strand,
Our friends are passing over;
And just before, the Shining Shore
We may almost discover!

NAUMANN. C. M.

1. There is an hour of hallowed peace, For those with cares oppressed, When sighs and sorrow-ing shall cease, When sighs and sor - row-ing shall cease, And all be hushed to rest :—

509   *"Sow in tears."*   W. B. TAPPAN.

THERE is an hour of hallowed peace,
  For those with cares oppressed,
When sighs and sorrowing shall cease,
  And all be hushed to rest :—

2 'Tis then the soul is freed from fears
  And doubts, which here annoy;
Then they, who oft have sown in tears,
  Shall reap again in joy.

3 There is a home of sweet repose,
  Where storms assail no more;
The stream of endless pleasure flows,
  On that celestial shore.

4 There, purity with love appears,
  And bliss without alloy;
There, they, who oft have sown in tears,
  Shall reap again in joy.

COVENTRY. C. M.   ENGLISH MELODY.

1. Oh, could our thoughts and wish - es fly, A - bove these gloom - y shades, To those bright worlds, be - yond the sky, Which sor - row ne'er in - vades!—

510   *"Things not seen."*   A. STEELE.

OH, could our thoughts and wishes fly,
  Above these gloomy shades,
To those bright worlds, beyond the sky,
  Which sorrow ne'er invades!—

2 There, joys, unseen by mortal eyes
  Or reason's feeble ray,
In ever-blooming prospect rise,
  Unconscious of decay.

3 Lord! send a beam of light divine,
  To guide our upward aim;
With one reviving touch of thine,
  Our languid hearts inflame.

4 Oh, then, on faith's sublimest wing,
  Our ardent hope shall rise
To those bright scenes, where pleasures spring
  Immortal in the skies.

WOODLAND. C. M. N. D. GOULD.

1. There is an hour of peaceful rest, To mourning wand'rers giv'n; There is a joy for souls distressed, A balm for ev-ery wounded breast: 'Tis found a-bove—in heaven.

511 *"No more death."* W. B. TAPPAN.

THERE is an hour of peaceful rest,
To mourning wanderers given;
There is a joy for souls distressed,
A balm for every wounded breast:
'Tis found above—in heaven.

2 There is a home for weary souls,
By sin and sorrow driven,—
When tossed on life's tempestuous shoals,
Where storms arise, and ocean rolls,
And all is drear—but heaven.

3 There faith lifts up her cheerful eye
To brighter prospects given;
And views the tempest passing by,
The evening shadows quickly fly,
And all serene—in heaven

4 There fragrant flowers immortal bloom,
And joys supreme are given;
There rays divine disperse the gloom;
Beyond the confines of the tomb
Appears the dawn of heaven!

VICTORY. 8s, 7s, 4s. H. H. BEADLE.

1. { Christ is coming! let cre-a-tion Bid her groans and travail cease; Let the glorious procla-ma-tion Hope restore and (Omit) .... } faith increase; Christ is coming! Come, thou blessed Prince of peace!

512 *"Christ is coming."* J. R. MACDUFF.

CHRIST is coming! let creation
Bid her groans and travail cease:
Let the glorious proclamation
Hope restore and faith increase;
Christ is coming!
Come, thou blessed Prince of peace!

2 Earth can now but tell the story
Of thy bitter cross and pain;
She shall yet behold thy glory
When thou comest back to reign;
Christ is coming!
Let each heart repeat the strain

3 Long thy exiles have been pining,
Far from rest, and home, and thee:
But, in heavenly vesture shining,
Soon they shall thy glory see;
Christ is coming!
Haste the joyous jubilee.

4 With that "blessed hope" before us,
Let no harp remain unstrung;
Let the mighty advent chorus
Onward roll from tongue to tongue;
Christ is coming!
Come, Lord Jesus, quickly come.

BEULAH. 7s. D.   E. IVES.

1. Who are these in bright array, This in-nu-mer-a - ble throng Round the altar, night and day
D. S.—Wis-dom, riches, to ob-tain,

Hymning one triumph-ant song?—"Worthy is the Lamb, once slain, Blessing, honor, glo-ry, power,
New do-min-ion ev - ery hour."

513   *"Who are these?"*   J. MONTGOMERY.

Who are these in bright array,
  This innumerable throng
Round the altar, night and day
  Hymning one triumphant song?—
"Worthy is the Lamb, once slain,
  Blessing, honor, glory, power,
Wisdom, riches, to obtain,
  New dominion every hour."

2 These through fiery trials trod;
  These from great afflictions came:
Now, before the throne of God,
  Sealed with his almighty name,

Clad in raiment pure and white,
  Victor-palms in every hand,
Through their dear Redeemer's might,
  More than conquerors they stand.

3 Hunger, thirst, disease unknown,
  On immortal fruits they feed;
Them the Lamb, amid the throne,
  Shall to living fountains lead:
Joy and gladness banish sighs—
  Perfect love dispel all fears—
And for ever from their eyes
  God shall wipe away the tears

I'M A PILGRIM. P. M.   ANON.

1. I'm a pilgrim, and I'm a stranger; I can tar-ry, I can tar-ry but a night! { Do not de - tain me, for I am go - ing }
D. C.—I'm a pilgrim, &c.   { To where the fountains are ever flow - ing: }

514   *Pilgrimage.*   M. S. B. DANA.

I'm a pilgrim, and I'm a stranger;
I can tarry, I can tarry but a night!
Do not detain me, for I am going
To where the fountains are ever flowing:
  I'm a pilgrim, etc.

2 There the glory is ever shining!
  Oh, my longing heart, my longing heart is
    there!

Here in this country so dark and dreary,
I long have wandered forlorn and weary:
  I'm a pilgrim, etc.

3 There's the city to which I journey;
  My Redeemer, my Redeemer, is its light!
There is no sorrow, nor any sighing,
Nor any tears there, nor any dying!
  I'm a pilgrim, etc.

LOWRY (or HILLSDALE). L. M.   GEO. F. ROOT.

1. Now let our souls, on wings sub-lime, Rise from the van-i-ties of time,

Draw back the part-ing vail, and see The glo-ries of e-ter-ni-ty.

515   *"Eye hath not seen."*   T. GIBBONS.

Now LET our souls, on wings sublime,
Rise from the vanities of time,
Draw back the parting vail, and see
The glories of eternity.

2 Born by a new celestial birth,
Why should we grovel here on earth?
Why grasp at transitory toys,
So near to heaven's eternal joys?

3 Should aught beguile us on the road,
When we are walking back to God?
For strangers into life we come,
And dying is but going home.

4 To dwell with God—to feel his love,
Is the full heaven enjoyed above;
And the sweet expectation now
Is the young dawn of heaven below.

516   *"A Rest."*   RAY PALMER.

Lord, thou wilt bring the joyful day!
Beyond earth's weariness and pains,
Thou hast a mansion far away,
Where for thine own a rest remains.

2 No sun there climbs the morning sky,
There never falls the shade of night;
God and the Lamb, for ever nigh,
O'er all shed everlasting light.

3 The bow of mercy spans the throne,
Emblem of love and goodness there;
While notes to mortals all unknown,
Float on the calm celestial air.

4 Around that throne bright legions stand,
Redeemed by blood from sin and hell;
And shining forms, an angel band,
The mighty chorus join to swell.

5 O Jesus, bring us to that rest,
Where all the ransomed shall be found,
In thine eternal fullness blest,
While ages roll their cycles round!

517   *"Many mansions."*   RAY PALMER.

Thy Father's house! thine own bright home!
And thou hast there a place for me!
Though yet an exile here I roam,
That distant home by faith I see.

2 I see its domes resplendent glow,
Where beams of God's own glory fall;
And trees of life immortal grow,
Whose fruits o'erhang the sapphire wall.

3 I know that thou, who on the tree
Didst deign our mortal guilt to bear,
Wilt bring thine own to dwell with thee,
And waitest to receive me there!

4 Thy love will there array my soul
In thine own robe of spotless hue;
And I shall gaze, while ages roll,
On thee, with raptures ever new!

5 Oh, welcome day! when thou my feet
Shalt bring the shining threshold o'er,
A Father's warm embrace to meet,
And dwell at home for evermore!

1. { Bride of the Lamb, a - wake, awake! Why sleep for sorrow now? }
   { The hope of glo - ry, Christ, is thine, (Omit).................. } A   child of glo - ry   thou.
D. C.—Hath sighed for one that's far a-way,—(Omit)... .... The Bridegroom of thy heart.

Thy   spir - it   through the   lone - ly   night,   From   earth-ly   joy   a - part

---

518   " The Lamb's Wife."   E. DENNY.

BRIDE of the Lamb, awake, awake !
 Why sleep for sorrow now ?
The hope of glory, Christ, is thine,
 A child of glory thou.
Thy spirit, through the lonely night,
 From earthly joy apart,
Hath sighed for one that's far away,—
 The Bridegroom of thy heart.

2 But see ! the night is waning fast,
 The breaking morn is near;
And Jesus comes, with voice of love,
 Thy drooping heart to cheer.
Then weep no more; 'tis all thine own,
 His crown, his joy divine;
And, sweeter far than all beside,
 He, he himself is thine !

519   " Behold, I come quickly."   ANON.

SOON will the heavenly Bridegroom come;
 Ye wedding-guests, draw near,
And slumber not in sin, when he,
 The Son of God, is here !
Come, let us haste to meet our Lord,
 And hail him with delight;
Who saved us by his precious blood,
 And sorrows infinite !

2 Beside him all the patriarchs old,
 And holy prophets stand;
The glorious apostolic choir,
 And noble martyr band.

As brethren dear they welcome us,
 And lead us to the throne,
Where angels bow their vailéd heads,
 Before the Three in One;—

3 Where we, with all the saints of God,
 A white-robed multitude,
Shall praise the ascended Lord, who deigns
 To bear our flesh and blood !
Our lot shall be for aye to share
 His reign of peace above:
And drink, with unexhausted joy,
 The river of his love.

520   " Come, Lord Jesus."   E. DENNY.

HOPE of our hearts, O Lord, appear,
 Thou glorious Star of day !
Shine forth, and chase the dreary night,
 With all our tears, away.
No resting-place we seek on earth,
 No loveliness we see;
Our eye is on the royal crown,
 Prepared for us—and thee !

2 But, dearest Lord, however bright,
 That crown of joy above,
What is it to the brighter hope
 Of dwelling in thy love?
What to the joy, the deeper joy,
 Unmingled, pure, and free,
Of union with our living Head,
 Of fellowship with thee?

NORTHFIELD. C. M. J. INGALLS.

1. Lo! what a glorious sight appears, To our be-lieving eyes!

The earth and seas are

earth and seas are passed away, And the old rolling skies.

The earth and seas are passed a - - - way, And the old roll - ing skies.
The earth and seas are passed away,

passed away, The earth and seas are passed a - - way,

521 *"Your descending King."*   I. WATTS.

Lo! WHAT a glorious sight appears,
　To our believing eyes!
The earth and seas are passed away,
　And the old rolling skies.

2 From the third heaven where God resides—
　That holy, happy place,—
The New Jerusalem comes down,
　Adorned with shining grace.

3 Attending angels shout for joy,
　And the bright armies sing,—
"Mortals! behold the sacred seat
　Of your descending King:—

4 "The God of glory, down to men,
　Removes his blest abode;
Men, the dear objects of his grace,
　And he their loving God:—

5 "His own soft hand shall wipe the tears
　From every weeping eye;
And pains, and groans, and griefs, and fears,
　And death itself shall die!"

6 How long, dear Saviour! oh, how long
　Shall this bright hour delay?
Fly swifter round, ye wheels of time!
　And bring the welcome day.

522 *Messiah's Reign.*   M. BRUCE

BEHOLD, the mountain of the Lord
　In latter days shall rise

On mountain tops, above the hills,
　And draw the wondering eyes.

2 The beam that shines from Zion's hill
　Shall lighten every land:
The King who reigns in Salem's towers
　Shall all the world command.

3 No strife shall vex Messiah's reign,
　Or mar the peaceful years;
To ploughshares men shall beat their swords,
　To pruning-hooks their spears.

523 *"Come, blessed Lord?"*   E. DENNY.

LIGHT of the lonely pilgrim's heart!
　Star of the coming day!
Arise, and with thy morning beams
　Chase all our griefs away.

2 Come, blessèd Lord! let every shore
　And answering island sing
The praises of thy royal name,
　And own thee as their King.

3 Jesus! thy fair creation groans,—
　The air, the earth, the sea,—
In unison with all our hearts,
　And calls aloud for thee.

4 Thine was the cross, with all its fruits
　Of grace and peace divine;
Be thine the crown of glory now,
　The palm of victory thine.

MT. BLANC. P. M.   OLD ENGLISH MELODY.

1. We are on our journey home, Where Christ our Lord is gone; We shall meet around his throne,

When he makes his people one, In the new, In the new Je - ru - sa - lem.

In the new Je-ru-sa-lem.

524   " The Holy City."   C. BEECHER.

WE are on our journey home,
  Where Christ our Lord is gone;
We shall meet around his throne,
  When he makes his people one,
    In the new Jerusalem.

2 We can see that distant home,
  Though clouds rise dark between;
Faith views the radiant dome,
  And a lustre flashes keen
    From the new Jerusalem.

3 Oh, holy, heavenly home!
  Oh, rest eternal there!
When shall the exiles come,
  Where they cease from earthly care,
    In the new Jerusalem!

4 Our hearts are breaking now
  Those mansions fair to see;
O Lord, thy heavens bow,
  And raise us up with thee,
    To the new Jerusalem.

RUTHERFORD. P. M.   CHAS. D'URHAN.

1. The sands of time are sink - ing, The dawn of heav-en breaks; The summer morn I've

sighed for, The fair, sweet morn a - wakes: Dark, dark hath been the mid - night, But

day-spring is at hand, And glo - ry, glo - ry dwell - eth In im-man-uel's land.

BETTER LAND. 7s. 6l. WM. F. SHERWIN.

1. Life has many a pleasant hour, Many a bright and cloudless day; Singing bird and smiling flower, Scatter

sunbeams on our way; But the sweetest blossoms grow In the land to which we go.

·525 *The better land.* F. C. VAN ALSTYNE.

LIFE has many a pleasant hour,
  Many a bright and cloudless day;
Singing bird and smiling flower,
  Scatter sunbeams on our way;
    But the sweetest blossoms grow
    In the land to which we go.

2 Earth has many a cool retreat,
  Many a spot to memory dear;
Oft we find our weary feet
  Lingering by some fountain clear;
    Yet the purest waters flow
    In the land to which we go.

3 Like a cloud that floats away,
  Like the early morning dew,
Here the fairest things decay;
  There, are pleasures ever new.
    Only joy the heart will know
    In the land to which we go.

4 'Tis the Christian's promised land;
  There is everlasting day;
There a Saviour's loving hand
  Wipes the mourner's tears away;
    Oh! the rapture we shall know
    In the land to which we go.

526 P. M. *Immanuel's Land.* A. R. COUSIN.

THE sands of time are sinking,
  The dawn of heaven breaks,
The summer morn I've sighed for,
  The fair sweet morn awakes:
Dark, dark hath been the midnight,
  But day-spring is at hand,·
And glory, glory dwelleth
  In Immanuel's land.

2 Oh, Christ, he is the fountain,
  The deep sweet well of love;
The streams of earth I've tasted,
  More deep I'll drink above.

There to an ocean fullness
  His mercy doth expand,
And glory, glory dwelleth
  In Immanuel's land.

3 The bride eyes not her garment,
  But her dear bridegroom's face;
I will not gaze at glory,
  But on my King of Grace—
Not at the crown he gifteth,
  But on his piercéd hand;—
The Lamb is all the glory
  Of Immanuel's land.

E. P. PARKER, arr.

1. This is not my place of rest-ing,— Mine's a cit-y yet to come;

On-ward to it I am hast-ing— On to my e-ter-nal home.

527　　*Not our Rest.*　H. BONAR.

THIS is not my place of resting,—
　Mine's a city yet to come;
Onward to it I am hasting—
　On to my eternal home.

2 In it all is light and glory;
　O'er it shines a nightless day:
Every trace of sin's sad story,
　All the curse, hath passed away.

3 There the Lamb, our Shepherd, leads us
　By the streams of life along,—
On the freshest pastures feeds us,
　Turns our sighing into song.

4 Soon we pass this desert dreary,
　Soon we bid farewell to pain;
Never more are sad or weary,
　Never, never sin again!

528　　*"The sea of glass."* C. WORDSWORTH.

HARK! the sound of holy voices,
　Chanting at the crystal sea,
Hallelujah, hallelujah,
　Hallelujah, Lord, to thee!

2 Multitudes, which none can number,
　Like the stars in glory stand,
Clothed in white apparel, holding
　Palms of victory in their hands.

3 They have come from tribulation,
　And have washed their robes in blood,
Washed them in the blood of Jesus;
　Tried they were and firm they stood.

4 Mocked, imprisoned, stoned, tormented,
　Sawn asunder, slain with sword,
They have conquered death and Satan
　By the might of Christ the Lord.

5 Love and peace they taste for ever,
　And all truth and knowledge see
In the Beatific Vision
　Of the blessèd Trinity.

529　　*The City.*　S. BARING-GOULD.

DAILY, daily sing the praises
　Of the City God hath made;
In the beauteous fields of Eden
　Its foundation-stones are laid.

2 In the midst of that dear City
　Christ is reigning on his seat,
And the angels swing their censers
　In a ring about his feet.

3 From the throne a river issues,
　Clear as crystal, passing bright,
And it traverses the City
　Like a sudden beam of light.

4 There the wind is sweetly fragrant,
　And is laden with the song
Of the seraphs, and the elders,
　And the great redeemèd throng.

5 Oh, I would my ears were open
　Here to catch that happy strain!
Oh, I would my eyes some vision
　Of that Eden could attain!

TAPPAN. C. M.

GEO. KINGSLEY.

1. On Jor-dan's rug - ged banks I stand, And cast a wish - ful eye To Canaan's

fair and happy land, To Canaan's fair and happy land, Where my pos-ses - sions lie.

530 *"Let me go over!"* S. STENNETT.

On Jordan's rugged banks I stand,
  And cast a wishful eye
To Canaan's fair and happy land,
  Where my possessions lie.

2 Oh, the transporting, rapturous scene,
  That rises to my sight!
Sweet fields arrayed in living green,
  And rivers of delight!

3 O'er all those wide extended plains
  Shines one eternal day;
There God, the Son, for ever reigns,
  And scatters night away.

4 No chilling winds, or poisonous breath,
  Can reach that healthful shore;
Sickness and sorrow, pain and death,
  Are felt and feared no more.

5 When shall I reach that happy place,
  And be for ever blest?
When shall I see my Father's face,
  And in his bosom rest?

6 Filled with delight, my raptured soul
  Can here no longer stay;
Though Jordan's waves around me roll,
  Fearless I'd launch away.

531 *. Jesus exalted.* I. WATTS.

Behold the glories of the Lamb,
  Amid his Father's throne;
Prepare new honors for his name,
  And songs before unknown.

2 Let elders worship at his feet,
  The church adore around,
With vials full of odors sweet,
  And harps of sweeter sound.

3 Now to the Lamb that once was slain,
  Be endless blessings paid!
Salvation, glory, joy remain
  For ever on thy head!

4 Thou hast redeemed our souls with blood,
  Hast set the prisoners free;
Hast made us kings and priests to God,
  And we shall reign with thee.

532 *"A building of God."* I. WATTS.

There is a house not made with hands,
  Eternal, and on high:
And here my spirit waiting stands,
  Till God shall bid it fly.

2 Shortly this prison of my clay
  Must be dissolved and fall;
Then, O my soul, with joy obey
  Thy heavenly Father's call.

3 We walk by faith of joys to come;
  Faith lives upon his word;
But while the body is our home,
  We're absent from the Lord.

4 'Tis pleasant to believe thy grace,
  But we had rather see;
We would be absent from the flesh,
  And present, Lord, with thee.

THE REST OF HEAVEN.

MIRIAM. 7s & 6s. D.   J. F. HOLBROOK.

1. Je - ru - sa - lem, the glo - rious! The glo - ry of th'e - lect,— O dear and future vis - ion
D. S.—To thee my thoughts are kindled,

That ea - ger hearts ex - pect! Ev'n now by faith I see thee, Ev'n here thy walls discern;
And strive, and pant, and yearn!

533   *"A City."*   J. M. NEALE, *tr.*

JERUSALEM, the glorious!
    The glory of the elect,—
O dear and future vision
    That eager hearts expect!
Ev'n now by faith I see thee,
    Ev'n here thy walls discern;
To thee my thoughts are kindled,
    And strive, and pant, and yearn!

2 The Cross is all thy splendor,
    The Crucified, thy praise;
His laud and benediction
    Thy ransomed people raise;—
Jerusalem! exulting
    On that securest shore,
I hope thee, wish thee, sing thee,
    And love thee evermore!

3 O sweet and blessèd Country!
    Shall I e'er see thy face?
O sweet and blessèd Country!
    Shall I e'er win thy grace?
Exult, O dust and ashes!
    The Lord shall be thy part;
His only, his for ever,
    Thou shalt be, and thou art!

534   *"Lamps trimmed."*   J. BORTHWICK, *tr.*

REJOICE, rejoice, believers!
    And let your lights appear!

The shades of eve are thickening,
    And darker night is near;
The Bridegroom is advancing;
    Each hour he draws more nigh;
Up! watch and pray, nor slumber;
    At midnight comes the cry.

2 See that your lamps are burning,
    Your vessels filled with oil;
Wait calmly your deliverance
    From earthly pain and toil.
The watchers on the mountains
    Proclaim the Bridegroom near,
Go, meet him, as he cometh,
    With hallelujahs clear.

3 The saints, who here in patience
    Their cross and sufferings bore,
With him shall reign for ever,
    When sorrow is no more:
Around the throne of glory
    The Lamb shall they behold,
Adoring cast before him
    Their diadems of gold.

4 Our hope and expectation,
    O Jesus, now appear!
Arise, thou Sun so looked-for,
    O'er this benighted sphere!
With hearts and hands uplifted,
    We plead, O Lord, to see
The day of our redemption,
    And ever be with thee.

EWING. 7s, 6s. D.   ALEX. EWING.

1. Je - ru - sa - lem, the gold - en, With milk and hon - ey blest! Be - neath thy contem-

pla - tion Sink heart and voice oppressed: I know not, oh, I know not

What social joys are there, What ra - dian - cy of glo - ry, What light beyond compare.

535 *The New Jerusalem.* J. M. NEALE, *tr.*

JERUSALEM, the golden,
　With milk and honey blest !
Beneath thy contemplation
　Sink heart and voice oppressed:
I know not, oh, I know not,
　What social joys are there,
What radiancy of glory,
　What light beyond compare.

2 They stand, those halls of Zion,
　All jubilant with song,
And bright with many an angel,
　And all the martyr throng;
The Prince is ever in them,
　The daylight is serene;
The pastures of the blessèd
　Are decked in glorious sheen.

3 There is the throne of David;
　And there, from care released,
The song of them that triumph,
　The shout of them that feast:
And they who, with their Leader,
　Have conquered in the fight
For ever and for ever
　Are clad in robes of white.
15 ✎

536 *"Short toil."* J. M. NEALE, *tr.*

BRIEF life is here our portion;
　Brief sorrow, short-lived care;
The life, that knows no ending,
　The tearless life, is there:
Oh, happy retribution !
　Short toil, eternal rest;
For mortals, and for sinners,
　A mansion with the blest !

2 And there is David's fountain,
　And life in fullest glow;
And there the light is golden,
　And milk and honey flow;
The light, that hath no evening,
　The health, that hath no sore,
The life, that hath no ending,
　But lasteth evermore.

3 There Jesus shall embrace us,
　There Jesus be embraced,—
That spirit's food and sunshine;
　Whence earthly love is chased:
Yes ! God my King and Portion,
　In fullness of his grace,
We then shall see for ever,
　And worship face to face.

ST. GEORGE. 7s. D. GEORGE J. ELVEY.

1. Come, ye thankful people, come, Raise the song of Harvest-Home! All is safely gathered in, Ere the winter storms begin:

God, our Maker, doth pro-vide For our wants to be sup-plied: Come to God's own temple, come, Raise the song of Harvest-Home!

537 *Song for Harvest.* H. ALFORD.

COME, ye thankful people, come,
Raise the song of Harvest Home!
All is safely gathered in,
Ere the winter storms begin:
God our Maker doth provide
For our wants to be supplied:
Come to God's own temple, come,
Raise the song of Harvest Home!

2 We ourselves are God's own field,
Fruit unto his praise to yield:
Wheat and tares together sown,
Unto joy or sorrow grown:
First the blade, and then the ear,
Then the full corn shall appear:
Grant, O Harvest-Lord, that we
Wholesome grain and pure may be!

3 For the Lord our God shall come,
And shall take his harvest home:
From his field shall in that day
All offences purge away:
Give his angels charge at last
In the fire the tares to cast:
But the fruitful ears to store
In his garner evermore.

4 Then, thou Church Triumphant, come,
Raise the song of Harvest Home!
All are safely gathered in,
Free from sorrow, free from sin:

There, for ever purified,
In God's garner to abide:
Come, ten thousand angels, come,
Raise the glorious Harvest Home!

538 *The close of the year.* RAY PALMER.

THOU who roll'st the year around,
Crowned with mercies large and free,
Rich thy gifts to us abound,
Warm our praise shall rise to thee.
Kindly to our worship bow,
While our grateful thanks we tell,
That, sustained by thee, we now
Bid the parting year—farewell!

2 All its numbered days are sped,
All its busy scenes are o'er,
All its joys for ever fled,
All its sorrows felt no more.
Mingled with the eternal past,
Its remembrance shall decay;
Yet to be revived at last
At the solemn judgment-day.

3 All our follies, Lord, forgive!
Cleanse us from each guilty stain;
Let thy grace within us live,
That we spend not years in vain.
Then, when life's last eve shall come,
Happy spirits, may we fly
To our everlasting home,
To our Father's house on high!

BENEVENTO. 7s. D.   S. WEBBE.

1. While, with ceaseless course, the sun Hasted through the former year, Many souls their race have run,
D. S.—We a lit - tle longer wait,

Nev - er-more to meet us here: Fixed in an e - ter - nal state, They have done with all be-low;
But how little none can know.

---

539   *New Year.*   J. NEWTON.

WHILE, with ceaseless course, the sun
  Hasted through the former year,
Many souls their race have run,
  Nevermore to meet us here:
Fixed in an eternal state,
  They have done with all below;
We a little longer wait,—
  But how little none can know.

2 As the wingéd arrow flies
  Speedily the mark to find;
As the lightning from the skies
  Darts, and leaves no trace behind,
Swiftly thus our fleeting days
  Bear us down life's rapid stream;
Upward, Lord, our spirits raise,
  All below is but a dream.

3 Thanks for mercies past receive;
  Pardon of our sins renew;
Teach us henceforth how to live,
  With eternity in view:
Bless thy word to young and old;
  Fill us with a Saviour's love;
And, when life's short tale is told,
  May we dwell with thee above!

540   *Independence Day.*   N. STRONG.

SWELL the anthem, raise the song;
Praises to our God belong;
Saints and angels join to sing
Praises to the heavenly King.

Blessings from his liberal hand
Flow around this happy land:
Kept by him, no foes annoy;
Peace and freedom we enjoy.

2 Here, beneath a virtuous sway
May we cheerfully obey;
Never feel oppression's rod,
Ever own and worship God.
Hark ! the voice of nature sings
Praises to the King of kings;
Let us join the choral song,
And the grateful notes prolong.

541   *Thanksgiving.*   A. L. BARBAULD.

PRAISE to God, immortal praise,
For the love that crowns our days !
Bounteous Source of every joy,
Let thy praise our tongues employ.
For the blessings of the field,
For the stores the gardens yield;
For the fruits in full supply,
Ripened 'neath the summer sky;—

2 All that spring with bounteous hand
Scatters o'er the smiling land;
All that liberal autumn pours
From her rich, o'erflowing stores;
These to thee, my God, we owe,
Source whence all our blessings flow;
And for these my soul shall raise
Grateful vows and solemn praise.

1. O God, be-neath thy guid-ing hand, Our ex-iled fa-thers crossed the sea,

And when they trod the win-try strand, With prayer and psalm they worshiped thee.

542   *Forefathers' Day.*   L. BACON.

O God, beneath thy guiding hand,
  Our exiled fathers crossed the sea,
And when they trod the wintry strand,
    With prayer and psalm they worshiped
      thee.

2 Thou heardst, well pleased, the song, the
    prayer—
Thy blessing came; and still its power
Shall onward through all ages bear
  The memory of that holy hour.

3 What change! through pathless wilds
    no more
The fierce and naked savage roams:
Sweet praise, along the cultured shore,
  Breaks from ten thousand happy homes.

4 Laws, freedom, truth, and faith in God
  Came with those exiles o'er the waves,
And where their pilgrim feet have trod,
  The God they trusted guards their graves.

5 And here thy name, O God of love,
  Their children's children shall adore,
Till these eternal hills remove,
  And spring adorns the earth no more.

543   *The New Year.*   P. DODDRIDGE.

Great God! we sing that mighty hand
By which supported still we stand;
The opening year thy mercy shows;
Let mercy crown it till it close.

2 By day, by night, at home, abroad,
Still we are guarded by our God;
By his incessant bounty fed,
By his unerring counsel led.

3 With grateful hearts the past we own;
The future, all to us unknown,
We to thy guardian care commit,
And peaceful leave before thy feet.

4 In scenes exalted or depressed,
Be thou our joy, and thou our rest;
Thy goodness all our hopes shall raise,
Adored through all our changing days.

5 When death shall interrupt our songs,
And seal in silence mortal tongues,
Our Helper, God, in whom we trust,
In better worlds our souls shall boast.

544   *The New Year.*   P. DODDRIDGE.

Our Helper, God! we bless thy name,
Whose love forever is the same;
The tokens of thy gracious care
Open, and crown, and close the year.

2 Amid ten thousand snares we stand,
Supported by thy guardian hand;
And see, when we review our ways,
Ten thousand monuments of praise.

3 Thus far thine arm has led me on;
Thus far we make thy mercy known;
And while we tread this desert land,
New mercies shall new songs demand.

4 Our grateful souls, on Jordan's shore,
Shall raise one sacred pillar more;
Then bear in thy bright courts above,
Inscriptions of immortal love.

BRYANT. C. M. D.   WM F. SHERWIN.

1. As shadows, cast by cloud and sun, Flit o'er the summer grass, So, in thy sight, Almighty One, Earth's

gen-er-a-tions pass. And as the years, an endless host, Come swiftly pressing on, The brightest names that

earth can boast Just glisten and are gone.

545 *Anniversary.* W. C. BRYANT.

As SHADOWS cast by cloud and sun,
Flit o'er the summer grass,
So, in thy sight, Almighty One,
Earth's generations pass.
And as the years, an endless host,
Come swiftly pressing on,
The brightest names that earth can boast
Just glisten and are gone.

2 Yet doth the star of Bethlehem shed
A lustre pure and sweet;
And still it leads, as once it led,
To the Messiah's feet.
O Father, may that holy star
Grow every year more bright,
And send its glorious beams afar
To fill the world with light.

546 *The Seasons.* I. WATTS.

With songs and honors sounding loud
Address the Lord on high;
Over the heavens he spread his cloud,
And waters vail the sky.

His steady counsels change the face
Of the declining year;
He bids the sun cut short his race,
And wintry days appear.

2 He sends his word and melts the snow,
The fields no longer mourn;
He calls the warmer gales to blow,
And bids the spring return.
The changing wind, the flying cloud,
Obey his mighty word;
With songs and honors sounding loud
Praise ye the sovereign Lord.

547 *God's Mercies.* H. F. LYTE.

The mercies of my God and King
My tongue shall still pursue:
Oh, happy they, who, while they sing
Those mercies, share them too!
As bright and lasting as the sun,
As lofty as the sky,
From age to age, thy word shall run,
And chance and change defy.

2 The covenant of the King of kings
Shall stand for ever sure;
Beneath the shadow of thy wings
Thy saints repose secure.
In earth below, in heaven above,
Who, who is Lord like thee?
Oh, spread the gospel of thy love,
Till all thy glories see!

PILOT. 7s, 6L   FINE.   J. E. GOULD.   D. C.

1. Je - sus, Sav-iour, pi - lot me Over life's tempestuous sea; Unknown waves before me roll, Hiding rock and treacherous shoal;
D. C.—Chart and compass came from thee: Jesus, Saviour, pi-lot me.

548   *Life's Sea.*   E. HOPPER.

JESUS, Saviour, pilot me,
Over life's tempestuous sea;
Unknown waves before me roll,
Hiding rock and treacherous shoal;
Chart and compass came from thee:
Jesus, Saviour, pilot me.

2 As a mother stills her child,
Thou canst hush the ocean wild;
Boisterous waves obey thy will

When thou say'st to them "Be still!"
Wondrous Sovereign of the sea,
Jesus, Saviour, pilot me.

3 When at last I near the shore,
And the fearful breakers roar
'Twixt me and the peaceful rest,
Then, while leaning on thy breast,
May I hear thee say to me,
"Fear not, I will pilot thee!"

AND CAN IT BE? L. M. 6L.   OLD MELODY.   FINE.

1. { And can it be that I should gain An int'rest in the Saviour's blood? }
   { Died he for me, who caused his pain? For me, who him to death pur-sued? }
D.C.—A - maz-ing love! how can it be, That thou, my Lord, shouldst die for me?

A - maz-ing love! how can it be, That thou, my Lord, shouldst die for me?

549   *"No condemnation."*   C. WESLEY.

AND can it be that I should gain
  An interest in the Saviour's blood?
Died he for me, who caused his pain?
  For me, who him to death pursued?
Amazing love! how can it be,
That thou, my Lord, shouldst die for me?

2 He left his Father's throne above;
  (So free, so infinite his grace!)
Emptied himself of all but love,

And bled for Adam's helpless race;
'Tis mercy all, immense and free,
For, O my God, it found ont me!

3 No condemnation now I dread,—
  Jesus, with all in him, is mine;
Alive in him, my living Head,
  And clothed in righteousness divine,
Bold I approach the eternal throne,
And claim the crown, thro' Christ my own.

ASSURANCE. 10s.　　　　　　　　　　　　　　　WM. F. SHERWIN.

1. Why is thy faith, O child of God, so small? Why doth thy heart shrink back at duty's call? Art thou o-bey-ing this—"Abide in

me," And doth the Mas-ter's word a-bide in thee?

550　　　*"Abide in me."*　W. F. SHERWIN.

WHY is thy faith, O child of God, so small?
Why doth thy heart shrink back at duty's
　　call?
Art thou obeying this—"Abide in me,"
And doth the Master's word abide in thee?

2 Oh, blest assurance from our risen Lord!
Oh, precious comfort breathing from the
　　Word!
How great the promise! could there great-
　　er be?　　　　　　　　　　　　　[thee!"
"Ask what thou wilt, it shall be done for

3 "Ask what thou wilt," but, oh, remem-
　　ber this,—
We ask and have not, for we ask amiss
When, weak in faith, we only half believe
That what we ask we really shall receive.

4 Increase our faith, and clear our vision,
　　Lord;
Help us to take thee at thy simple word,
No more with cold distrust to bring thee
　　grief;
Lord, we believe! help thou our unbelief.

AMERICA. 6s, 4s.　　　　　　　　　　　　　　　H. CAREY.

1. My country! 'tis of thee, Sweet land of lib-er-ty, Of thee I sing: Land where my fa-thers died! Land of the

Pilgrims' pride! From every mountain side Let freedom ring!

551　　　*National Song.*　S. F. SMITH.

MY country! 'tis of thee,
Sweet land of liberty,
　　Of thee I sing;
Land where my fathers died!
Land of the Pilgrims' pride!
From every mountain side
　　Let freedom ring!

2 My native country, thee—
Land of the noble, free—
　　Thy name I love;
I love thy rocks and rills,
Thy woods and templed hills;
My heart with rapture thrills
　　Like that above.

3 Let music swell the breeze,
And ring from all the trees
　　Sweet freedom's song;
Let mortal tongues awake;
Let all that breathe partake;
Let rocks their silence break,—
　　The sound prolong.

4 Our fathers' God! to thee,
Author of liberty,
　　To thee we sing;
Long may our land be bright
With freedom's holy light;
Protect us by thy might,
　　Great God, our King!

CUTTING. 6s, 4s.   W. F. SHERWIN.

1. Christ for the world we sing; The world to Christ we bring, With loving zeal; The poor, and them that mourn, The faint and overborne,

Sin-sick and sorrow-worn, Whom Christ doth heal.

552   *Christ for the World.*   S. WOLCOTT.

CHRIST for the world we sing;
The world to Christ we bring,
  With loving zeal;
The poor, and them that mourn,
The faint and overborne,
Sin-sick and sorrow-worn,
  Whom Christ doth heal.

2 Christ for the world we sing;
The world to Christ we bring,
  With fervent prayer;

The wayward and the lost,
By restless passions tossed,
Redeemed, at countless cost,
  From dark despair.

3 Christ for the world we sing;
The world to Christ we bring,
  With one accord;
With us the work to share,
With us reproach to dare,
With us the cross to bear,
  For Christ our Lord.

4 Christ for the world we sing;
The world to Christ we bring,
  With joyful song;
The new-born souls, whose days,
Reclaimed from error's ways,
Inspired with hope and praise,
  To Christ belong.

GREEN PASTURES. P. M.   WM. F. SHERWIN.

1. Tell me, whom my soul doth love, Where thy flock are feeding; Where the pastures which they rove—Thou their footsteps leading?

553   *Cant.* 1: 7.   S. WOLCOTT.

TELL me, whom my soul doth love,
  Where thy flock are feeding;
Where the pastures which they rove—
  Thou their footsteps leading?

2 Tell me, sheltered from the heat,
  Where at noon they rest them;
Where at night their safe retreat—
  Fold, where none molest them?

3 Strong is thy protecting arm;
  Richly thou providest;
Feeding, resting—kept from harm—
  Blest the flock thou guidest.

4 Noon and night be my defence;
  Let no foe ensnare me;
Bring me to the Shepherd's tents—
  In thy bosom bear me.

INDEX OF TUNES.

It is to be understood that most of the Music included in this Collection is introduced "by permission," either purchased or given. It must, therefore, not be used in any other, without the consent of the authors or of those who hold the copyright of the Tunes.

INDEX OF SUBJECTS.

THE FIGURES REFER TO THE HYMNS.

INDEX OF FIRST LINES OF HYMNS.

234

INDEX OF FIRST LINES OF HYMNS.

HYMN.

Holy and reverend is the name 165
Holy Father, hear my cry 86
Holy Father, thou hast taught me.... 390
Holy, holy, holy Lord 87
Holy, holy, holy, Lord God Almighty. 421
Holy Ghost ! with light divine 199
Hope of our hearts, O Lord, appear.. 520
How beauteous on the mountains.... 450
How blest the righteous when he dies. 481
How charming is the place.......... 28
How condescending and how kind... 187
How firm a foundation, ye saints of the 309
How gentle God's commands ! 300
How pleasant, how divinely fair...... 33
How pleased and blest was I 1
How precious is the book divine..... 147
How shall I follow him I serve....... 181
How shall the young secure their hearts 148
How sweet, how heavenly is the sight. 11
How sweet the name of Jesus sounds.. 344
How vain is all beneath the skies !.... 493

I AM coming to the cross........... 270
I ask not now for gold to gild....... 394
I have a home above................ 501
I hear the Saviour say.............. 228
I hear thy welcome voice........... 229
I lay my sins on Jesus 254
I love thy kingdom, Lord.......... 35
I love to steal awhile away 65
I love to tell the story 231
I'm a pilgrim, and I'm a stranger 514
I'm not ashamed to own my Lord.... 292
I need thee, O my God............. 256
I once was a stranger to grace and to.. 350
I saw One hanging on a tree........ 186
I saw the cross of Jesus............ 232
I stand on Zion's mount 296
I would not live alway ; I ask not to.. 476
If God is mine, then present things .. 376
If on our daily course our mind...... 370
If you cannot on the ocean......... 409
In all my Lord's appointed ways..... 424
In all my vast concerns with thee 160
In heavenly love abiding........... 302
In the cross of Christ I glory........ 192
In the dark and cloudy day......... 386
In time of fear, when trouble 's near.. 287

JERUSALEM ! my happy home ! .. 507
Jerusalem, the glorious !........... 533
Jerusalem, the golden 535
Jesus,—and didst thou leave the sky .. 227
Jesus! and shall it ever be......... 327
Jesus calls us, o'er the tumult....... 442
Jesus, engrave it on my heart 211
Jesus! I love thy charming name.... 343

Jesus, I my cross have taken 275
Jesus, Jesus! visit me.............. 37
Jesus, keep me near the cross....... 59
Jesus ! lover of my soul............ 274
Jesus, Master, whose I am 349
Jesus, my All, to heaven is gone..... 195
Jesus only, when the morning 321
Jesus, Saviour, pilot me 548
Jesus shall reign where'er the sun.... 473
Jesus spreads his banner o'er us...... 441
Jesus, still lead on................. 308
Jesus, Sun of Righteousness 4
Jesus, the very thought of thee...... 345
Jesus, these eyes have never seen 339
Jesus, thou Joy of loving hearts...... 328
Jesus, thy blood and righteousness... 331
Jesus ! thy church with longing eyes.. 471
Jesus ! thy love shall we forget 179
Jesus, thy name I love............. 335
Jesus, we look to thee 49
Jesus, where'er thy people meet...... 74
Jesus, while our hearts are bleeding.. 391
Jesus, who knows full well 70
Jesus, who on his glorious throne 342
Jesus, whom angel hosts adore 183
Joy to the world,—the Lord is come.. 173
Just as I am, without one plea 252

KEEP silence, all created things ! 100

LEAD, kindly Light ! amid the encircling 392
Lead us, heavenly Father, lead us.... 135
Let me but hear my Saviour say..... 284
Let party names no more 50
Life has many a pleasant hour 525
Light of the lonely pilgrim's heart !.. 523
Light of those whose dreary dwelling. 401
Like sheep we went astray 213
Lo ! on a narrow neck of land 209
Lo ! what a glorious sight appears.... 521
Look from thy sphere of endless day. 463
Lord, as to thy dear cross we flee 178
Lord, at this closing hour 124
Lord, at thy mercy-seat 5
Lord, before thy throne we bend 257
Lord, dismiss us with thy blessing.... 136
Lord God of Hosts, by all adored !.... 85
Lord, how mysterious are thy ways .. 157
Lord, I am thine, entirely thine...... 436
Lord, I believe ; thy power I own.... 359
Lord ! I cannot let thee go 62
Lord, I hear of showers of blessing.. 53
Lord, it belongs not to my care...... 288
Lord, my weak thought in vain would 158
Lord of all being ; throned afar...... 156
Lord of earth ! thy forming hand.... 88
Lord ! thou hast searched and seen me 135